ISLAM AND POLITICS
IN THE CONTEMPORARY WORLD

Beverley Milton-Edwards

polity

First published in 2004 by Polity Press Ltd.

Polity Press
65 Bridge Street
Cambridge CB2 1UR, UK

Polity Press
350 Main Street
Malden, MA 02148, USA

ISBN: 0-7456 2711-0
ISBN: 0-7456 2712-9 (pb)

A catalogue record for this book is available from the British Library and has been applied for from the Library of Congress.

Typeset in 10.5 on 12 pt Palatino
by Kolam Information Services Pvt. Ltd, Pondicherry, India
Printed and bound in Great Britain by MPG Books, Bodmin, Cornwall

The publisher has used its best endeavours to ensure that the URLs for external websites referred to in this book are correct and active at the time of going to press. However, the publisher has no responsibility for the websites and can make no guarantee that a site will remain live or that the content is or will remain appropriate.

For further information on Polity, visit our website: www.polity.co.uk

CONTENTS

Preface   vii

INTRODUCTION   1

1 ISLAM AND POLITICS DEFINED   9

2 ISLAM AND THE STATE   34

3 THE POLITICS OF PROTEST   62

4 THE DEMOCRACY DEBATE: INTRACTABLE
   PATHS?   88

5 BRINGING DOWN THE BARRICADE: THE GENDER
   DEBATE   118

6 GUN BARREL POLITICS: ISLAM AND POLITICAL
   VIOLENCE   149

7 THE MAKING OF MUTUAL ANTAGONISM:
   ISLAM AND THE WEST   180

CONCLUSION: ISLAM AND POLITICS,
A TWENTY-FIRST-CENTURY CHALLENGE   208

Glossary   218

Bibliography   221

Index   227

PREFACE

The theme of this book is both timely and significant for any individual seeking to understand the dynamic of global politics in the twenty-first century. The correlation between Islam and politics is representative of a major phenomenon that has been made manifest across the globe as an intellectual and political force in a myriad of political contexts or locales. The roots of the current phenomenon are found in the twentieth century as a response to the major upheavals experienced in a variety of Muslim domains as a result of the European colonial adventure. Although elements of the past and Islam's 'golden age' are reflected in current discourses, the political interaction and manifestation of Islam by Muslims is very much a modern creation in tune with the major ideological forces of our times.

This study is designed to articulate a vision of a range of Islams as political forms as expressed through thinkers, movements, states and other actors across the reach of the modern globe. Thus, there is no geographic restraint, and the transnational nature of modern political Islam is demonstrated. The themes addressed provide historical depth and an outline of Islam as a faith system within the monotheistic family rooted in the Middle East. Variety and context are illustrated in the breadth of the political as perceived and understood by Muslims across the globe, as forms of protest politics, a reaction to injustice, as terrorism and violence, and a blueprint for political systems. This requires a reflection on the conversations and dialogues which take place within Islam and their heterogeneous character.

This book, then, takes a modern spin on Islam and politics, and demands that the formal as well as the informal dimensions of the political arena be addressed. In this respect the voices of diversity are reflected from a variety of geographic locales, making possible a contextualization of Muslim political activities under wider political themes and philosophical debates about modern politics. This demonstrates the argument that Islam and politics are solidified and marked not by bearded fundamentalist men who set the limited parameters of the debate, but by a myriad of voices often representing the genuine grievances of otherwise silenced populations.

The research for this book was greatly facilitated by the award of a grant from the Arts and Humanities Research Board (AHRB) as well as visiting fellowships at the Centre for Islamic Studies at Oxford University and the Centre for Muslim–Christian Understanding at Georgetown University. I would like to express my gratitude to these institutions as such assistance facilitated my work greatly and allowed me to explore my ideas and develop my research alongside scholars of excellence. There are many individuals who through my encounters with them have shaped and informed this work and who for reasons of security may not be named. Nevertheless I extend my sincere thanks to them and appreciate the encounters that we shared. I would also like to thank the following for their assistance: Mari Palmer and Mark Donnan. Special mention goes to Major Tony Pfaff who offered much valuable comment from the 'other side of the pond' and the 'deserts of Arabia' – his insights were important to much that transpires in this book. My editor at Polity, Andrea Drugan, and David Held have been a great support. The written content of this book has been improved upon by Jean van Altena and production-managed by Sue Leigh. I truly appreciate their immense skill and expertise. Finally thanks to Graham, Josh and Cara for the usual forbearance.

Belfast, 6 October 2003

INTRODUCTION

When Muslim terrorists steered civilian passenger planes into the World Trade Centre in New York and the Pentagon in Washington, and a fourth failed to reach its target but also crashed on September 11th, 2001, the unfolding horror was broadcast across the globe to an incredulous television and radio audience. The attack on America by Muslim terrorists from the al-Qaeda network headed by Osama Bin Laden established a new sense of fear across the globe. Here Islam was instantaneously and visually associated with brutal terrorism. The genesis of this book lies in the ever-deepening interest in the dynamic of the politics that engage and concern Muslims. The issues that are raised and addressed here have been given an added potency in the wake of the attacks on America and the subsequent US-declared War on Terror. The book is designed to serve as an introduction to the political issues and themes which motivate and engage Muslim believers into activism, opposition, rule, reform, violence and power seeking in a variety of contexts in the contemporary world. My *modus operandi* is to look at the issues which motivate and engage a variety of organizations and movements that cross continents. It is my contention that without acknowledging these issues it is impossible to understand the dynamics of a modern-day phenomenon known variously as Muslim or Islamic politics. I hope to avoid myopic stereotype by illustrating the issues with empirical examples from across the globe. In this respect I want to make it clear that this book is not about political Islam as a monolithic phenomenon, but rather the many dimensions of politics that form a connection and dynamic with Islam in its plural form as well. Each chapter addresses a variety of Islamic perspectives on the kind of political issues that dominate and engage other political movements across the globe.

Much of what is understood about contemporary Islam in the West is also portrayed as inherently political in the sense that Western audiences are encouraged to view Muslims as a challenge to what they in the West have and which the Muslims want to do away with and replace with their own divinely inspired order. In other words, Western views of Islam are informed by prejudices (some of them quite deep) about Islam that are generated in the context of the cultures in which they grow up or are located. In the West these cultures are often resistant to and / or experience difficulty with the place that Islam should and does occupy in such contexts. This has created tensions and is given weight by the way in which contemporary Islam and political Islam are portrayed. The role of the mass media, including Internet technology, in 'telling the story' of Islam has been shaped by an agenda that predominantly associates Islam with fanaticism, violence and terror. The media, for example, have often covered Islam as if it were a religious, cultural, political, legal and economic exception to the rules of normative liberalism which apparently govern the rest of the world. Yet I would contend that Islam is unique only in the same way that any religious faith is unique. For the former approach fails to reflect that within Islam, as a faith system, that is part of a broader fabric of political protest, political thinking and philosophical norms in the twentieth and twenty-first century. Muslims who engage with political issues do so bringing with them a variety of world views which would sit across an entire spectrum of opinion. Additionally, Muslims are not unique in this respect, but are similar to others such as socialists or environmentalists who contest the processes and effects of modernization, the lack of opportunities in their own societies for political participation, poor economic growth, indebtedness and lack of rights in the multitude of societies in which they live and play a part. In February 2003 a global anti-war coalition which comprised CND protestors, ordinary people, Greens, Muslim students, national politicians, literary and cultural figures marched across the globe to demonstrate the depth and breadth of public feeling against the prospect of engaging in a war against Iraq. Those Muslims who embraced the views of the coalition were happy to fall under its multi-organizational umbrella in organizing the largest global anti-war protest of 11 million people. Yet, by and large, Muslim engagement with politics is yet to be seen as part of, rather than apart from, other political movements and organizations that grew and were a visible part of broader political landscapes across the globe in the late twentieth century. In this respect a number of myths grew up around such political mobilization which served to perpetrate a fear that Muslim engagement with politics or political issues – particularly in terms of any encounter with the West – was threatening, dangerous and tinged by the fanatic moniker.

The main purpose of this book is to introduce the major themes and analyses of Islam and politics in the contemporary world. By the contemporary world I mean the patterns of global politics which characterized the twentieth century and continue to shape and influence the twenty-first. My approach is to look at the debate about Islam and politics and the Muslim world more generally through a number of important issues. These issues have shaped and characterized modern and contemporary responses within the Muslim polity to political changes of global proportions. Thus, as well as incorporating themes which have emerged at specific historical junctures in response to global phenomena, such as European colonialism, the book will address major issues such as the relationship between Islam and democratization/liberalization, gender-based politics and Islam and the state. I hope to avoid reductive generalizations of Islam and its political guises. In this way we will avoid falling into the familiar trap of assuming that all politics associated with Islam is similar in root and manifestation.

Islam and politics in the contemporary world are frequently portrayed as threatening, extreme, violent and barbaric. Islam's religious and political leaders and those, referred to as Islamists, who advocate a mix of the two approaches, are regularly depicted as bearded hoods brandishing a gun in one hand and a Qur'an in the other. Journalists and news people regularly report events and stories of Muslims that reinforce negative stereotypes. To many news organizations and their editors there is a perception that the Muslim world and Muslims in general, whether they reside in Lyon or Lahore, are a newsworthy threat to the West. In such coverage there is often a failure to recognize Islam's diverse character. Ultimately the demands of the 30-second soundbite or 60-second piece to camera establishes reductive stereotypes as the norm. Yet, as authors such as Eickleman and Piscatori have highlighted, Muslim manifestations of politics are as broad as any manifestation of liberal-democratic politics in the twentieth century, and 'the need to place Muslim politics into multiple and shifting contexts thus becomes apparent' (Eickleman and Piscatori, 1996, p. 20). In this respect a major perception needs to be exploded. This perception is based on the belief that Islamic politics represents a rigid pattern of activity undertaken by a bitter religious group with a major grudge against the rest of the world.

The task here is to explore the issue and present a multi-faceted account of Islamic politics in a manner that is useful to students who are new to the subject. The majority of such students already carry with them a generalized, and often stereotypical, view of Muslim politics. Such views are not atypical as long as the prejudice behind such a position is acknowledged and the further acquisition of knowledge on the subject takes on board a wider variety of views. For the novice, Islamic politics, Islamism and manifestations of Muslim politics are represented in the following ways: bearded, violent, terrorists, veiled women, beheadings and suicide bombers. Such preconceptions are natural; as Edward Said has acerbically asserted, 'knowledge of Islam and of Islamic peoples has generally proceeded not only from dominance and confrontation but also from cultural antipathy' (Said, 1997, p. 163).

In the West followers of Islam and, more generally, the image of Islam have never been a good news topic. It is futile, therefore, to deny a preconception of Islam and politics—particularly in the contemporary era dominated by mass media and technological wonders. Opinions and views will have been shaped from a variety of diverse sources, but primarily through the representation of Muslims in the media of films, news, art, music, books and television programmes. The purpose of this text, then, is to begin the task of challenging such preconceptions, seeing how they differ in the many political realms in which Muslims live and participate, and to build a new store of knowledge that is more balanced and informed, free of the bias and prejudices we hold. Bias, in this context, is a passionate and emotive term. For when all is said and done, it is difficult, in this day and age, for any scholar of Islamic politics to present an account of this modern and contemporary phenomenon that is a model of value-free neutrality. Writing and researching the subject have become a form of politics and interaction itself, with Western and non-Western, Muslim and non-Muslim, orientalist and 'apologist' scholars, activists and camp-followers, falling on either side of a political fence which has been constructed around the subject. This book will strive to address these debates and the way in which the forces of modern political Islam are perceived and understood at a global level.

Too often the politics of Islam has been portrayed as the politics of extremes and associated with instability, revolution and violence. This text, while acknowledging such activities, also sets out to illustrate the other agendas which reflect political Islam in its contemporary manifestation. In so doing, it will reflect on the immutable essences of the faith, which in turn have been interpreted and applied in the contemporary era to a breath-taking breadth of contexts and events. In the contemporary era, dimensions of Islam and politics have entered public consciousness in both Muslim and non-Muslim societies. Coupled to the phenomenon of religious resurgence that has been triggered in a variety of faith systems in response to secularized orders, Islam as faith and then politics has become present in a myriad of ways. Islam has become the hallmark of states in Iran, Sudan and Afghanistan – states that have emerged from revolution, conflict and upheaval previously ruled by secular authoritarian elements. Where revolution has failed to install Islam at the head of the state, dimensions of Muslim politics are found to both legitimate and oppose diverse forms of rule across the globe. In this sense Islam is labelled as a transnational opposition phenomenon of importance. The threat that is perceived as implicit to this phenomenon has led Western governments to stand in the way of such opposition for the sake of what is believed to be global security.

The Muslim immigration phenomenon in both Western European states and North America also reinforced the notion of Islam as a political, military and existential threat. This issue has grown in certain policy-making circles and is evident in the emergence of a discourse about immigration, race and the threat from within. The presence of Muslim Europeans or Muslim North Americans has become perceptible, adding a new dimension to the debate about Islamic politics. For previously such discourse was coloured by a popular association with the Arab world, in ignorance of the fact that the majority of Muslims live outside the geographic reach of the Middle East in a variety of other locales.

Islamic revivalism and resurgence are translated and found in public domains across the globe and perceived as deliberately undermining the status quo. In this respect the status quo is found in a myriad of state types. Islamist and fundamentalist movements and their leaders are understood as opposing secular rule, Communist rule, democratic rule, liberal rule, plural rule and the 'wrong' kind of Muslim rule. The alternative is understood as a very narrowly defined, fundamentalist, totalitarian and backward-looking phenomenon.

A number of important themes, therefore, require addressing in reflecting on this important factor in contemporary global politics and international relations. The first theme is Islam as a faith and its manifestation as a modern political phenomenon. In this respect important distinctions between spiritual dimensions of practising adherents and those otherwise labelled Muslim as a category of political allegiance need to be made. It has been argued that Muslims have increasingly fallen under the spell of revivalism and the particular political orientation that accompanies it. This means a lot in terms of internal political dynamics in a variety of Muslim domains, as well as patterns of contemporary transnational and global politics. For it is important to state that traditional approaches to international relations failed to recognize the portent of Islam as a modern political force. Islamists take inspiration from a variety of forces in fashioning a vision of statehood shaped by Muslim tenets. It is this variety, which is both historical and modern in inspiration, that is perhaps most surprising. In theory a number of principles or characteristics may be identified. Yet in reality, statehood, Muslim style, is manifest in a number of different hues. Such examination will also reveal the dynamic of political institutions that characterize so-called Islamic state structures, including the legislative function and the role of leaders. This should shed light on the discourse of some scholars who argue that Islamic statehood is inherently totalitarian and despotic. Islamist discourse can also be seen to wrestle with these issues. This is the case particularly in terms of a form of opposition politics that seems at odds not only with the tempo of many modern nation-states but with the increasingly globalized norms and values of liberal democracy.

Oppositionism, then, is a dimension of Muslim politics that needs acknowledgement. This has taken the form of protest politics in a variety of domains where plural politics is absent or the Muslim voice is marginalized from the political mainstream. This is the case in a variety of contexts and in relation to a variety of issues that may be more or less Muslim or Islamic in focus. Indeed, I would argue that the dynamics of Muslim protest share much in common with protest politics and movements from other cultures and earlier eras. Such protest may be rooted in particular traditions within the Islamic spectrum or may be part of the reactive process experienced by Muslim populations living in authoritarian regimes. This in turn points to the debate about the absence of democracy in Muslim domains and the anti-democratic credentials that some argue characterize Islam. Such positions can be tested empirically and measured in terms of the modern political dynamic. For whether Muslim discourse can be considered as possessing democratic credentials impacts on a variety of political activities, including opportunities for ordinary citizens, women included, to participate in the political life of their country. The resort to terrorism certainly changes the debate about democratic norms and behaviours as they relate to Muslim domains. Hence the very political culture of Islam is highlighted, with contrasting positions and arguments outlined. The gender debate as a facet of Muslim or Islamist politics has become a major motif in the contemporary era. The image of the Muslim woman as veiled and secluded (and thus excluded) is dominant, relaying particular understandings of the contemporary political phenomenon. In reality the picture or image is not one-dimensional and addresses a variety of themes as they relate to the experience of women in a variety of political arenas.

The chapter on Islam and violence provides an important focus for much of the current interest and morbid fascination with Islam in the contemporary world. I do not believe that there is much to be gained by seeking to regard and reflect Islam and its political manifestations as inherently violent. Islam has been labelled as violent and dominated by an atavistic embrace of a particular kind of violence, that being terrorism. Authors such as Samuel Huntington in his employment of the 'clash of civilizations' thesis does indeed expound this perspective of Islam – with particular attention to its 'bloody borders'. Of course this perspective makes sense in light of the 'senselessness' motivating the violence of the men who steered civilian airliners into the Twin Towers in New York and the Pentagon in Washington. It helps make sense of a new international uni-polar order where significant challenge has been mounted by mainly non-state actors as a transnational force. The Cold War may indeed be over, yet this approach is problematic in that I believe it reflects the same kind of simplistic division of the world into two opposing sides, with Islam replacing the Communist East as the new threat to the West. I have acknowledged the value of this approach, but it is also flawed and narrow. It reduces the complexities of a multi-actor international order, and in particular the role of Muslims in it, to a two-sided division where diverse communities are 'lumped together'. In this sense, then, the manifestation of violence or terror by one group targeted at the other does create negative stereotypical and hostile understandings. The chasm between Islam and the West thus appears to deepen – fuelled by mutually reinforcing suspicion of the other and exploited by political and religious leaders. The absence of differentiation ignores much of the reality fuelled by the *realpolitik* and economic necessity of global orders founded on trade relationships and increasing interconnection and interdependency. For many Islamists the West is reduced to a symbol of American power as it is understood in a limited and restricted fashion. The diversity of European power and politics often remains entirely lost in such analyses, perpetuating a myth of mutual reductions, mutual stereotypes and mutual antagonism, rather than the reality of the rich history and diverse present.

The political Islam to which this book refers is far from one-dimensional, but a plural phenomenon that demands careful delineation. For the dissonance and myth sustained in the myopic views of certain leaders from both sides of the chasm that appears to divide the contemporary global system into 'Islam and the Rest' is difficult to overcome without careful distinction and exploration.

1

ISLAM AND POLITICS DEFINED

Introduction

Islam is a faith system, a religion and identity for over one billion Muslims across the contemporary globe. The word 'Islam' is Arabic and means to submit – submit one's will to God (Allah). Arabic is regarded as the language of Islam. When Muslim schoolchildren in Bradford learn of their faith and read its texts, they are encouraged to do so in Arabic. Islam is the major religion of the Middle East, and in addition there are major Muslim populations in South-East Asia, Central Asia, India and Africa and minority Muslim populations in Europe and North America. Indeed, it is important to note that the majority of Muslims live outside the Middle East. Nevertheless, the Middle East is perceived among many Westerners as somehow synonymous with Islam, and the fact that the majority comprise populations elsewhere is regularly overlooked. This is because the region has some of the most homogeneous Muslim states and the longest history of Islamic rule, and is considered central to the faith of Muslims through both prayer and pilgrimage. Moreover, it is the case that some Muslim states of the Middle East have been significant funders of Muslim communities and activities globally.

Contemporary Islam represents a dynamic thread of faith and identity that promotes a set of beliefs established in the seventh century by the son of a merchant from the deserts of Arabia and known as Mohammad. Following the prophetic tradition of others such as Abraham, Moses and Jesus, Mohammad experienced his first divine revelation from God – Allah – as a middle-aged and fairly prosperous married man. From this point on, and as a result of other divine revelations, the Prophet Mohammad preached a new message and a new set of ideas for organizing society, power, economy and politics that challenged the status quo and prevailing power-holders. It is not considered apt to think of contemporary parallels to great historic figures, but it is not difficult to imagine the impact that this promotion of a new way of thinking, interacting and living together would have in a society used to the worship of more than one god, that was familiar with foreign rule through the powers of Byzantium and maintained tradition through strict adherence to tribal lore and norms. Islam as a new system of faith, following in the monotheistic tradition of Judaism and Christianity, would become more than just a group of faithful followers.

All of these developments have played a part in shaping myriad manifestations of Islam and Muslim identities in the contemporary world. Through the interface with power, Islam was always regarded as a political religion or as religio-political, and as made manifest in a broad variety of forms. Additionally, as a religio-political phenomenon it is argued that Islam affects, shapes or is responsive to any number of contemporary political issues. These include gender, the environment, economy, conflict, the search for peace, local politics, human rights, anti-globalization and so on. In fact, it is difficult to think of a contemporary political issue that does not animate particular adherents to Islam.

In seeking to frame a response, take the initiative, or ascertain a position, Muslim believers turn to the text in which what was divinely revealed by Allah to the Prophet Mohammad is recorded: the Qur'an. The Qur'an is also the primary source of all law in Islam. Islamic law is known as the *shari'a*. Additionally, Muslims have the sayings and pattern of the Prophet's own life as recorded in literature known as the *sunna* and *hadith*. The sunna means the way of life as led by the Prophet Mohammad and in recorded form is the second source of Muslim law and jurisprudence. The hadith are the narrated texts and literatures that relate the life of the Prophet Mohammad and the example he set for others to follow. Those others include the close companions and followers of Mohammad who succeeded in leading the new faith after his death. Such sayings and examples were not directly recorded at the time, but were the output of Muslim scholars in the seventh and eighth centuries who sought to commit to written form what was divinely revealed or inspired in the life and the sayings of the

Prophet Mohammad. In the twenty-first century the religion and its scriptures have the potential to remain as contemporary or as modern as the scholars of Islam choose them to be. While modern phenomena that could never have been envisaged in seventh-century Arabia have arisen, such as web-based communication, the AIDS crisis and broadcast media, Muslims still turn to their faith to define what is permitted and what is forbidden (*halal* and *haram*). For those Muslims to whom their faith remains an important dimension of their whole identity, then, the ancient texts will always have a modern or contemporary resonance.

Islam as a faith system

The basic tenet of the faith and the Qur'an is the oneness of God and the belief that the Prophet Mohammad was God's messenger and divinely inspired. A Muslim is born into the faith; there is no practice of baptism or other rituals associated with inclusion in the faith. There are many 'kinds' of Muslim in the same way as there are many kinds of Christians. There are denominational schisms between Sunni and Shi'a, Alawite and Ismaili, and Druze. There are orthodox Wahabi Muslims and reformist Sunni Muslims. There are quietist Muslim sects such as the variety of Sufi brotherhood or *tariqa* that focuses on the development of a close spiritual bond with God. There are observant Muslims and non-observant Muslims, Muslims who are liberal and others who are described as fundamentalist, Muslim men and women, Muslim feminists and Muslim terrorists. One way or another they are all bound by a fundamental link to the faith of the religion founded in the seventh century by the Prophet Mohammad, yet they represent many types of Muslim. One young American Muslim woman describes her experiences, enriched not just by an opportunity for higher education but by the interconnection that transcends borders through the web thus: 'In college, we meet so many different Muslims – they are all of different backgrounds, cultures and most importantly, thought systems. Then, there's Internet. A lot of Muslims surf the net ... these are also places where you see the most diverse group of Muslims' (Pervez, 2002).

Famous contemporary Muslims include Malcolm X, a Black-African criminal who converted to Islam while in prison; Mohammad Ali, probably one of the most famous sports personalities in the world, who converted to Islam during his career and was imprisoned for five years after refusing the draft to Vietnam because of his religious principles. Principled conscientious objection by this anti-war Muslim led to Ali's vilification in the American media and accusations of treachery. Prince Naseem, the British boxing sensation of the 1990s, has made no secret of his attachment to Islam. Others include Chris Eubank, Yousef Islam – formerly 1970s' pop hero Cat Stevens – and Ayatollah Khomeini. In the United States of America Islam is the fastest-growing religion, and Muslims there include a number of hip-hop stars such as Mos Def (Dante Smith) and Rapper Q-Tip. These people are public figures for whom their 'Muslim-ness' is core to their identity. In the United Kingdom, Muslims serve in the House of Lords and the House of Commons, as well as constitute their own forums through community organizations and the Muslim parliament. In Africa, Asia, the Middle East and the former central Soviet Republics, Muslims serve in governments that rule over Muslims and non-Muslims alike. In sum, being Muslim is a multi-faceted phenomenon that can transcend race, language and culture in the same way that being European can. Like being European, too, dimensions of Muslim identity can be unpicked and made sense of in localized ways.

At a fundamental level, observant Muslims recognize and respect the revelations of other monotheistic traditions. Abraham is as important to the Muslim as he is to the Jew. Jesus is recognized as a prophet (but not the son of God); the difference in Islam lies in the belief that God's revelations are the final revelation, yet, as a prophet, Mohammad follows in the footsteps of Moses, Abraham and Jesus. The Muslim holy day is Friday. All Muslims are obliged by their faith to maintain five duties which are referred to as the five 'pillars' of Islam. These are as follows.

1   The *Iman*, or *Shihada* – profession of faith. This involves saying with full acceptance 'There is no God but God and Muhammad is his prophet'. Upon this act an individual becomes a Muslim. Profession of faith is a fundamental act that is neither unique nor specific to Islam. It is a verbal attestation of an identity shaped by faith rather than profane or secular influences. The profession of faith defines a Muslim by his or her faith.

2   *Salat* – prayer. This is a commitment to pray five times a day, according to the call to prayer, facing Mecca and saying Friday noonday prayers at the mosque. The call to prayer is issued from the mosque by the muezzin. In bygone days the muezzin climbed to the highest point in the mosque and through the power of his

melodious voice issued the call to the faithful to make their prayers. In the contemporary era, modern technology means that the call to prayer can be broadcast from a loudspeaker with the effect remaining the same. While all around may change, there is a five times daily reminder that Islam can remain as a constant in often turbulent and chaotic lives. In 1989 I asked a leading activist and fundamentalist Islamist leader in the Gaza Strip what the call to prayer meant to him. His response embodies Islam's appeal during a period of major upheaval: 'For me, it reminds me what our struggle is all about, it keeps me fixed to my faith when all around may be a sea of chaos, destruction and death. My enemies may be at the door but the *salat* alerts me to my faith as something that is always there' (Saftawi, 1989). The call to prayer is broadcast from mosques throughout the Muslim world to remind the faithful of prayer times. Muslims, however, do not have to attend the mosque to pray; the prayers may be recited almost anywhere – in a house, a workplace, out-of-doors, etc. Prayers should be made on a special prayer mat which is rolled out to face Mecca. Ritual washing (hands and feet in particular) along with certain postures as well as specific verses of the Qur'an are prescribed for these prayers. Friday, the Muslim holy day, is when special prayers are recited at the mosque – particularly the noonday prayer which most obser-vant Muslims will endeavour to attend. Prayers are led by the Imam. In the contemporary era, as religious observance has in-creased, Friday prayer is one of the most visible signs of the impact that Islam now has on public life in general. In the early 1980s in the Jordanian capital of Amman, Friday prayers were a modest affair in the downtown central mosque; yet twenty years later, Friday prayer now draws a crowd of faithful adherents who not only fill the mosque and its courtyards but spill out on to the pavement outside and the side roads beyond. A demonstrable attachment to Islam is made visible in the massed ranks of prostrate worshippers.

3   *Zakat* – charity tax or alms. This involves the payment of a certain percentage of earned income to assist the poor, the widowed and orphaned children in particular, and is considered the third obligation of the faith. The payment of *zakat* becomes obligatory on Muslims whenever wealth is created. The Qur'an states: 'Prosperous are the believers who in prayers are humble and from idle talk turn away and at almsgiving are active' (Sura XXIII: 4). The Zakat Foundation of India, for example, disburses alms from Muslim donors to a variety of projects, including small business assistance, house repairs, assisting people to find employment, dowries for girls and assistance for widows and their

families. In states where social assistance is poor or subject to disruption, this obligation of faith has been used to maintain and protect vulnerable communities. This view is echoed by British Muslim scholar and legal expert Zaki Badawi: 'Zakat funds should plan to achieve the aim of the Shari'a – that is, to find a long-term solution to poverty and dependence ... The imposition of an organised Zakat collection system should be the objective of every Islamic state, both for the benefit of social peace and religious fulfilment' (Badawi, 2001, p. 2). Here *zakat*, in a modern context, is constructed as meaning more than almsgiving. It is interpreted by modern scholars as having an important function in terms of poverty reduction, welfare and the function of the state in such issues. *Zakat* becomes a means for development and assistance to the most vulnerable elements of society.

4   Ramadan. This means keeping a fast (*sawm*) from dawn to dusk during the holy month of Ramadan. Certain people are excepted – such as travellers, breast-feeding mothers, or children. The fast is an abstinence from all food and drink, including water. The fast is broken (break-fast) at dusk each day. Ramadan is an event shared by observant Muslims across the globe, an individual, yet communal act that underlines the notion of community (*umma*) and oneness (*tahwid*) that underpins Islam. The end of Ramadan is celebrated by a feast known as *Eid al-Fitr*. For Muslims Ramadan is perceived as a time for reflection about their faith and relationship as individuals with God. British former WBO champion and convert to Islam Chris Eubank explains what Ramadan means to him: 'Because my career is about fighting I understand what fasting can achieve and what it does ... It gives you an inner strength ... looking into yourself, for at the end of the day that is where God is, not in the synagogue or the church, but yourself. It makes you reflect on yourself' (BBC, Faces of Islam transcript). Ramadan, therefore, roots observant Muslims in their faith and creates a focus back on to the community of believers to which they belong. It establishes a communal sense of belonging in so many contexts, in many of which modern society works against such principles. Ramadan and its feast are a celebration of Muslim identity.

5   *Hajj*. The *hajj* or pilgrimage, if possible, should be undertaken at least once in a lifetime to Mecca, Medina and Islam's other holy sites in Saudi Arabia or additionally cities like Jerusalem, where the third most holy site in Islam – the Haram al-Sharif and al-Aqsa mosque – is located. In contemporary times the *Hajj* is manifest in an annual gathering at Mecca in Saudi Arabia. Mecca assumes

importance because the Prophet Mohammad was born there. Muslims are also obligated by their faith to face Mecca five times a day for prayer in recognition of its spiritual centrality. At Mecca pilgrims gather at a shrine, the Kaba, to perform the rituals of *Hajj*. Around two million Muslims from across the globe arrive in Saudi Arabia for the *Hajj*. Their journeys are diverse, and a great literature has been generated from the stories of pilgrims from far-off lands undertaking the most important journey of their lives. Indeed, from the point of embarkation the journey becomes imbued with import-ant rites and rituals, and pilgrims attest to a heightened sense of spirituality. Malcom X, the Black Muslim convert, describes this experience in his famous autobiography. Describing his journey from Cairo to the Saudi airport of Jeddah he reflects: 'Planeloads of pilgrims were taking off every few minutes, but the airport was jammed with more...those not going were asking others to pray for them at Mecca...Packed in the plane were white, black, brown, red and yellow people, blue eyes and blonde hair, and my kinky red hair – all together, brothers! All honouring the same God Allah, all in turn giving equal honour to each other' (X, 1965, p. 436).

Meeting, perhaps for the first time, so many Muslims of different races, cultures and domains under the guise of full equality is symbolic of the 'equalizing' of the pilgrim experience. Thus, all pilgrims are simply and similarly attired: 'we took off our clothes and put on two white towels...a pair of simple sandals,' remarks Malcolm X, 'Every one of the thousands...was dressed this way. You could be a king or a peasant and no one would know' (X, 1965, p. 435). Mecca itself is prohibited to all non-Muslims, a site of Muslim exclusivity. There the apex of the rite of pilgrimage is reached. 'Then I saw the Ka'ba,' writes Malcolm X. 'It was being circumambulated by thousands upon thousands of praying pil-grims, both sexes, and every size, shape, colour, and race in the world' (X, 1965, p. 450). The *Hajj* then represents an important dimension of faith which is shared in other religious traditions in the present day. Its emphasis on equality in the eyes of each other as well as God underlines a fundamental tenet of Islam as a con-temporary phenomenon.

These five pillars of faith combine to make a comprehensive commitment to faith by observant Muslims. They also impact on the shaping of Muslim identities as they relate to the discourse on power and, therefore, politics in their own societies and beyond. Oftentimes such issues are codified or reflected through the four major orthodox schools of Islamic jurisprudence – they are named after their founders – the Hanafi, Hanbali, Maliki and Shafi. *Shari'a* (Islamic) law is based on the Qur'an and the *hadith*. In some Muslim countries it is contended that the entire legal system and legal administration is Islamic, and the only courts of law to be found are *Shari'a* or Islamic courts. There courts are presided over by Qadi's – Muslim judges. In countries such as Iran and Saudi Arabia, all legal issues, including commercial or business matters, are, in principle, interpreted through Islamic lenses, and thus modern legislation is grafted on to traditional Muslim legal statutes. In other countries, however, the Islamic law applies to all personal status issues concerning Muslims – such as divorce and inheritance – while secular civil law is applied to all inhabitants. In 1998 following a military putsch, the new Prime Minister of Pakistan, Nawaz Sharif, announced that under his new administration Shari'a law would be fully introduced into the country. Women's groups and human rights activists were among those 'who... accused him of using the Shari'a as an excuse to amend the constitution and give his government sweeping powers that threaten freedom of expression and the judiciary's independence' (Bhatia, 1998).

Eternal internal difference

As in other faith systems, internal difference – that which is sectarian – characterizes Islam. The major sectarian difference within Islam is that between Sunni and Shi'a. The division or split originally came during a battle over succession upon the death of the Prophet Mohammad. On Mohammad's death, Abu Bakr was chosen as Caliph (successor). He held office from 632 to 634, and was succeeded by Omar (634–44) and then Othman (644–56). Those who formed themselves as Shi'a, however, believed that Ali, the prophet's son-in-law, was the true and legitimate successor to the Prophet Mohammad. For them, qualification for such an important post included recognition of the importance of the blood line. In fact, Ali became Caliph in 656 in succession to Othman, but he in turn was defeated at the battle of Siffin by the Syrian-based Mu'awiya, who in claiming victory became Caliph. Later, in 680, Ali's son Hussein, who was a grandson of the Prophet Mohammad, organized a leadership claim for Islam but was killed by his Arab Ummayad opponents near Karbala (in modern-day

Iraq). Hussein's death was understood by his followers as a martyrdom in the name of Islam – and is still commemorated as a day of mourning and repentance (*ashura*).

The Shi'a supporters of Ali and Hussein also viewed leadership of the Muslim community through an alternative lens. Such alternative thinking combined with historical experience would greatly influence the discourse within Shi'a Islam with regard to power, politics and leadership in Muslim domains. Their successors, those who led the Shi'a community, believed that legitimate leadership rested in the notion of imamate – the omniscient authentic descendant of the Prophet reflecting both the spiritual and the political dimensions of leadership. This represented an oppositional stance in relation to the attempt at orthodoxy promoted by the Sunni Arabs. Hence, opposition has been cited as a characteristic of Shi'a Islam, yet there is much evidence in the historical records that suggests as much capacity for quietism as opposition in such domains. There is an additional element to this schism that has been introduced by some. This reflects on the geographic locus of Iran as the home of Shi'ism. Hence, ethnic difference between the 'Persians' and the 'Arabs' is represented as a dimension of this issue, although, 'ethnic conflict between the Arabs and the *mawalis* (non-Arab Muslims) was not itself the origin of the Islamic schism between Sunna and Shi'a. Rather', argues Tibi, 'this ethnic conflict deepened the schism in the course of history' (Tibi, 2001, p. 41). Yet it could be similarly argued that while sectarian/ethnic difference exists in modern-day states like Iraq between the Shi'a majority and the ruling Sunni minority, it certainly does not do so to the extent that it has led to conflict and civil war, as in Northern Ireland. When Shi'a Muslims, encouraged by the West, rose against Saddam Hussein in the ill-fated rebellion of 1991 (and the Kurds in the North revolted too), it was because the Ba'th regime and the leader of that regime promoted a reign of terror that affected every Iraqi citizen. Saddam Hussein did use the pretext that the 'Persian presence' in reference to his own Shi'a population represented a threat from within and persecuted its clerical establishment. This should be seen, however, as no more than another excuse for oppression irrespective of ethnic, religious or political background. Sectarian difference has thus been utilized by political leaders to legitimate antipathy or particular plays for power in contemporary contexts. Just as Saddam Hussein 'rediscovered' his faith and utilized it in his ideological positioning against the West – even to the extent that in 1990 he ordered a change to the national flag of Iraq changing it with an assertion of the Muslim profession of faith, so too have others across the sectarian divide. Ayatollah Khomeini, the leader of Iran from 1979 to his death in 1989, established a discourse for politics and governance *vilayat al-fiqh* which took a new perspective on the tradition of the imamate of Shi'a Islam, with the task of leadership placed in the hands of the clerical establishment. In this way he laid the religious and ideological foundations for the principle of clerical rule (theocracy) that would characterize the political structures of the post-revolutionary state, colouring its politics in every dimension. Difference in both these cases was a reflection of leadership rather than societal relations, tension, pattern and proximity to the other. Making a virtue out of difference, generating group loyalty or identity by maintaining an insider/outsider stance – particularly within the realm of religious identity – a 'chosen people' syndrome is not uncommon, or specifically unique to Islam. In manifestations of unionist and loyalist identity in the civil conflict that unfolded in Northern Ireland, religious destiny and identity became powerful factors in the interface between politics and faith. In Iraq the Sunni–Shi'a difference has never been historically exploited.

Islam as political

The notion that faith no longer had a public political role and its removal from the public arena in this guise grew with Enlightenment thinking in Europe. The historical relationship between Christian faith and politics – particularly in relation to concepts of divine kingship, rule or governance, or more specifically the alliance of church and state through powerful theocratic frameworks – had defined many dimensions of politics in Europe for centuries. Enlightenment thinking, however, with its focus on principles of the sovereignty and democracy of man, made manifest in revolution and republic in countries like France and later allied to the forces of developing capitalism and industrialization, succeeded in undermining religious influence in the political domain. The absolutist doctrines of faith were undermined by 'new truths' and philosophies that accounted for a disconnected political space. What then is the linkage between the religion and political thought in Islam? And why is it so important?

Esposito believes that the integral relation in Islam between religion and politics has meant that almost any social or political event becomes a 'religious issue'. Political rulers were, therefore, also a kind of religious leader; they had to make sense of reality against the 'normative ideal' of Islam. And 'Muslim jurists and theologians (during Abbasid rule) had a twofold purpose: to maintain the divine origin and purpose of the Islamic community and to legitimate the claims and rule of the caliphs' (Esposito, 1984, p. 29). This makes quite explicit the connection between the religious and the political, with an implicit distinction between political and clerical rule in the name of Islam. Moreover, from this period onward the essential theme of Islamic political thought may be identified: Allah has absolute authority over the state.

Authority is delegated to the people as God's instrument to the world. The caliphate serves as God's and the people's servant – elected or nominated by the people – and has certain moral character. The caliph must uphold and defend the *shari'a*. Based on these fundamental themes a diverse body of work has emerged over the centuries representing Islamic political thought and records of the historic practice of politics in Muslim domains. In the contemporary era such political thought has engaged with social revolution, the colonial experience, secularization of the state, globalization, conflict resolution and terrorism. Yet for all this diversity, Islam has maintained an immutable core that has important consequences for political dynamics. The impact of the political on the religious, and vice versa, has resulted in a complicated history where the political hue of Islam assumed greater importance usually as a result of, or in response to, a challenge or contest for authority. The history of Islam and its political dimension is one of ebb and flow and periods of revivalism and renewal. Islam's followers have challenged corrupt authority and rebelled against the despotic in a battle against injustice. Dynamic, turning and reaching out to respond to the imperative of the 'here and now', the followers of Islam have contributed to the development of political systems which dominate large parts of the contemporary world. In the twentieth century, the revival of Islam as a political response to the oppressive downturn of Muslim-dominated societies exploited by colonial leaders compelled religious leaders into action. Colonial rule and the accompanying experience of modernization also meant that the impact of Western-inspired secularism requiring the breaking of the bonds between Islam and politics clashed jarringly with the hitherto held notions of political, religious, economic and social norms and authority that played their part in the governance of Muslim domains.

Resurgence and revival as a contemporary phenomenon

In the latter half of the twentieth century, Islamist movements, groups and ideologues appeared to sweep through Muslim domains. The notion that with globalization and the end of ideology and history a more homogenized global politics might emerge appeared to be severely challenged by the Islamist phenomenon. By Islamist here I mean to refer to the broadest dimensions of faith and politics across a spectrum of thought and opinion. This concept is not state-centric, nor is it a tool for exclusive analysis that ignores other forces and contexts. Indeed, it is these forces and contexts that give rise to much that is inherently responsive rather than proactive within Islamist discourse. As a product of the revivalist programme alongside changes in other dynamic forces internal and external to Muslim domains, the religious aspect of the political is recognized through the conception of Islamism. This does not necessarily entail one engaging in a reductive exercise where everything is essentialized; in fact, I would contend that it is for its breadth and diversity that the Islamist phenomenon should be recognized.

Islamism must be recognized. All too often policy-makers and politicians have been seen to engage in attempts to 'wish the problem away' in the vain hope that through strategies of overkill, repression and security crackdowns, Islamists and the message that they preach will go away. Others contend that Islam must be taken out of the picture in terms of confronting anti-democratic or authoritarian tendencies across the developing world. Yet how can analysis and understanding of the politics of Muslim domains such as Nigeria, Afghanistan, Pakistan, Indonesia or Chechnya be constructive if policy-makers, politicians, soldiers and academics limit the scope of inquiry to narrow definitions predicated on one-dimensional perspectives? For in ignoring historical, cultural, economic and other dynamic factors, what constitutes Islam for more than a billion people is limited, rigid and fixed. Geographic, ethnic, linguistic, economic, cultural and other factors coalescing in particular specificities unique to time and place are lost. The West, by essentializing Islam, also reduces itself.

The growing presence of an Islamist global trend, whereby Muslims are generalized as engaged in a political struggle to overthrow political leaders and use any means possible to achieve their goal, was underscored in the West when al-Qaeda flew American airliners into the Twin Towers in New York and the Pentagon in

Washington. Hence the belief that Islam and its adherents represent a major if not *the* major threat to contemporary global politics. Up to this point in September 2001 it was widely believed in the West that the Islamist phenomenon would never be visited so directly on the doorstep of the West. There was a belief that, despite successive policy agendas promoted by a variety of Western governments, resulting in major interference in the political, cultural and economic dynamics of Muslim domains, the West was somehow protected by its principles of democracy, equality and liberty. And while Muslims believed that such an act of terror was unrepresentative of Islam and the Muslim belief system, Bin Laden's political complaints resonated in many Muslim domains. ———

In these ways Islamism has begun to alter – not necessarily dominate – but at least blur the focus of society–state relations from the bottom upwards in locales as diverse as Kandahar, Cairo and Chicago. Under revivalist programmes, some of which have even been spearheaded by the state in an attempt to undercut the Islamist competition, the place of religion, and more specifically Islam, in people's lives has been reassessed and consciously deliberated. Thus, in some contexts the place of religion in people's lives – as both a public and a private issue – has increased, either voluntarily or through coercion. In these contexts society, particularly in public manifestation, becomes more Islamic. We can see that this was the case of Afghanistan under the Taliban. Under the extreme fundamentalist strictures of the Taliban-led government in Kabul, Afghan society was Islamified from above, codified through law and imposed with force. For women this meant that they were denied an education and were virtually banished from the public sphere. For men, enforcement of the growing and wearing of a Taliban-approved beard was one of the most obvious manifestations of coercion. Far from Afghanistan, the Islamization of society in the Palestinian Gaza Strip was the result of a number of factors, including the spearheading of Islamization supported and funded by Gulf state organizations. In addition, the Israeli government and its apparatus of military occupation tacitly encouraged Islamization as a much-hoped for foil to Palestinian nationalist sentiment and anti-occupation fervour.

Revivalism, or the resurgence of faith, was not unique to Islam in the latter decades of the twentieth century. Faith resurgence and revivalism have become an important dimension of analysis for those seeking to explain changing political and public discourses in places like the United States of America and India. In these contexts religious revivalism was a reflection of a growing tension in modernizing societies between the secular perspective dominating public discourse and the marginalization of religion to private realms and practice. For some groups, movements, organizations and ideologues, revivalism was explicitly linked to aspirations for control of the state and its apparatus. This, for example, helps to explain the rise of Hindu fundamentalism in India and the way in which ideologues of the movement have focused on the need to obtain state control to determine the nature of modern-day India as a Hindu product. Control would surely mean an opportunity to remake the state as Islamic, Hindu, Christian, Jewish or whatever. Revivalism, though, reflects more than a political agenda. It is important to remember that revivalist/resurgence groups are active in more than just political arenas and that there are dimensions of revivalism that have no political bearing at all. Part of this general phenomenon are the Islamists. For many of them, an Islamic state, the resurrection of the caliphate, theocracy, democracy under Islamic leadership, Islam and monarchy, and so on are but a few dimensions of this particular manifestation of the phenomenon. Universality is not a hallmark of it. This can be illustrated by a small but powerful example. In December 2002, at a much-postponed and hastily arranged conference in London, in the full glare of the world's media, the representatives of more than fifty exiled Iraqi groups spanning its ethnic, religious and political spectrum met. Within the confines of the conference, many visions of a future Iraq, including some with an Islamist dimension, were debated. Iraq's Shi'a opposition was represented by more than one group – some with links to Iran and others not. Even within the Islamist fold, therefore, more than one vision was promoted. The specificity of Islamism was further epitomized by a small but noisy demonstration outside the conference centre that included other Islamists who objected to the conference altogether. Representing the Islamist *Hizb al-Tahrir* (Liberation Party), demonstrators denounced the delegates at the conference for undermining Islamic principles. The visual juxtaposition of a variety of Muslim Shi'a clerics in the garb of their office inside the conference differing vehemently with each other and noisy Muslim demonstrators outside should not be overlooked.

Of course an Islamic state system or a resurrection of the caliphate has the potential to alter the nature of politics in Muslim domains. Geo-strategic considerations, prevailing cultural and other traditions such as those of tribe, competing faith systems and class structures impact and ameliorate the impact of such attempts at political influence and governance. In contemporary

Nigeria the impact of a revivalist agenda has been made manifest in regional rather than central structures. This is explicable by the nature of the federalism in Nigeria, the geographic distribution of the population with a Muslim preponderance in the north and a Christian preponderance in the south, as well as tribal, patriarchal and economic factors. Here Islamic revivalism is federalized, working within and exploiting the advantages offered by federal approaches to politics, particularly in relation to ethnically diverse societies. A federal system is a form of governance with two levels: one central, the other provincial. This allows for some autonomy in governance and was manifest in the arrangements for state and government in the United States of America in 1774. In principle, governance is about parity rather than the centre coming before the province. Separate spheres of jurisdiction are thus maintained. Thus federal states maintain their independence in specific political and economic domains as well as judicial and security (internal) functions. In 1999, after more than fifteen years of military rule, there was a return to democratic federalism in Nigeria. In its wake the force of Islamic revivalism was apparent. In this new democratic federal structure, twelve of Nigeria's northern states adopted Islamic law (*shari'a*) as the new legal code for their domains. High-profile cases, including those of Safiya Husseini and Amina Lawal, demonstrated the unease at the coercive rather than voluntary nature of *shari'a* law. Additionally, a fear has grown, exacerbated by inter-religious tensions, that the introduction of *shari'a* in such states is the first step on a slippery road to a radical fundamentalist take-over.

Such moves towards greater Islamist governance and involvement in politics are thus experienced as a set-back. It is the fear of revolutionary, radical, fanatic and fundamentalist Islamism that has also motivated the current Western conditions of both fascination and repulsion at this phenomenon. Political Islam, Islamism, Islamic fundamentalism, Islam and politics, Muslim politics, as it is variously and popularly referred to, have become central to the study and analysis of global politics at a variety of levels. Whether scholars are trying to assess the impact of Islamist trends on politics, stability and the economy, cultural representation, or patterns of global politics and ideology, global security challenges, the war on terrorism, dimensions of conflict and ethnic violence, the Islamist dimension figures far more prominently than it ever did before. In the 1970s the discourse on modern terrorism and paradigms of terrorology were informed by analyses of left-wing violence and nationalist demands, not on the way in which Islam impacted on political discourses from left to right, or from the moderate to the extreme end of the political spectrum. Likewise, the media, particularly in the West but also at a global level, have generated thousands upon thousands of 'news' stories, articles, think pieces, editorials, live debates, documentaries, interviews, books, journal articles and new artworks that focus on Islam in all its dimensions, but particularly in the political. An image of Islam as a political phenomenon (rather than phenomena) now dominates public consciousness, particularly in the West. Policy-makers, economists, politicians, risk analysts, security experts, legislators, defence specialists and diplomats in the twenty-first century now feel compelled to take serious account of a political manifestation that was really only brought to their attention in the latter decades of the twentieth century. A 'new' dimension of political discourse that appears to eschew Western norms, values, philosophies and patois appears to have crept up at an alarming rate in an assault not just within Muslim domains but also as part of a trans-global movement of terrifying proportions.

Additionally it is contended that within the Islamist spectrum radicals have reinforced the current Western fixation. Islamist fanatics appear to have urged their followers, from Finsbury Park to Grozny, to return to the 'straight path' and adhere to their religion in its most fundamental and orthodox form. It is these fanatics who are empowered by the notion of the millions of enraged Muslims under the banner of Islam. Such 'fundamentalists' are accused of running campaigns within immigrant Muslim communities to enforce their orthodox approach at the expense of all other expressions of Islam. Some also maintain that it is Islamists themselves who have manipulated and exaggerated the so-called Western threat in a variety of Muslim domains. Islam is accused of playing on the fears posed by its own revival. Thus the perpetuation of mutual suspicion and hostility is self-reinforcing (Halliday, 1996, p. 110).

Political Islam, described by Dessouki as 'increasing political activism in the name of Islam by governments and opposing groups alike' (Dessouki, 1982, p. 4), then, is one part of a larger revival of Islam which became a dominant phenomenon for much of the latter half of the twentieth century. Islamism and Islamist movements are those perceived as significantly active on the political front but often engaged in activities embracing welfare, education and military activities. Islamists are often perceived as oppositional elements, and the term is not regularly deployed to refer to governments of Muslim hue. The resurgence of faith, the increased demonstration of religiosity in public, new churches, synagogues and mosques, more debate on the importance of religion in society are not perceived in the Muslim context, however, as the same as the revival of faith in Christian or other faith contexts. The majority of Christian evangelical movements, for example, work within the system, and almost all confine their activities to legitimate means of persuasion; they contest elections and are not generally perceived as a threat to any regional or international order. Thus it appears that 'it has been a long time since Christianity was Islam's other. Even if there is a religious revival among Christians and Jews, it is in no way parallel to that of the [Islamic] fundamentalists' (Roy, 1994, p. 203). The revival of Islam is understood in the West and among the ruling elites of pro-Western states as a new menace, replacing old fears about the Communist threat with a new one with an Islamic hue. Revivalism in the guise of Islam is discussed with a huge sense of fear.

How Ahmed got his groove: resurgence as radical

A pervasive perspective of Islam is associated with fear, terror and violence. Newspaper headlines reflect an image of Islam that is dominated by what appears to be a political manifestation that is anti-democratic, hostile if not deeply antipathetic to secular states, and anti-Western. As Miller contends, 'in Islam's war against the West and the struggle to build Islamic states at home the end justifies the means ... radical political Islam placed atop these societies in the Middle East has created a combustible mixture ... They are, and are likely to remain, anti-Western, anti-American and anti-Israeli' (Miller, 1993, p. 33). From this perspective, Islamic politics is rigidly defined by just one dimension – one that sits at the extreme of the political spectrum epitomized by bearded clerics like Abu Hamza or Sheikh Omar Rahman, or terrorist bombers like Ramzi Yousef, who was one of the individuals responsible for the first bomb attack on the World Trade Centre in the early 1990s. Sheikh Rahman was imprisoned by the American authorities after he was found guilty of seditious conspiracy against the USA, solicitation to murder Egyptian President Hosni Mubarak, conspiracy to bomb and solicitation to bomb a military installation. Abu Hamza, a well-known firebrand cleric in north London, has been an unrepentant and outspoken critic of the West, calling on his supporters to maintain Islam in all aspects of their lives. Such figures give the lie to the belief that political Islam is merely a modern-day manifestation of a bloodthirsty obligation that Islam puts on all Muslims – that of *jihad*. In fact, *jihad* is often referred to as the sixth obligation of Islam. Hence the resurgence movement in Islam is apparent in the violent impulses at the heart of the faith, as Lewis declares: 'the Muslim world is again seized by an intense – and violent – resentment of the West. Suddenly America has become the arch-enemy, the incarnation of evil, the diabolic opponent of all that is good, and specifically, for Muslims, of Islam' (Lewis, 1990, p. 53). Thus, for authors like Lewis, the notion of an inextricable link between faith and violence marks Islam out from other religions. Although adherents or followers of fundamentalist Christianity or Hinduism may engage in acts of terror and violence as part of their agenda, the difference between them and the Muslims, it is contended, is that other religious traditions eschew such a central role for force and violence.

The view that Islam and therefore dimensions of politics were founded through the sword rather than pacifist platitudes, and that the leader of the new faith was a radical, has become a new way in which Islam in general is understood as a twenty-first century phenomenon. Muslims as political creatures thus appear to eschew normative democratic and non-violent political interaction in favour of violent, thuggish, terrorist assaults on states, both their institutions and innocent citizens. Leaders of Islamist movements are perceived as culpable for establishing in a generation of young people the 'roots of rage' that appear to typify the faith system in the contemporary era.

Historic resonance has become increasingly apparent in the clashing discourse between Islamists and Western political leaders where the Crusader past has been resurrected as a tool of useful divination about the other in the contemporary era. On both sides this has been tailored and twisted to promote understandings of the other as political creatures. Yet some Islamists reject the thesis that Islam is a religion of violence. One Hizballah leader argues that 'Islam is not a religion of violence. Islam is a religion which gave its followers the legitimacy to resist the aggressors based on justice and preciseness.... After all, Islam is a religion of love, mercy, dialogue and acceptance of others and a religion that calls for wisdom, good advice. This is the basis of Islam' (Fnaysh, 2001). In Western popular culture, however, political Islam remains defined by the negative, whether in the pages of magazines, films, television, photos or in the statements of leading politicians. It becomes difficult to perceive of the matrix embedding Islam and politics as being anything other than radical, fanatic and fated as violent. The endurance throughout the 1990s of this monolithic vision of Islam dominated analysis of the contemporary situation.

The notion of Islam as a radical political movement of global proportions was reinforced by the radicals themselves. Radical maximal positions or stances appeared to characterize the fanatic fringe populated by the likes of the Arab-Afghan rebels, Algerian hotheads and Palestinian suicide bombers. Hence the image so prevalent in the Western imagination of masked Muslim terrorists brandishing the Qur'an in the right hand and a kalashnikov in the left. These images reinforce a knowledge of political Islam within and outside Muslim domains, however, that tells only one part of the story. They reinforce the notion that Islam threatens not just Western interests abroad but the West itself.

Alternative dimension of the spectrum

Knowledge, then, of political Islam was based on an image of Islam as radical and violent. Here the perception, rather than the multi-dimensional reality which offered a vista in which many dimensions of the political were present, was what really mattered. The re-emergence of Islam as a dynamic political and social force came at a time of immense change in Muslim domains. In the Arab world in the early 1970s, politics and political solutions to contemporary problems were being thought anew in the wake of the Arab defeat in the war with Israel in 1967 and the 'crisis of confidence' that appeared to afflict nationalist discourse. As nationalist secular ideologies were questioned and undermined, the idea that 1967 served as a turning point in the waxing/waning fortunes of Islamist agendas in competition with nationalist secularist ones emerged. Indeed, it appeared that Islam as a polit-ical tool was being examined anew, and new movements for change were established. The movement's thinkers were given prominence, and a sense of resurgence was palpable. Moreover, in places like the former Soviet Central Asian republics, resurgence grew, and Islam had an impact on the new political frameworks that were established in the wake of the collapse of the old ideo-logical order of communism. A 'rediscovered' faith lost in the past to the anti-religious structures of communism was apparent in the unfolding struggle for power and new political systems and frameworks in states like Tajikistan, Azerbaijan, Kazakhstan and Uzbekistan.

Resurgence, even within the twentieth century, had taken place before. What is referred to and maintained as the modernist or reformist trend in Islam is empirically far more representative than the radical one in terms of political Islam or the Islamist agenda. In the Middle East the modernist/reformist trend was spearheaded by great thinkers and important clerics attached to one of the most prestigious institutions in the Muslim world – the al-Azhar University. The ideas and approaches of modernist thinkers such as Mohammad Abduh or Jamal a-din al-Afghani reflected a response to the project of modernity that maintained its Islamic credentials. This demanded interpretation and innovation. Although there were major differences among these thinkers in their approaches and at that time they, as individual leaders, failed to arouse populist movements, their ideas, and those of other modernists such as Sayyid Ayub Khan in India, have established the intellectual grounds for successive generations of Islamists to connect with the political once again. For such individuals and movements, whether in Tunisia or Indonesia, the connection between contemporary circumstance and faith as an input into political identity is central. Yet Western authors have continued to promote a thesis that Islam's failure (something which Muslims themselves recognize) to confront modernity and secularism gave rise to ordeal and discord (*mihna wa fitna*), compelling the faithful into 'pitched battle' against the evil of their own societies. This in turn led them to argue that radical Islam is the 'cutting edge of the Islamic resurgence', and therefore represents the 'revival movement as a whole' (Sivan, 1985, p. xi). Since the 1980s, radical Islamist elements have been discovered across nearly every Muslim and non-Muslim domain. These dangerous elements of political Islam seem to be everywhere in a loose, transnational network of modern and more lethal terror. They have been 'discovered' and described in every country of the Middle East and beyond. The threat that these groups pose is both to internal political systems and increasingly to the global order. The radical dimension of the political spectrum is now understood as representative of Islam's revival more generally. Hence the expression of Islam in a political or any other guise is in the contemporary era increasingly described as radical.

Yet a new generation of Islamist thinkers have continued to seek what may be labelled as more mainstream liberal, moderate or modernist approaches to political issues that animate ordinary Muslims across the globe (Utvik, 2003, p. 45). Their ideas indirectly challenge the monolithic assumptions behind the way in which political Islam is understood. This may be problematic both for the state and for radical elements in Muslim domains. Egypt is a case in point. First, the liberal-reformist-modernist agenda has character-ized the contemporary debate within Islam throughout the twenti-eth century. Today Muslim liberal authors and intellectuals such as Nasser Hamid Abu Zayd, Fu'ad Zakariyya, Mohammad Ahmad Khalafalla, and Mohammad Said al-Ashmawi have opened up new debates within political Islam that undermine the assumed domin-ance of the radicals or fundamentalists. They, and others like them in Indonesia, Malaysia, Tunisia, Pakistan and the USA, have gener-ated internal debates in which the political and the radical are not automatically assumed. Indeed, it has been remarked that 'Islamic liberals, and the liberal Muslims, have started to answer the chal-lenge of the fundamentalists, and many of them are conducting this debate in Islamic terms, which must add substantially to the cred-ibility of their argument' (Ayubi, 1991, p. 212).

Fundamentalism

In the early 1980s, fundamentalism was identified as central to the resurgence of Islam. Islamic fundamentalism was described as 'essentially anti-democratic, anti-accommodationist, and anti-plur-alist and that it violates, as a matter of principle, the standards of human rights defended...by Western democracies...(and is) under assault by the forces of resurgent religious radicalism' (Marty and Appleby, 1993, p. 5). Religious revivalism or resurgence within the Islamic faith was understood or labelled as a new phe-nomenon: a radical modern reworking of traditions yet advocating a return to a past utopia as a political project upon which to shape future state entities. Fundamentalism was also represented as a reflection of literal and core values of the faith system. The fripper-ies of faith, fringe worship, rites and rituals with localized rather than purely Islamic hues were criticized and rejected as significant in the weakening of Islam as a political, economic, cultural and religious force in modern societies. Fundamentalist movements and their leaders sought to mount campaigns that would reassert and achieve the prominence of Islam that they believed it deserved. This meant the embrace of some rigid and orthodox views regarding scientific development and modern technology, as well as social mores and values. Yet this was juxtaposed against the utilization of modern technology to disseminate their message.

The ideologues of fundamentalist Islamism, however, contended that the rejoinder to what they believed to be a crisis of identity and the offensive by the West on Muslim universal values should be a revived, orthodox adherence to Islam. According to such a perspective, fundamentalist Islamism offers a solution more dynamic than traditional Islam and inclusive of every other aspect of a heightened sense of Muslim identity. If Muslims would return to the straight path of Islam, adhering strictly to the fundamental tenets of the faith as a blueprint for all aspects of contemporary life, the nation of Islam would ascend and achieve its goal in the face of the opposition. The ideological thrust of the fundamentalists centred on the crisis of identity, the crisis of the Muslim soul that had lost touch with its religion, and the project to recover it. This is highlighted in a variety of writings by Islamist figures such as Sayyid Qutb.

Western scholarship on the fundamentalist phenomenon in the early 1980s was coloured by the tumultuous events and revolution that took place in Iran in 1979 and was harnessed by Shi'a clerics. The revolution in Iran was not just about replacing one political order with another. It also touched very directly on the relationships between particular Western governments and the new Islamist domain of Iran. For the old regime and its Shah, much popular dissent was focused on the Westernized policies of his governance. In essence, the problems of the Shah were perceived as rooted in the deep tie to the West, and to the USA in particular. As a focus for anger, the events of the revolution deepened an emerging breach between pre- and post-revolution Iran and the states of the West. The seizing of American hostages in November 1979 at the American Embassy in Tehran prompted a major crisis for the Carter Administration and betrayed a change of attitude between this new form of fundamentalist Islam and the West. The revolution led to a crisis in US–Iranian relations that has never truly been healed. This breach has also affected dimensions of scholarship on the topic, particularly in the immediate aftermath of the revolution and the break with the West. It altered the way in which modern fundamentalism was represented to many Western audiences. Most scholarship on fundamentalist Islam, Hunter contends, 'tended to view the Islamist trend as a mainly Shi'a and Persian phenomenon.... According to this school of thought, certain characteristics of the Shi'a faith, along with the structure of the Shi'a clerical establishment, made Shi'ites more susceptible to extremist Islamist tendencies' (Hunter, 1995, p. 319). Thus, the study of fundamentalist Islamism presupposed an anti-Western and reactionary or backward-looking character to Islam and politics more generally, and often with good reason. The problem, however, lay in the extent to which the same perspective was offered in response to the emergence of a whole variety of movements, thinkers and organizations across Muslim domains and across the spectrum of political Islam. Additionally, fundamentalist elements exploited this perspective, presenting themselves as returning to an earlier utopia.

One problem with such accounts, however, lay in the limited perspectives that emerged in interpreting any expression of Muslim politics as evidence of a resurgence of Islam that embraced many more Sunni than Shi'a Muslims. The objective of much of such research was to demonstrate to the West, and the USA in particular, the threat implicit in Islam, a threat that was violent and divine in inspiration. Islam became symbolically linked to a threat and to politics only through the expression of violence, which in reality meant terror. Authors such as Halliday argue that such scholarship betrayed a hostility to Islam that is explained as a form of 'anti-Muslimism' (Halliday, 1996, p. 162). Additionally, these early representations of Islamism as fundamentalist and violent did little to reveal the doctrinal, spiritual and religious differences between Sunni and Shi'a Islam, particularly as they relate to issues of governance, leadership and the nature of the Islamic state. The complexity within Islam and its political dimensions were often eschewed in favour of studies for Western readers that stressed a simplistic image of the faith. Hence the easy visual association of Islam in the majority of Western media with images such as veiled women and bearded 'fundamentalists'.

The image of Ayatollah Khomeini and the revolutionary masses of Iran had a major impact in shaping contemporary understanding of political Islam in the latter half of the twentieth century. The threat posed by such a regime to geo-strategic and geo-political realities in the oil-rich Middle East, for example, was translated in very bald terms as one between good and evil – the West and Islam. The fundamentalist dimension was understood as an anti-modern trend that championed a return to barbarism. Martin Kramer contends that

> for most of the 1980s, those who saw Islamic fundamentalism for what it is saw groups as violent and dogmatic as any in the world. These were people who mixed nostalgia with grievance to produce a millenarian vision of an Islamic state – a vision so powerful that its pursuit justified any means. Angry believers invoked this Islam

when they executed enemies of the revolution in Iran, assassinated a president in Egypt, and detonated themselves and abducted others in Lebanon. Their furious words complemented their deeds. They marched to chants of 'Death to America' and intimidated all opponents with charges of espionage and treason. They did not expect to be understood, but they did want to be feared, and feared they were, by Muslims and non-Muslims alike. (Kramer, 1993, p. 35–6)

There were other representations of the contemporary phenomenon of political Islam and analysis of its import globally which made a case for a multi-faceted resurgence of Islam in which fundamentalist Islam was but one element. By the early 1990s, Islamist modernism, liberalism and other political agendas and platforms were identified as emerging in Muslim domains. Nevertheless, this process of identification and analysis, while part of mainstream research on political Islam, failed to permeate the popular psyche.

The manifestation of Islam and Islamist politics in the contemporary world also has it roots in early and historical Islam, elements of which are relevant and others defunct. Those which are relevant to the contemporary experience are considered the 'immutable' fundamentals of the faith coupled to visions of political power that manifests itself in Islam as an ascending force in a myriad of political realms. Furthermore, that which is relevant is often subject to interpretation and conscious or unconscious mythologizing to make it relevant to the political agendas of the present – particularly as they relate to power. As I have argued elsewhere, past, present and future political Islam are a fusion of influences, experiences and thinkers that attempt to shape, reinforce and sometimes make redundant what seemed important to faith and identity only a decade before. Islam in this contemporary manifestation has many dimensions that relate to the political environments that Muslims experience.

In the twenty-first century Islam is labelled as a peculiar political phenomenon. Political Islam is understood as on a crash course with Western civilization and any Muslim regime of occidental-leaning rulers. The threat that is perceived as inherent to political Islam and Islam more generally dominates debate on both sides and between both sides whenever it takes place. Dimensions of political Islam dominate knowledge of the Muslim world and Muslim domains, whether the focus is on post-conflict politics in Afghanistan or social exclusion in Bradford. On the Islamist side, the charge that moderates have allowed the fanatics to dominate internal agendas is relevant in societies like Pakistan or Nigeria. Unless additional factors, such as the nature of the state, the contemporary debate about terrorism, human rights, the socio-economic, political and cultural contexts within which these phenomena occur, are also accounted for, Islamic politics will be objectified through a myopic vision of a fanatic fringe as representative of an entire spectrum of thought and opinion. For this reason the labels must always be questioned. The alternative thesis fails to explore the other causes of Muslim political engagement in societies which have experienced totalitarian government, socio-economic deprivation, limited political rights and ethno-national conflict, the ravaging effects of globalization, demands for secession, social exclusion, marginality or racism. The issue to be identified here is why certain Muslim communities view politics in the ways they do. Political Islam can be seen as a response to the project of modernity spearheaded by the West and its impact on Muslim domains across the globe. Islamists have become the drivers of certain social changes that have political import for the politics of the contemporary age.

2

ISLAM AND THE STATE

Introduction

State formation and the emergence of nation-states was a major feature of global patterns of politics in the twentieth century. Admittance to the important international forums such as the League of Nations and then the United Nations has depended on statehood. Statehood in turn became dependent on the so-called modern attributes of the nation-state, including flag, borders, capital, international recognition and legitimacy. Economic assistance for less developed economies in the latter half of the twentieth century, from international lenders and financial institutions such as the World Bank and the IMF, has often been tied to statehood (nascent, developing or under repair), and statelessness has made it all the more difficult to obtain the important benefits associated with such international legitimacy and recognition. Failed states, population movements and statelessness made manifest in the immigration and asylum phenomena in the twenty-first century, including many Muslim populations, also highlight the importance of the state to any debate about Muslim identity and politics.

The state is a much studied institution of politics. The state is recognized as a locus and institution of authority and sovereignty. The state, its institutions and those who run or rule the state have power. Sovereignty is commonly associated in contemporary studies of the state with territory – a tract of land, shaped and defined by borders that keep the citizens of a state in and foreigners out. Hence states are also about exclusivity – the provision of a sense of belonging and designed, therefore, to generate a sense of identity focused on the state and those who live in it. There are, however, many contested definitions of the state as a modern or contemporary phenomenon in Western literatures. Theories of the state have preoccupied many Western political theorists over the past century, contributing to the growth of a body of literature that reflects on themes such as sovereignty, power, citizenship, economic factors, laws, accountability and so on. The state is also an institution that is not exclusive to any one political ideology. Therefore, it is not dependent on a particular theory or approach enshrined by liberal-democratic theory. And while it may be true that increasingly the modern state is recognized by secular rather than religious arrangements, there is no single argument that favours one arrangement over another. The state is an important focus in the majority of modern societies, irrespective of their cultural or geographic domain; hence it is acknowledged as shaping, altering and becoming a focus for identity and identity-related politics. Additionally, while traditionally associated with formal institutions, rules and regulations, I would argue that the boundaries between state and society are sometimes fuzzy. The coercive power of the state is also worthy of some reflection. For rulers of the state often see themselves as the ultimate locus of force, with responsibilities for law and the maintenance of order. They enjoy the power of coercion over their citizens.

The state, then, is an important dimension of politics that attracts the attention of those who seek power, have power and wish to maintain power in the political arena. The state has become an important locus for Islamist movements across the globe. State power has largely been denied to Islamists; indeed, Islamists are often regarded as *a* if not *the* major threat to the international state system of the twenty-first century, dominated as it is by Western liberal-democratic secular states such as the Republic of France, the United States of America and the United Kingdom. These states, and states both like them and different from them, have also become a target of Islamist ire. Islamist ideologues advocate the reform or overthrow of states across the globe. Osama Bin Laden has advocated the overthrow of the Saudi state, the state of Israel and the United States of America. Radical ideologues and activists in Egypt, Algeria, Nigeria and Pakistan have argued that prevailing state orders and their rulers must be eradicated, reformed and remade in the image of a true Islam. One goal, then, of a variety of radical and non-radical Islamist elements is either state reform or overthrow and reconstruction around principles and practices considered inherent to the faith. In order to reform or remake the state in the contemporary era, Islamists and Muslim thinkers have become preoccupied with past interpretations as well as ambitions for the future. Some reflections are utopian, some look at certain though not all historic moments within Islam for inspiration and other approaches or arguments speak more of the future than the past. Hence, like Western approaches and theories about the state, Muslim deliberations on this subject are not singular but multiple. Additionally, it is disingenuous to argue or suggest that a Muslim fifth column exists and is united around a single theory of the state, and that the political system and institutions that should be arranged and organized in its name.

While it is true that particular themes or texts appear to resonate in a variety of positions and views, this is not the same as believing that if all Muslims gained control over their own destinies through statehood tomorrow, a single system of governance would emerge. In reality, a variety of historic examples and concepts are introduced and examined in any reflection on Islamic or Muslim statehood and its institutions. Some of those historic examples or concepts may enjoy parallels with other traditions or theories, yet others may differ. The conceptual dimension of the Islamic state and Muslim states is of the most interest in the contemporary debates that animate Islamists and their opponents. Such dimensions alert us to aspiration and the ideal vision of a faith system that contains texts and commandments to certain perceived political behaviours and identities that matter in the present as well as the past context. In this chapter the impact of the past – how earlier Muslim states and empires handled statehood and related issues and the variety of actual as opposed to theological outcomes – will be examined along with an analysis of how for many decades in the contemporary era established and establishing states, such as Saudi Arabia, Pakistan, Afghanistan and Tajikistan, have used Islamic themes to control and legitimate their particular type of rule. Such an approach demonstrates that sometimes Islamization or revivalism of the active kind can come as much from above as below. The purpose of this chapter, then, is to highlight variety, not singularity, and to reflect on the debates that are core to Islamist as well as Islamic conceptualizations of the modern-day state as a locus of power and control in any society.

Making the model

The opportunity for state creation is not an everyday event. State creation, or the establishment of new territories with sovereign and internationally recognized borders, is not what could be called an ordinary phenomenon. Throughout the twentieth century, however, many new states were established as old orders dissolved in wars and conflicts and occasional transitions in rule occurred. Territorial units were made anew, created from scratch or altered by dispute with neighbours and those considered to be enemies. In the late 1980s the collapse of the Soviet Union – a state born out of the act of revolution in 1917 – and of successive Communist-ruled East European states appeared, according to some rhetoric, to signal the 'end of history' and the end of ideological confrontation that was responsible for much rivalry and conflict between modern states. In reality, the events that unfolded over the following decade demonstrated that things – particularly as they relate to the (nation-) state – were far from simple. From 1991 to 2001, thirty-one states joined the United Nations. Of that number, over half were 'new' states that emerged after the historic breakup of the Soviet Union, including Estonia, Latvia, Armenia, Azerbaijan, Kazakhstan and Kyrgyzstan. Historically also, states, irrespective of their religious dimension, tend to be born, altered or created out of settlements surrounding turmoil, instability and conflict.

Hence the context of state creation is important. Those who engage in state creation, the organization of tasks and institutions associated with political as well as coercive power, matters to those who fall under the aegis of a particular state. For Muslims, an initial point of inspiration and reflection on the concept of the state usually rests in the state established by the Prophet Mohammad in the seventh century in the Arabian trading town of Medina in the area of the Hijaz, now one of Islam's most holy and venerated sites. Some narrative about those events is necessary here. The engagement with the political domain by a religious leader in the seventh century was hardly unusual. Considering the circumstances, the future of the 'new religion' depended on creating a unit of organization that included a coalescence of the spiritual with the dimension of power that was understood as the 'political'. It should be noted, however, that in Arabia political power was not manifest in institutions of the state as we know it today. Political power, allied with economic and coercive force, rested in the hands of tribal chiefs, religious figures and soldier-warriors.

When the Prophet Mohammad and his band of followers were ejected from Mecca, as a threat to local power, they arrived in Medina seeking to protect themselves from further assault. Protection came in the form of self-organization around the provision of power within the community and defence against others. Things did not go smoothly, and many conflicts resulted from these attempts to forge a distinct community of believers whose lives were also shaped by new codes relating to power – the political, economic and military manifestations of it. The point here is that statehood arose out of context, not simply from specific, divine commandment. Additionally, the Prophet Mohammad did not establish a particular blueprint for the organization of any entity to be known as an Islamic state. In practice, of course, there are many who believe that in Medina the first Islamic state was established. This model embodied the symbiosis between faith and power headed by the spiritual leader of the new faith who also acted as its political leader in external and internal relations, as well as its military commander. The nearest any scholar has to a blueprint from this model moment is the *al-sahifa*, or constitution, of Medina. Yet to regard the constitution as representative of some pure Islamic formulation would be misleading. For there is general consensus that the model reflected pre-Islamic tribal and Byzantine norms, along with the Prophet's own divinely revealed inputs.

The notion of constitution as recorded in a later historical era recognized the important tribal norms and values that governed societal relations in Arabia. This factor was acknowledged within certain suras of the Qur'an, where reference to the 'tribe' and its importance as an organizational unit of power is made. I believe it can be argued that the new model based on the Medinan experience took the best of the old to merge with the new. The constitution recognized that a particular unit of organization – the *umma* – was important alongside relations with other groups, such as the Jewish tribes of Arabia. Some believe that the constitution was an endorsement of a pan-Islamic universal pledge, while others reflect that provision for smaller units of organization and responsibility was also advocated. Incorporation would, however, figure as a dominant motif in this vision of something that may in the contemporary era be called statehood. Yet those who were incorporated into state structures were not converted if they were already attached to the Jewish or the Christian faith. The constitution, however, demonstrates the explicit linkage between faith and state. The believer is central to the outline of responsibilities and duties. A kind of social order and its rules and taboos are also revealed. Yet there is little that is explicit to the organization of institutions that can be recognized as an Islamic state in the modern dimension. What, then, appeals in this model to Islam's theorists and political activists?

Ibn Taymiyya, the medieval Hanbali scholar and jurist, attached great importance to the Medinan model in reflecting on Muslim power and statehood. In this model he recognized the importance of consensus to any state organization (legitimacy). This is a theme that is reflected by modern-day opinion-formers in the Muslim world. In an article by Hamza Alavi published in the Pakistani paper *The Dawn* in 2001, the relevance of this seventh-century document to twenty-first-century political debates was emphasized. 'The Prophet resolved the crisis of Medina by replacing the traditional...system with a new state of Medina [that] was both democratic and tolerant. This has much to teach us in Pakistan, not least in the light of the widespread bigotry, intolerance and the reign of terror that is let loose in our country' (Alavi, 2001, p. 3). For this author and other Muslim scholars, this document, albeit a brief one, is important because for them it represents an acknowledgement of Muslim attachment to consensus and diversity (ethnic and religious) within the state long before corporatist documents such as the Magna Carta or the Constitution of the United States of America. Additionally, the constitution is read as a document that enshrines the principle of 'equal citizenship' long before others. As Rodinson remarks, 'Muhammad came as an arbiter, without assuming the power of a chief of state...(He) acted as a Bedouin sayyid (chief), *primus inter pares*...deriving his power entirely from his moral ascendancy. He treated his disciples as his equals, with courtesy and respect' (Rodinson, 1971, p. 24). Thus, the Prophet Mohammad is credited with creating for a decade something known as a 'city-state,' though not a 'state' in the conventional sense of the contemporary West. He led his community and forged pacts and agreements that created new political and power bases in Medina. He is said to have demonstrated Muslim democracy in practice, not just in principle, countering the allegations in Western literatures that the Medinan model created a foundation for Muslim authoritarianism and was an anti-plural set of state institutions and arrangements. Some Muslim scholars and activists find in the model an example of equal citizenship, pluralism and consensus in legitimating a political leader; yet no matter how generous the interpretations, the document combined with particular sura of the

Qur'an gives limited rather than generous outline and guidance about the nature of the Islamic state and its institutions, including its leadership. Indeed, the Prophet Mohammad failed to make explicit even whether leadership of the community should be located within a principle of succession through blood, religious or other ties.

This lack of explicit direction led to the succession crises and the first schism within Islam, between Sunnis and Shi'as, following the death of the Prophet. Indeed, from this point onward, the 'Islamic state' would emerge in a variety of forms and guises. It should be remembered as well that Islam and nation were always intertwined concepts as the extension of Muslim rule resulted in territories in Asia, Africa and Europe governed according to the principles of Islam.

As an ideal or theory, the Islamic state has some core immutable elements with everything else subject to historical, geographic, social and other contexts. Islamic theorists writing about the state have spanned a number of centuries and covered wide ideological ground. To begin with, the term 'state' (*dawla*) in the Islamic sense is actually described as the *umma* (community) or the caliphate. Any discussion by Islamic theorists of the *dawla*, the state, is a relatively recent innovation linked in large part and in response to the rise of the European nation-state and associated political thinking and theorizing. In the twentieth century much Islamist discourse on the Islamic state was a response or rejoinder to the European domination of political thinking on this subject, an attempt to reclaim the Muslim body politic and a result of a particular, specific experience of the nation-state through colonialism and European domination of the Muslim world. In addition, while Western theorizing of the state and government was largely realized for contemporary Muslim thinkers addressing the subject of an Islamic state, the ideal remains the norm. Although many states and their rulers may claim Islamic credentials, very few, if any, are accepted as Islamic within the Muslim fold. The practical examples are few and far between.

Historic manifestations

The nature of Muslim governance, following the death of the Prophet Mohammad, from the seventh century to the end of the nineteenth century, was made manifest in a variety of locales and ways. Some epochs of Muslim governance were characterized by empires of Islam with territories subject to the central authority of one ruler and his elite. Muslim governance has been limited to smaller territories in locations remote from the cosmopolitan heart of power; outpost Islamism is compelled to maintain functions of governance through political power that has been cognizant of other cultures and their potency. Muslim governance and Muslim-ruled states have been subject historically to both internal and external threat, dissension and competition. Muslim state forms have been variously dominated by military elites, family or tribal elites, clerical elites, urban elites, the empowerment of slave classes turned rulers, revenue-raising functions, territorial expansion, state contraction, development of culture, learning, science, public works and infrastructure, state protectionism and internecine conflict.

Leadership, along with other functions of the state such as the legislative function, citizenship and tax raising, has always been considered an important dimension of the Islamic or Muslim-ruled state. As I have already indicated, the question of leadership in succession to the Prophet Mohammad led to the emergence of a major schism within Islam that persists to the present day. On one side of the battlefield were the blood relatives of the Prophet – Ali (his son-in-law) and his sons. On the other side were the Rashidun companions of the Prophet who enjoyed status through their attachment to him and to his religious ideals. They ruled in succession (Abu Bakr, Omar and Othman) over expanding Muslim state forms that broke out of the territorial confines of the Arabian desert northwards and elsewhere to other territories of the Middle East. These successors – caliphs – would serve as the ultimate mortal authority under that of Allah. Additionally, the caliphs and the institutions of the caliphate that developed around them and survived until the collapse of the Ottoman Empire at the end of World War I came to signify dimensions of state rule through military command, religious leadership and public office. The Caliph did not simply grasp power and the command of leadership by force, but was elected to the position of successor and bound by the divinely revealed laws and norms of Islam.

Each leader put his own particular stamp on the emerging state form of the newly established and expanding community of believers. Secession, however, became apparent in the minds of Ali and his supporters as they chafed under the demands imposed by contested rule. Ali's dissension resulted in his assassination and the ascension of a new Caliph, Mu'awiya, the former governor of Syria.

Civil strife, rather than harmony, became the hallmark of the Islamic state form – manifest in where and how state revenues were raised and what type and strength of state force was deemed important. Yet, as has been noted, the civil strife that resulted in bloodshed within the community 'created permanent divisions... Henceforth, Muslims were divided over who had the legitimate right to occupy the Caliphate' (Lapidus, 1988, p. 58). The martyrdom of Ali's son, Hussein, in the battle of Karbala in 680, at the hands of Mu'awiya's successors, fractured Islam, with important repercussions for state rule made manifest in leadership and notions of legitimacy. Force, in the form of military prowess, was often an important feature of such states and empires, perhaps best illustrated in the case of a reflection on Mamluk rule and Sultan Baybar and his successors in the thirteenth century.

The historic domain of thirteenth-century Islam incorporated many territories across Arabia, Asia, Africa and Spain. The Abbasids of Egypt, the Seljuks, the Persians and the Mongols vied for leadership and control over these domains. The Abbasid heirs of the famous Saladin ruled their empire from the confines of their stunning fortress in medieval Cairo. Their fortress mentality was largely responsible for their demise at the hands of their own military corps, in the form of the Mamluk (slave) officers and regiments. Force begets force, violence begets violence, and Mamluk governance of their domains, including Egypt, consisted of a state system built around a privileging of the military over other realms. This policy proved its worth in terms of beating their enemies on the battlefield. The Mamluks succeeded in defeating both Mongol and Crusader foes on the battlefield and in securing political control over territory that extended beyond the border of Egypt to Palestine, Syria and even Armenia. The Mamluks, the warrior slave caste that turned on its Ayyubid overlords, acquired a reputation for ruthless rule, yet unification over a significant territorial expanse was achieved in the name of a faith and its rulers. The state elite was military based and drawn almost exclusively from the slave caste. The Mamluk state raised revenues for its defence and other expenditures through taxes levied across their domains and administered by the bureaucratic elite.

Under the Mamluk state, the Islamic faith was employed as a legitimator of rule through the appointment of four chief judges, along with other dimensions linked to the obligations of the faith. Islam, however, was but one dimension of the Mamluk claim to legitimacy of rule and leadership that also included their monopoly of force. Trade became an additional dimension of power in this

Muslim state. There were Mamluk rulers who took the form rather than the substance of Islam more seriously than others as a means to demonstrate their credentials – such as al-Mu'ayyad Sheikh. Sunni revivalism, much like its twentieth-century counterpart, found expression in extreme as well as moderate ways. *Shari'a* law was the legislative foundation of the state, and revivalism inspired a spread of Islam's message from urban locales such as Cairo and Damascus to the rural heart of the Mamluk Empire. State-sponsored Islam – the establishment of a clerical core (*ulama*) in the pay of the state and under its dictat – ensured that religion would be tied to the state through more than just a spiritual or legal dimension. The Mamluk state, however, is also criticized for the hypocrisy and 'rapacity' of its ruling elite, for stasis and eventual decline, with a ruling elite described as 'more promiscuous than monkeys, more larcenous than mice, and more destructive than wolves' (Rodenbeck, 1998, p. 138). Ottoman conquest of Cairo in 1517 may have ended Mamluk rapacity, but the connection between state and religion remained.

Hence the leadership of a Muslim or Islamic state has been a dynamic and oft-contested phenomenon. Some assert, however, that leadership norms and values in such contexts emerged with a principal tendency towards authoritarian or despotic rule over subject peoples. Islam is charged with shaping and dominating discourse in government and statehood for all the wrong reasons. Thus Kedourie claims that Arab Muslim rulers 'very speedily transformed an unsophisticated tribal polity into one of the most sophisticated and most durable kinds of rule, that of oriental despotism, the methods and traditions of which have survived in the Muslim world to the present day' (Kedourie, 1992, p. 12). Norms of just and consensual rule are considered absent in the phenomenon of Muslim statehood and leadership. Muslim tendencies towards the despotic are thus regarded from a Hobbesian perspective as providers of absolute power to contain the 'natural condition of mankind . . . a state of nature . . . [of] war of all against all . . . [where] life in the state of nature is nasty, brutish and short'. Indeed, in interesting contrast, Hobbes was motivated to provide an alternative to the prospect of internal civil conflict through the notion of a strong sovereign leader. It would appear that certain Western historians of Muslim rule, such as Kedourie, share the Hobbesian perspective in their reflections and evidence-gathering attempts to prove the despotic nature of Islamic leadership. Significant Muslim philosophers such as Ibn Taymiyya and al-Ghazali also reflected on the import of leadership and the leader to the Islamic state system, advocating a centralized and strong leader. This is interpreted as an advocacy of the rule of a dictator or a despot to overcome the prospect of internal strife or disorder (often referred to as *fitna*), and indeed this is an oft-invoked theme in such writings.

Additionally, philosophers such as al-Ghazali were at great pains to point out the duties of a ruler to be just and fair in the name of Allah. In many respects the primary duty of the ruler is to uphold principles of justice in the name of Islam. An unjust ruler is 'ill-starred' and endangers the sovereignty of God. Furthermore, historically strong leadership and absolute sovereigns were a political norm across the known world. The critique of Islamic state systems in relation to the popular mandate emerges with more potency in the twentieth century. The tradition-setting and backward-looking view of many contemporary Islamist thinkers when addressing the issue of Islamic statehood is cited as important evidence of a symbiotic relationship between the belief system and its impact on political authority that tends for historical and theological reasons towards tyranny. It is also clear, as the Mamluk era highlights, that the close relationship between the state and Islam ensured that a check on power (at least within majority Sunni Islam) was sometimes absent, with the clerical class in the pay of the state eager to dance to the tune of the piper.

The Ottoman state – the last intact 'caliphate' within Islam – was a major player for more than 500 years. It presided over the final decline of a Muslim dynasty (or civilization, as Ibn Khaldun might have referred to it) eventually dominated by non-Muslim European powers. The Ottomans are described by Hourani as establishing 'stable and lasting policies, militarily powerful, centralized and bureaucratically organised, able to collect taxes and maintain law and order over a wide area for a long time. The Ottoman Empire was one of the largest political structures that the western part of the world had known since the Roman Empire disintegrated' (Hourani, 1991, p. 215). State authority was absolute and in the hands of the ruling family in the name of Islam. Power was centralized and amassed in the hands of the few (known as *vizirs*), and once again the traditional tie to the military was an important dimension of the state. Decision making, formation of policy and legislation were in principle based on the *shari'a*. The most fundamental claim to legitimacy as an Islamic political unit or authority was authenticated through this function. The clerical classes, established under the Mamluks, were strengthened under successive Ottoman sultans. In reality, the noble clerical classes knew that their status and privilege came at a price, and that this meant a compromise between what was divinely ordained and the more temporal tasks of power maintenance by the Sultan. The clerical class was empowered in some ways and seen very much in alliance with the state, the court and its military elite. Whether in Constantinople or in the provinces, the Ottoman era gave rise to the expansion of the Sunni clerical establishment. In Jerusalem, for example, where the Ottoman rulers were obligated by faith to act as custodians of the al-Aqsa mosque and Dome of the Rock, the clerical establishment began to grow and flourish – in relative terms. This was an important dimension of statehood that would stand in stark contrast to the unfolding impact of European colonization in a variety of Muslim domains. For although modern colonial advances in Muslim domains such as the holy lands of the Middle East may have been inspired partly by Christian fervour, the Christian clerical elite had been disestablished from the state and was no longer tied into it at an elite level.

Modern musings on Muslim statehood

Over 1 billion Muslims live in nation-states that define and give character to the modern international system. While supranational and international organizations, such as the EU, the UN and the OIC (Organization of Islamic Conference), give body to the aspiration for identity that transcends the boundaries of nation-states, in reality Muslims, like other religious or ethnic groups, find themselves living in a variety of nation-state forms that cross the ideological spectrum. Statehood, Islamic style, has become an aspiration for many of those Muslims. It is important to remember, however, that such an aspiration is not shared by all those labelled Muslims, whether they live in Western secular liberal-democratic states or otherwise. Islamic statehood, the aspiration for a territorial unit of political authority governed by the theocratic injunctions and commandments of Islam, is already a reality in some cases, and in other domains is part of secessionist demands, a critique of existing state orders (that are primarily secular in nature) and civil strife. A state governed by the laws of Islam – the Shari'a – is, however, the product of more than one vision, related to the context in which the aspiration is located. Hence, for a secessionist movement like the Chechen movement, the religious dimension of the demand for statehood is altered by the context of the conflict with the central authority in the guise of Moscow. Those states that claim Islamic credentials as also subject to critique and cannot be categorized as all the same. Of course, there are elements of *shari'a* that these states enforce at an extreme level, such as the death penalty, which are represented in the international media as a way of understanding them as one and the same thing. Moreover, those who advocate the application of *shari'a* in the contemporary context have struggled to find a liberal interpretation of a canon of law that is rooted in very specific instructions from a much earlier time. In contrast, in Christianity there are few specific instructions regarding Judaic law and thus fewer obstacles to the process of interpretation or reinterpretation. It is true, for example, that in relation to the rights of women, these Islamic states manifest the same legislative position of extremism in contrast to the universalism of human rights agendas as they relate to women's empowerment. Yet, the explanation, as many writers themselves have highlighted, has also to demand that patriarchal norms – which appear to cross religious boundaries – be examined for a fuller account of the phenomenon. There is also some degree of issue as it relates to what factors define a state as Muslim or Islamic. In terms of defining a nation or state as Islamic or Muslim, state instrumentalism can often be inconsistent and subject to other pressures that impact on the definition.

Nevertheless, throughout the twentieth century a new generation of Islamist thinkers – those who seek to emphasize the fusion between religion and politics with politics taking as much primacy in the equation – often became apparent. The development of new discourses or reassessments of the role and functions of the Islamic state should be seen very much as part of the revivalism phenomenon that in turn sought to take Islam from the private fringe of modern societies and nation-states and make it more central to political authority, institutions and methods of modern governance. This discourse is not singular in dimension. In fact, it would be more judicious to argue that particular dichotomies have emerged in this debate. Some may be identified along a breakdown of sectarian lines – for example, the difference in Shi'a and Sunni discourse regarding political authority and leadership through governance in modern nation-states. In other respects the dichotomy can be represented as breaking down modernist and traditionalist perspectives and promotion of discourse on the subject. The debate about the state and its Islamic dimensions is also motivated by what many Islamists consider to be their emasculation in relation to the state authority under which they live – even if in those states the leadership or ruling authority claims legitimacy in the name of Islam. Indeed, it is in this realm that we see another chasm emerge that has historic echoes of the critique and rejection of Muslim leadership in the tenth century that gave rise to the Assassin sect. Here the controversy between those who believe that the 'unjust' ruler must be pulled down from within and those who adhere to al-Ghazali's assertion that in Muslim states 'the tyranny of the sultan for a hundred years causes less damage than one year's tyranny exerted by the subjects against each other' becomes apparent. In this respect there has always been much debate within contemporary discourse of the means to statehood of the Islamic ideal type. Ultimately, as the *mujahideen* of Afghanistan were exhorted to remember, 'all roads lead to Jerusalem, Mecca and Medina', reminding Muslims that irrespective of the route, the end result is the same. Such assertions should be tested against contemporary manifestations of state and visions of statehood.

The debate about the means matters, because international legitimacy is dependent on the route to liberation and new statehood. In the 1980s popular revolution in Iran and the ascension to power of the *ulama* on an agenda for a new state that was theocratic and anti-Western resulted in a rupture in international relations. The growing perception was that foreign 'domination', occupation or corruption of a ruling Muslim elite increasingly became the foundation for a new call to arms from radical Islamist elements such as Osama Bin Laden. In his earlier statements Bin Laden declared,

> Our youths knew that the humiliation suffered by the Muslims as a result of the occupation of their sanctuaries cannot be kicked and removed except by explosions and Jihad. As the poet said: The walls of oppression and humiliation cannot be demolished except in a rain of bullets. The freeman does not surrender leadership to infidels and sinners. Without shedding blood no degradation and branding can be removed from the forehead. (Bin Laden, 1996a)

In the 1990s, when Algerians who had rejected the secular-nationalist mantra of the past and embraced Islamism as a route to reshaping the state began the process of transformation through the electoral system, the process was effectively scrapped as a result of international pressure because of fear of an Islamic state form. Indeed, many dimensions of international politics, conflict and tension that characterized the later decades of the twentieth century could be said to, in essence, boil down to the ways in which the international community reacted to the prospect of Muslim or Islamic statehood. Somalia, Afghanistan, Bosnia-Herzegovina,

Iran, Algeria, the Israeli–Palestinian conflict, Egypt, Saudi Arabia, Bangladesh, Lebanon, Sudan, Pakistan, Kashmir, Iraq, Indonesia, East Timor, Chechnya, Nigeria and Libya were all increasingly vulnerable to the threat that Islamist ambitions for statehood posed and the effects that attainment would have on the international system.

For by the late twentieth century a variety of Islamist organizations emerged with the ambition to change or achieve state power. Some proposed the establishment of states that were more Islamic, and others theocracies with the clerics holding the reins of power. It is asserted that theocratic rule is a Muslim norm of governance. Past examples are cited as evidence for the contention that theocracy is natural to Islam. The Medinan state, established by the Prophet Mohammad, was a theocracy in which the Prophet stood as figurehead of both the state and faith. There is, however, no single blueprint for the organization of contemporary Muslim theocracies; nor is it clear whether such forms of rule are fundamental to the organization of modern Muslim polities and states. Evidence of past episodes of such arrangements demonstrate that there is no established rule. Historically, Muslim statehood has not been intrinsically tied to the theocratic model. In the twentieth century there have been few examples of theocratic statehood in Muslim domains. In Iran and Afghanistan (under the Taliban) political power has been in the hands of the clerical elite. In other Muslim domains the case for theocracy has been addressed to Muslim audiences living in failed or failing states, where both nationalism and the Western paradigm have been seen as bankrupt. Moreover, the extent to which the debate centres on authentic theocratic governance or rule in a more Islamic fashion is contested. Yet, in principle, the state form that is aspired to as an end goal is broadly similar though not always theocratic. Hamas ideology, that of the Palestinian Islamist movement founded in the late 1980s, for example, reflects dimensions of Islamic nationalism with a stated goal of statehood for a people without a state. Achievement of statehood for Hamas, however, necessitates the destruction of the state of Israel. Hamas calls for a state, a government, a people and a flag. As the Covenant of the movement declares,

> The goal of the Islamic Resistance Movement, therefore, is to conquer evil, crushing it and defeating it, so that truth may prevail, so that the country may return to its rightful place, and so that the call may be heard from the minarets proclaiming the Islamic state. And aid is sought from God.... Nationalism from the point of view of the

IRM is part and parcel of religious ideology. Nothing is loftier in nationalism or deeper in devotion than this: If an enemy invades Muslim territories, then Jihad and fighting the enemy becomes an individual duty on every Muslim. (Articles 9 and 12)

Hassan al-Turabi, the Sudanese Islamist leader, also views Islamic statehood as an important dimension of Muslim identity and rights,

> Is it true that the Muslims constitute an *Umma*, a community, and therefore there can be no territorial state? Can an Islamic state be based on a definite territory? And how will it relate to other Muslims beyond the territory? The model of the Prophet is also pertinent here. He organised a state in Medina, and it had definite frontiers; he set the frontiers, actually. But he related also to Muslims beyond... because Muslims don't really believe in frontiers. Anyway, these frontiers are not of their making; it was the British, French and Belgians who made them in the first place. (Hassan al-Turabi, 1998, p. 10)

For al-Turabi, the Medinan example is important in terms of certain dimensions of statehood, but he also believes that Islamic statehood should have thoroughly modern dimensions as well. Indeed, many Islamist thinkers cite the Medinan example as an ideal for their followers to aspire to. The appeal of such an image is not difficult to discern and interpret – new beginnings, chosen people, winning against the odds, new conquests and a harmony between faith and politics – and finally the emergence of a political community, a body politic, a state (*dawla*) headed by a just ruler legitimated by the community and faithful to the word of God. In such a political climate the endemic political problems which currently characterize many modern nation-states in which Muslims live today seem truly appalling. The theorists who develop their ideas of the state around this Medinan model, however, generally articulate their ideas from an orthodox, rigid and conservative mind-set, arguing that the problems which currently beset the modern Muslim world can only be resolved by a wholesale rejection of current approaches and thinking and a return/revival of this fundamental state type. The state type is fundamental inasmuch as it is limited by the known historical experience and limited blueprint of the Medinan constitution, and the tradition of interpretation is deemed less important than the prospect of fixed rules – Shari'a – that govern discourse on this approach. Additionally, such an approach to Islamic statehood can be interpreted as a rejection of the acculturated norms and accretions of twentieth- and twenty-first-century societies across the globe and an assertion of what is believed to be a more authentic state type underpinned by the basic foundations of Islam. The difficulty behind such a project and theorization of state type lies in the ability to compare the authenticity of the original project (of which there is relatively little remaining evidence) with the modern age – an act which in itself requires separation from the contemporary political arena. This in turn helps us understand why groups like the Egyptian radicalist Jihad organization led by, among others, Ayman Zahrawi sought to play their part in waging a *jihad* against Egypt's President Anwar Sadat. Sadat was perceived as the symbol of a state in which the legitimacy of Islam was, they believed, abused by the political elite. Sadat paid with his life when the jihadists assassinated him in October 1981. Their rejection of state authority as un-Islamic and *jahilli* was literal and included self-imposed isolation and removal from society.

The emergence of the modern *dawla* (state)

In the modern era, then, the Muslim state-builder has encountered a variety of difficulties in any attempt to re-establish political rule along the lines of the Medinan state – indeed, there are many Islamic theorists and state-builders who would and have avoided a literal re-establishment and point instead to the benefits of the general and universal rules underpinning any Muslim political project (the Medinan state included). Instead they urge followers to innovate, interpret and modify to meet the specific demands of the time. As a result of the modernizing project, which has been embraced by Muslims, the maintenance of more fundamentalist and prescriptive approaches to state building, as well as a number of types of political community (*umma*), government or state (*dawla*), can be identified in the Muslim domains. As a twentieth-century and post-World War I phenomenon a number of nation-states have been established or have achieved independence that may be referred to as Muslim or Islamic. For example, the Organization of the Islamic Conference (OIC), founded in 1969, has some fifty-seven members who represent dimensions of Islamic statehood or Muslim identity within nation-states. Hence member states of the OIC include Egypt and Iran alongside Benin with a Muslim population of only 20 per cent and recently independent new states of the former Soviet Union such as Tajikistan and Uzbekistan. Some state elites in these countries employ a narrow conception of Islamic statehood as it relates to their populations. Esposito (1984) would argue that a further distinction within the category needs to be drawn. He thus refers to three state types: totally secular, separating Islam from the state; Islamic, where the state has codified Islamic laws and consists of Islamic institutions of governance; and Muslim states that reflect both Western legislative and governance practices as well as some Islamic norms as well. Yet Muslim theorists, ideologues and Islamists would hold different perspectives on this process of categorization. According to Esposito's categorization, for example, Saudi Arabia and Pakistan qualify as Islamic rather than Muslim states, yet Islamists and others would contest this status. Additionally, the differences between such states as they relate to governance, institutions of the state and politics also vary considerably. In this respect I suggest we examine the ideas, the empirical evidence and the main forces or factors shaping and altering them.

Space does not permit me to give an overview of the ideological vision *vis-à-vis* each theorist or ideologue, so I will endeavour to provide snap-shots. In the contemporary era a variety of thinkers have emerged to influence the debate on the nature of the Islamic state in Muslim domains. Their views span a wide spectrum of opinion regarding the criteria for qualifying for the status of Islamic state. Most of the commentary, positions and literature offered is critical of current constructs and manifestations, particularly in relation to the way in which they seem open to the influences of other cultures and political systems, ideas and ideologies. This reflects an uneasiness with the somewhat haphazard and dynamic way in which states are formed and consolidated. Few contemporary thinkers legitimate the rule of those states that do claim Islamic credentials, such as the Kingdom of Saudi Arabia. Radical Islamist opponents of Saudi Arabia and its claim to Islamic credentials include Osama Bin Laden and also Sheikh Abu Hamza al-Misri, the London-based radical cleric and head of Supporters of the Shari'a (SOS). Literature available from SOS critiques the Islamic credentials of the state from a variety of positions—including education, tourism and, like Bin Laden, the vexing issue of the presence of foreign (US) troops on territory considered sacred and holy to Islam. For these extreme exponents of a vision of the Islamic state, there is no empirical evidence that any state on the contemporary globe qualifies for this honour. In this respect the debate about statehood and the way in which it is couched is designed to inspire the followers of Islam into action. In some ways these extreme voices of dissent echo the disappointed aspirations of millions of Muslims who live in states that are governed in the name of Islam or in which certain patterns of governance are legitimated in the name of Islam. In response, these voices add to contemporary debate that began in the late nineteenth century and at the turn of the early twentieth century, when Muslim domains experienced release from foreign control, occupation and rule.

Thus, a figure such as the India founder of the Jamiaat al-Islami movement, Muwlana Mawdudi, can be identified as one of the early critics of modern manifestations of Islamic state rule and governance. As a critic of the form of statehood made manifest following the partition of India in 1948 and the establishment of the new state of Pakistan, Mawdudi promoted his own vision. The vision that he articulated might well be labelled today as a fundamentalist aspiration for Islamic statehood not coloured or shaped by Western concepts of nation, nationalism and institutions of governance. Thus he was at odds with the proposal for an Islamic state form in the guise of Pakistan, and raised opposition to its leaders. Mawdudi, like other populist ideologues such as the Shi'a cleric Ayatollah Khomeini, have inspired change and harnessed political and social revivalism and even revolution to their particular vision of political practice.

Mawdudi's vision of divine statehood

I would argue that context matters in terms of understanding Mawdudi's notions of the state. He was a child of colonial India and an adult of the post-colonial and partition pain that gave birth to India and Pakistan in 1948. He experienced societal and political transformation of the most extreme and bloody kind. Born in 1903 in pre-partition India, he died in 1979 in the Islamic Republic of Pakistan. He was a leader and founding figure of Jamiaat al-Islami (the Islamic Association). He made a significant attempt to influence the debate about the nature of the state in Pakistan after its formation in 1948. Displeased at the outcome of partition and the rise of Muslim League figures such as Jinnah to the portals of power in the new state, Mawdudi advocated change from within to reach the goal of 'authentic' Islamic statehood. 'Islam,' he declared, 'is a revolutionary doctrine and system that overturns governments. It seeks to overturn the whole universal social order... and establish its structure anew.' In his authentic version of the state, Muslim institutions were central to governance, including a president (who must be a Muslim), a consultative council (*majlis al-shura*), Muslim courts and judges and advisory roles for others to create checks and balances on earthly authority. Sovereignty would remain with Allah, and not the people. The laws of Islam as an authentic way of life, and not just politics, remained Mawdudi's ambition. The notion of territorial units with sovereignty from the people, borders and nation-states was an obtacle to his goal of pan-Islamic statehood. Thus, he opposed 'Muslim nationalism', yet supported anti-colonial movements. He rejected nationalism and secularism as un-Islamic, threatening the sovereignty of God and his law.

According to Mawdudi, the first principle of an Islamic state was unity and the universal sovereignty of God. He declared that 'The belief in the Unity and the sovereignty of Allah is the foundation of the social and moral system propounded by the Prophets... The *shari'a* is a complete scheme of life and an all-embracing social order' (Esposito, 1984, p. 147). For Mawdudi there is absolutely no separation between the state and the mosque, religion and politics, public and private. Thus a community governed by the *shari'a* is an Islamic state (*dawla Islami*). Law is God-given, and all that people can do is 'create laws not covered by the *shari'a'*. Rule is the responsibility of every man and woman, yet the leader (the ruler / caliph, *amir*) may be selected by the people to represent God and their fellow Muslims. So powerful was the appeal of Mawdudi's ideas that he was able to establish and garner support for his movement to put his ideas into action. The state elite in Pakistan considered him a threat, imprisoning him on four occasions and even sentencing him to death for the apparently seditious content of his widely circulated writings. Mawdudi's vision of the state has been described as 'Islamic totalitarianism' (Kedourie, 1994, pp. 5–6). Yet Mawdudi would profess to totalitarianism for all the right rather than wrong reasons. His utopian motif is summed up in a vision of statehood that is authentic to Islam but also democratic. Mawdudi asserts, 'Islam and democracy are not contradictory to each other. ... But the values of western democracy are not identical with those of Islam' (Mawdudi, n.d., p. 198). Through revivalism and revolution, Mawdudi believed his goal would be achieved by a united Muslim community.

In Pakistan that project found many obstacles in its path. In this respect the challenge of putting the ideas, the programme for rule and the agenda for governance into practice, even in a system that appears at least disposed to Islamic governance, is considerable. When General Zia al-Haq seized power through a military *coup* against a leader with a popular mandate and imposed martial law on the country, he claimed that his programme would lead to the achievement of meaningful Islamic statehood in Pakistan. Influenced and inspired by Mawdudi, and through alliance with his Jamiaat al-Islami organization, Zia al-Haq opened the corridors of political power to his Islamist brethren. An Islamization programme was regarded as an important pillar of his iron grip on the country. Although the army remained the ultimate source of power in Pakistan, al-Haq promoted the notion of divine sovereignty through a variety of programmes and policies that affected substantive dimensions of society in Pakistan, including the judiciary, politics, education and human rights. Among the most compelling aspects of this experiment in Islamic statehood were the changes to the economy of the country demanded by the Islamization of the state on al-Haq's orders. One dimension of this included the establishment of a financial system that respected Islamic laws prohibiting the charging of interest on loans. General Zia al-Haq established the Islamic Ideological Council (IIC) to reform the law and the economy of the country. The IIC was successful in obtaining the President's support for the introduction of Islamic banking to Pakistan. Resistance was met in other quarters, however, and in practice a mixture of approaches to interest and its charge on loans emerged. Even in the wake of al-Haq's demise, Islamization of the economy remained an important platform for his successors, with the formation of state bodies such as the Islamization of Economic Commission. Under Benazir Bhutto, some reversals were apparent, but under Nawaz Sharif there was some attempt by state authorities to reflect on regulation of the economy through Islamic rules and norms. In theory the state approves such moves; in practice it has dragged its feet and fudged the issue of implementation.

For Mawdudi, in the realm of politics and governance, popular sentiment is reflected in the process of mutual consultation (*shura*), but the people are not sovereign. *Shura* may be conducted formally or informally through an assembly/parliament or *majlis* (council) consisting of 'adult Muslim males who are good Muslims and know their religion well'. According to Mawdudi, the four primary functions of the council would be:

1   to enact laws that embody the word of God and his Prophet Mohammad and regulations for their proper enforcement
2   to interpret the Qur'an and Sunna when required

3   to deduce laws and rules from the Qur'an and Sunna when none exists

4   to formulate law consonant with the Qur'an and Sunna.

Citizenship of the state derives from early Islamic practice. Two types of citizenship are envisaged. They are based on religion rather than ethnicity or other factors: Muslim and non-Muslim. Rights and privileges, as well as different responsibilities, for both groups are outlined. This distinction, however, underscores the principle of being separate and unequal in terms of the state. Religious affiliation thus becomes a point of differentiation and an obstacle to liberal democracy taking root in such environs. Unlike in liberal democracies, the same rights are not accorded to all people irrespective of race, religion or gender. The Islamic state has to be defended, by military means if necessary (*jihad*) – waging war when Islam and the Islamic way of life are threatened. As an ideologue of Islam in the contemporary era, Mawdudi had a vision of the state that can be viewed as utopian in the extreme; yet in practice he sought to provide a significant voice in the establishment of the state of Pakistan (a Muslim nation) and its constitution. He represented a way of thinking about Islam and politics in the modern world which eschewed attempts, which other Islamic theorists had engaged in, to accommodate Western ideologies of secularism, democracy, socialism, capitalism or communism. He did not wish to take any of these ideas 'on board' or reflect them in his prescriptions for Islamic rule, government and politics. Indeed, the impact of these ideologies, according to Mawdudi, had created an atmosphere of *jahiliyya* – ignorance and abandonment of values, which account for the decline of modern Muslim society and the corruption of its leaders. Mawdudi's message remains potent to the community of Muslim believers throughout the globe, and his influence on other thinkers such as Sayyid Qutb remains significant. One figure who can be seen as following in the footsteps of such revolutionary fervour of state renewal with an Islamic hue is Ayatollah Khomeini of Iran.

Theocracy in action? Khomeini and the state

Ayatollah Khomeini played a significant part in shaping the amorphous social forces behind the revolution in Iran in 1979 and in Islamifying the reformation and remaking of the state and its institutions. The establishment of the Islamic Republic in Iran was largely due to Khomeini's Shi'a-based but unique interpretation and vision of Islamic statehood. Khomeini's blueprint for Islamic government has remained distinct from other viewpoints held by figures like Mawdudi, Sayyid Qutb or Taki ad-din al-Nabahani. His vision resulted from a distinct marriage of ideas, drawing on Islamic tradition and jurisprudence and interpretation (*ijtihad*), and emerges as a unique notion of state. Like those of Mawdudi or Sayyid Qutb, Khomeini's vision of the state pays little or no attention to the West as a means of inspiration. His vision of leadership of the Islamic state, however, is quite different from that expressed by Mawdudi. Khomeini emphasizes the charismatic leader rather than the community. His doctrine of *vilayet al-fiqh* concentrates on the issue of leadership underpinning the state – linked to Shi'a traditions of *imamate*. In his lectures on Islamic government, Khomeini argues that 'Islam as a religion must include a governmental system'. According to Zubaida, he believed that the 'functions which are integral to the Islamic religion require a government' (Zubaida, 1993, p. 16). The head of this state must, in the absence of the Prophet or Imam, be a significant religious leader – the *faqih*. In this sense, as compared to Mawdudi, Khomeini distinguishes himself by proposing a theocracy.

Thus proponents of Islamic revivalism and resurgence such as Khomeini advocate a return to governance that appears alien in the post-modern secular age of nation states, popular sovereignty, democracy and capital-based economies. Rule in the name of God has become outdated and presupposes a backward-looking agenda. Theocratic forms of governance, irrespective of their religious complexion, are normally regarded as a historical phenomenon. The notion of a divine mandate was successfully contested from the late sixteenth century in Europe. The clerical elite soon lost ground to the forces of revolution, democracy and popular rather than divine sovereignty. For Khomeini the goal was to institute governance in the name of the divine and all that was sacred. While the separation of church and state may have been a historical inevitability within Christianity and other religious traditions, including Islam, cutting the threads that fuse the mosque and the state has neither been easy nor necessarily advocated as desirable. The re-establishment of theocratic governance was a goal of many Muslim revivalist movements in the latter part of the twentieth century, with major implications for thinking about the nature of the state. When the Prophet Mohammad established the Medinan community, tied by divine ordinance that transcended nation, ethnicity and even tribe as a marker for governance, a template for state and faith was established. For some Islamists this historical template has been hard to resist as a revived form in its purest sense. Yet one should be careful to avoid making theocratic rule – governance by the clergy or clerical elite – essential to Islam. For in practice this is just not the case. Nevertheless, Iran under Khomeini's vision and, more recently, Afghanistan under the short-lived rule of the Taliban were theocratic regimes with state power almost exclusively in the hands of the clerical classes or elite, with the sole function to order society in all its aspects according to the tenets of religious law.

Ayatollah Khomeini and other Iranian figures such as Ali Shari'ati were inspired to advocate revolutionary change because of the dispossession of ordinary Iranians along with the clerical classes of any power or sovereignty in relation to the state as ruled by the Pahlavi Shah, whom they succeeded in deposing in January 1979. They headed but one of a variety of Shi'a and Sunni Muslim movements, organizations and coalitions that, prompted by the misery of life under unpopular authoritarian and repressive regimes, began to argue that some form of Islamic theocratic rule might be a meaningful alternative to the secular, leftist, nationalist, monarchical dictators and their coteries that ruled them. Khomeini believed, in fact, that theocracy was the only form of governance appropriate to an authentic Islamic state. This struck a chord among the popular masses of impoverished and bankrupt regimes like Iran or Sudan.

Khomeini was explicit in his outline of this Islamic state system: 'It is not dictatorship: the leader must rule according to divine law, not his own will. It cannot be an elected system in which representatives of the people can legislate, nor a popular republic which makes people their own rulers. It is the rule of Divine law as interpreted and applied by the Just Faqih – the duty of the people is to obey in accordance with the Koran' (Zubaida, 1993, p. 17). From these general principles, the Islamic Republic was established, and the clergy dominated political rule, shaping the republic's constitution and appointing Khomeini as ruler. The clergy controlled the cabinet and the parliament, and *shari'a* became state law. The Islamization of politics and the state was to be a comprehensive process. The revolution, Khomeini and his vision of Islamic government were subsequently and successfully institutionalized throughout the 1980s. The death of Khomeini in June 1989 did not immediately trigger a change in ideological direction within the Islamic Republic. Yet in the absence of a strong charismatic figure, and as a result of internal power struggles within *ulama* circles between traditionalists and modernists, a second republic has emerged, Ehteshami claims (Ehteshami, 1995, p. xiv). The state elite and its hold on theocratic foundations of power have been challenged from below by an array of growing social forces. How tenaciously the clerics can cling to power remains to be seen.

In many ways this experiment in theocracy has thrown up some real dilemmas for those with any concern about theocracy in the secular age, democracy and the nature of regimes in the modern nation-state. It has been asserted that theocracies now tend to be fleeting phenomena, and in relation to Muslim domains there may be an element of truth in this assertion, particularly when examining Afghanistan or Sudan. Yet in Iran the sheer endurance of the state, with its clerical elite remaining at the top (despite more recent popular pressures that could just possibly force its collapse) for more than twenty years, appears to have defied popular wisdom in this respect. Of course Iran in the twenty-first century is a much-changed state that has become more outward-leaning and less dogmatic, but the state has not failed with the clerics at the helm. They have succeeded in Islamification (of sorts) of the Iranian economy. This is an economy that fares no better and no worse for its Islamic framework than others in developing Third World states. Where there is weakness, it lies in the growing pressure for a more pluralistic approach to governance demanded by elements of civil society such as students and women against policies of the state that undermine their freedom. This in turn has led to an over-dependence on state power to enforce or regulate – through violence – social protest and unrest. International isolation means that states like Iran and Sudan and Taliban-ruled Afghanistan became 'pariahs' in the international system. The prospect of an accommodation or relationship between liberal-democratic states and Muslim theocracies seems impossible.

The Crown and the Crescent, Saudi Arabia

While post-revolution Iran appeared to challenge contemporary thinking regarding Islamic states as entirely theocratic constructions that, if exported successfully, could threaten the stability of an entire region, it also had implications for those states across Muslim domains that claimed Islamic credentials and gained global legitimacy as such. One state in particular, the Kingdom of Saudi Arabia, would be thrown into sharp relief within Islamic and Islamist circles promoting the growth of a major opposition and critique born out of rethinking the state along the lines of the Iranian model. In Saudi Arabia the news of the revolution in Iran in 1979 was received with some foreboding and disquiet. The Kingdom, established in 1932 on principles of a fusion of funda-mentalist Sunni Wahabi orthodoxy and dominance of the al-Saud family/tribe through territorial conquest, claimed legitimacy as a fundamentally Islamic state. The territory of the new Kingdom included the most holy sites of Islam – Mecca and Medina – and legitimacy through the gift of custodianship of the two holy places for all Muslims. •The founding principles of the new state were essentially Islamic – with the *ulama* of the Wahabite clerical corps on their side, successive Saud rulers have maintained a nation-state underpinned by the *shari'a* and other principles of Islamic govern-ance. Indeed, as one author notes, 'Wahabism...becomes a state ideology [in Saudi Arabia].' (al-Azmeh, 1993, p. 112). While the tribal base of society through the dominance of one family is formalized in the way in which power and society is ordered by the al-Sauds, fundamental doctrines of Wahabi Islam permeate governance and the state. 'Wahhabism,' argues al-Azmeh, 'remains pervasive not only in the educational system, the media and public discourse in general ... [and] not to speak of its spectacular perform-ances in the shape of public punishment of errants and criminals, much reminiscent of the Roman circus' (1993, p. 113). In this Islamic state the clergy do not control the state, but rather legitimate and remain core to al-Saud positions, whether on internal opposition, the presence of foreign forces, the rights of women, or respect or toler-ation of other religions. The Saudi state has no written constitution. The Qur'an serves as the constitution of the Kingdom. There is no elected legislature, and no opportunity for the promotion of plural politics. All law is religious. There is no freedom of association. In principle, the state upholds the fundamental tenets of puritan Wahabi Islam in all aspects of life: society, politics, culture and the economy. In practice, is there evidence that these principles are maintained? How, then, does one explain the significant hostility and critique within radical Islamist circles against this state?

Before the issues that have been raised are addressed, it should already be evident that two parts of the Saudi–Islamic state equa-tion are missing. The first part is the impact of its vast oil resources; the second is the fact that Saudi territory, as I have already men-tioned, is the most holy in Islam. In this way Saudi Arabia is different from Brunei or Kuwait, which also enjoy immense wealth derived from oil revenues but are not symbolically linked with Islam in the same way that Saudi Arabia is. Revenue from oil has allowed Saudi Arabia to insulate itself from the pressures of external economies and global politics and hence devote more time and energy to its state-led fundamentalist Islamic model as directed from above with the support of the clerical elite and imposed on a subject population. Revenues received by the state can be said to have allowed them the luxury of pursuing Islamic statism. As manifest, this statism has been highly orthodox and rigid in interpretation.

One major problem that the radical clique faces, however, is the apparent inconsistency of approach in a universal form. One issue that highlights this is the presence of American troops in Saudi Arabia since 1990, when as a form of protection offered to the Kingdom in the wake of Iraq's occupation of neighbouring Kuwait, the USA sent its armed forces, at the invitation of King Fahd, to protect this vulnerable state. The presence of foreign troops has enraged radical elements, and become a target of their ire against the state and a cause for the denouncement of its Islamic character. The chief proponent of this critique has been Osama Bin Laden. Some of his early *fatwas* were a direct attack on the Saudi state for its failure to embody Islam in its most authentic form. This has resulted in attacks on the ruling family as well as the religious establishment, and in particular the late Sheikh Abdullah bin Baz Grand Mufti and the highest religious figure in Saudi Arabia. Additionally bin Baz was head of the state-established Committee for the Propagation of Virtue and Prevention of Vice, the body that became the arbiter of what would be deemed Islamic and un-Islamic in the Kingdom. Their rulings included the decision to prohibit women from driving. From Bin Laden's perspective, however, Sheikh bin Baz was a stooge of a corrupt, un-Islamic regime and an enemy of what he considered to be authentic Islam. He declared that, 'the regime enlarged the role of bin Baz because of what it knows of his weakness and flexibility and the ease of influencing him with the various means which the interior ministry practices through providing him with false information. So, a generation of youth were raised believing that the most pious and knowledgeable of people is bin Baz as a result of the media promotion through a well studied policy which had been progressed over twenty years' (Bin Laden, 1996b).

The critique of the al-Saud regime is two-sided. On one side stand those, not just in Saudi Arabia but elsewhere, who criticize the regime for its authoritarian and anti-democratic state form. Such critics bemoan the lack of rights, the absence of plurality, and repressive state behaviour. On the other side stand an increasing corps of religious fundamentalists who are infuriated by what they believe to be the moral and religious hypocrisy of the state. They also complain about its rampant culture of corruption, its unabashed consumerism, and the close relationship with the West, and the government of the United States of America in particular, that the ruling elite enjoys. Internally, the fate of these critics has been severe, with clerics and other opponents arrested along with their students and supporters. Moreover, the regime has been periodically compelled to engage in campaigns that provide public demonstration of their 'authentic' attachment to fundamentalist Islam. These have included attempts at creating distance in the relationship with the West, as well as accelerating its Islamic propagation activities at home and abroad. Ruthven contends that such behaviours are part of the condition of 'cultural schizophrenia from which Saudi Arabia suffers' (Ruthven, 2002, p. 149). Whether this is a question of cultural or other factors, Ruthven highlights the dimension of internal differences that alters and undermines the principle of Islamic statehood in modern-day Saudi Arabia. This underscores the difference between the ideal and the reality. Whether Saudi Arabia has much of a future, even as a non-theocratic yet Islamic state form, depends both on the complex interplay of religious and economic power dynamics in the kingdom as well as regional changes wrought from conflict and regime change in neighbouring states. In many respects, however, even were the al-Saud regime to collapse tomorrow, the very nature of the territory as Islamic and resonant with statehood of a Muslim kind would remain.

As this broad overview of the debate about the Islamic state has highlighted, central core themes emerge around issues of leadership or rule. They include whether or not the leader should be drawn from the clerical class, the role of the state/government in raising revenue, the duties of the citizen, the inclusiveness versus exclusiveness of the Islamic state, and the principles underpinning a variety of interpretations of what is immutably Islamic and what is not. While this survey has only touched the tip of the iceberg, it should help readers understand the entirely different religious values which underpin Islamic thinking on government and political systems the world over and the hostility expressed by many thinkers towards Western-inspired political values and systems of government.

3

THE POLITICS
OF PROTEST

Introduction

Dimensions of Muslim protest reveal new insights into how we might look at the configuration of political Islam in the contemporary era in a more holistic way. Hence the Islamic as political in this context can be part of the revival phenomenon, but not by necessity. The doctrinal and clerical link to political activity in such contexts is circumscribed by individual and community-based empowerment and mobilization around contemporary political issues. The politics of protest and opposition reveals a diversity that is appropriate to the subject matter and remains cognizant of global trends that were emergent throughout the twentieth century. The religious dimension of this manifestation of politics, however, cannot be ignored, but what it should highlight is a resonance with other faith systems and modern engagement with political issues rather than the unique case of Islam. Here religion acts to transcend the traditional boundaries of state borders as a transnational force. Thus Muslim protest, in terms of political issues, has assumed a global dimension. How this transnational dimension is interpreted by others, however, is crucial. If interpreted as a threat, then the notion of Muslims politically engaged in protest that goes beyond borders becomes a strategic and global issue. Rarely is Muslim protest interpreted in other ways. In this chapter a broad overview of the more usual manifestations of Muslim politics, including those of protest, contestation, adversarial and oppositional forms across the globe will be analysed. Through this prism the growth of this aspect of Muslim politics as a response to many forms of governance and rule across continents will be examined. This will lead to a reflection of the ongoing tension between secular-driven political agendas and ideologies and the emergence of Muslim opposition to such agendas. Additionally, however, Muslim opposition and protest will also be presented as resonant and consonant with a series of wider global issues that concern more than one population or group of people in terms of how power in modern societies is used and distributed. This reveals the dynamic of Muslim politics that takes place outside the confines of the state, in civil society and non-governmental organizations such as student groups, agricultural workers, women's groups and community-based politics. Opposition issues will be shown to reflect political concern and the generation of discourses that animate Muslims and affect Muslim identity as they relate to the role of the state in education, foreign policy, welfare, economy and human rights issues. It is useful also to ascertain whether schismatic differences within Islam – such as those between Sunni and Shi'a – account for differing experiences of engagement in the politics of protest and opposition. For such differences may be understood better in terms of dimensions of minority status or the politics of the subordinate. More importantly, from a theological viewpoint, I will examine the internal debate and discourse within Islam as it relates to internal revolt, civil strife and rebellion, and its import in contemporary Muslim domains.

Reclaiming the political

Following the September 11th, 2001, attacks by al-Qaeda on the World Trade Centre in New York and the Pentagon in Washington, there was a new interest in the West in Islam and Islamic fundamentalism as a political phenomenon in particular. Muslim countries were seen as the locus of a form of politics that had given rise to terrorism of an international variety that many Western political leaders were declaring as a global existential threat. Fear and confusion about Muslim politics gave rise to notions in many Western communities that their own immigrant Muslim populations were 'enemy aliens' harbouring hate-filled theological antipathy to them. Muslim politics were initially perceived as a single variant epitomized by figures like Osama Bin Laden and movements like the Taliban. While it is true that some forms of Muslim politics do echo and reflect radical anti-Western perspectives, it is question-able, as has been asserted elsewhere in this book, whether such groups are 'representative' of contemporary Muslim politics, and in particular protest politics across the globe. Radical Islamism reflects the same dimensions of religious resurgence as are evident in radical Hindu fundamentalism and in the Christian fundamen-talist Right in North America. It reflects a renewed political engage-ment in public and other political arenas that characterizes religious resurgence in general. In this respect, taking a more gen-eralized approach, Muslim protest politics is reacting to issues that define and confront the project of modernity and reflect concerns about justice, human rights, liberty, equality and freedom. Muslim social protest, in this respect, should be understood in the context of protest politics more generally, particularly as associated with the politics of the dispossessed, socially excluded and marginal in any modern society.

⋅ For in these contexts, and others in the rest of the world, the reason why Muslims engage in politics, and especially the politics of opposition and protest, often stems from their predicament as the poor, the oppressed and the powerless. Sometimes that protest targets aspects of a political system or a political elite that promote secular-based agendas, but it would be a mistake to believe that this dimension of Muslim politics is an attack on secularism *per se*. As a form of the politics of protest, Islamism is largely ignored in West-ern academic literature and in the media. It is only when the protest becomes violent that Muslims become the focus of attention. But their concerns are otherwise often overlooked. Muslim leaders have in the past exhibited a fear of internal disorder, and therefore have traditionally shied away from inciting rebellion within Muslim domains. The establishment of immigrant Muslim populations – mostly minority – in non-Muslim domains in the contemporary era presents alternative pressures for such leaders to grapple with. For Islamic politics, whether protest or not, is not understood as quiet-ist, passive or pacifistic in tradition or manifestation. This goes some way to explain why it is that the violent radicals appear to dominate the picture. Yet the disinclination to internal rebellion does not prevent opposition and protest as a dimension of politics against injustice and inequality – whoever perpetrates it. Evidence of such positions, and of individuals who have taken them, can be found in Asia, where Muslim thinkers and activists such as Badshah Guffar Khan, also known as the Muslim Gandhi, or non-Muslim activists like Martin Luther King have had an important impact on Muslim protest politics of the non-violent kind. Thus, while many commentators opine that Islam lacks such progressive trends in its politics, such a viewpoint ignores that rich tradition of addressing social injustice that has been advocated by people like Badshah Guffar Khan.

Social injustice is an issue deeply relevant to many Muslim populations. The motivation to engage with the political is related to blatant acts of injustice not just against or within their own communities, but outside them as well. Badshah Guffar Khan was a well-known social reformer who, alongside Gandhi, worked to reach a peaceful solution to the end of the British Empire in India and against injustices perpetuated against ordinary people. He argued that there was no tension between Islam and non-violence: 'There is nothing surprising in a Muslim or a Pathan like me subscribing to the creed of non-violence. It is not a new creed. It was followed 1,400 years ago by the Prophet all the time he was in Mecca' (Easwaran, 1999, p. 140). Hundreds of thousands of his followers became known as 'non-violent soldiers'. Their faith was invoked as a guide to protest, a call for justice and non-violent struggle. Their commitment was tested in 1930, when, following an unarmed demonstration against British misrule in India, more than 200 of these protesters were massacred on the orders of the British authorities. Badshah Khan promoted an Islamic position on protest underpinned by his theocratic understandings of Islam as a polar opposite of violence and injustice. For him the symbiotic nature of Islam and peace was more than a reaction to current conditions and injustice – it was an immutable element of Islam. As he declared, 'I cited chapter and verse from the Koran to show the great emphasis that Islam laid on peace, which is its coping stone...' (Easwaran, 1999, p. 146). For Khan, peaceful protest was not an oxymoron to Muslims engaging in political acts. In the case of Mohammad Iqbal, the poet and social leader, political consciousness among Muslims in relation to social injustice was also a key dimension of his life. This found expression when he spearheaded a campaign in the Indian province of the Punjab against feudal practices in the 1930s. He contended that it was a Muslim obligation to seek redress of Muslim impoverishment as a promotion of justice. His campaign struck a chord with the poor rural masses of the Punjab, who joined in protest activities for reform. Thus, although much of this early protest politics was directed against Western and particularly British colonizers and rulers, further depth and dimension were added in the way in which internal Muslim political issues became defined and mobilized around.

Political identity and consciousness were organized around important Islamic motifs and theological reflections on social justice, plurality and equality that have been echoed throughout Muslim domains, in demonstrations by Muslims as well as in opposition to the dominant political authorities. Community politics, in one sense, is an organic norm – part of what defines Muslims and creates their identity. The community (*umma*) is a feature of Islam that is held up as a model by enlightened leaders, as a vehicle to achieve change in the face of injustice and inequality.

The politics of protest and revolution

The Iranian revolution of January 1979 illustrates the power of Muslim political protest against an unjust, corrupt and authoritarian pro-Western regime which at times had been propped up and maintained in power by the CIA. Under the rule of the Shah, the state had failed, despite huge wealth generated from oil revenues, to truly address economic, social and political disparities between the 'haves' and 'have-nots' of Iranian society. Protest defined and shaped the pattern of political action that created the conditions for revolution. This was a revolution in which a diverse range of social and political forces agitated and mobilized for change but was ultimately harnessed by the Iranian clerical elite led by Ayatollah Khomeini. The new political order would be part of a project to Islamize society according to the unique theocratic vision of Khomeini and his supporters. The revolution was the culmination of decades of misrule, an abuse of power coupled with spiralling economic and social problems in this highly populous Muslim country. The majority of Iran's citizens were conscious of the wealth of the ruling elite and the indebtedness of the ordinary people. In this respect traditional class, ethnic and religious markers were irrelevant. Whether one was talking about a farmworker from the rural areas or a bus-driver in Tehran, the sense of injustice, inequality and, what appeared to be, Western-imposed backwardness was increasingly palpable. From this situation would rise a number of figures who would give a voice to the dispossessed, raising their concerns and mobilizing support for social, economic and political change that would in fact culminate in revolution. One figure, who in many respects was overshadowed by Khomeini, but was an important inspiration for Iranian protest politics, was Ali Shariati, who along with other figures like Mehdi

Bazargani took a new perspective on Muslim politics in the modern age. For them Islam could serve as an important political vehicle for the ferment of protest against an internal order shaped by the global reorientation of the contemporary order according to Western-inspired norms and values.

Such norms and values, as experienced by mass Muslim populations in countries like Iran and Egypt and Indonesia, were largely about lack of liberty, poverty and limited political rights. In this respect Muslim protest has fixed and focused on the same kinds of issues that have motivated more secular protest movements associated with race, anti-globalization and environmentalism (Barry, 1999). In the contemporary era, however, many Muslims have turned to Islam as a means to express an identity through which their voices can be raised. For many, a previous attachment to secularist Marxist or socialist ideologies was abandoned in favour of a new attachment to Islam. Many other Muslims, however, remain attached to nationalist-socialist and other secularist identities.

The new protest politics

The economic impulse behind contemporary globalization remains in many respects unchanged from the liberal economic motives that were influential in eighteenth- and nineteenth-century imperial and colonial projects made manifest in a variety of Muslim domains throughout Africa, the Middle East and Asia. In the latter decades of the twentieth century the international political economy was dominated by liberalism and capital-based economies. In terms of America as the global superpower that sits astride the globe, such values shape the predominant orientation of foreign policy and global positioning, which is more Jacksonian than Wilsonian. The 'New World Order' declared by President George Bush Senior is understood in many developing states as one in which economics matters more than the principle of democracy, justice and human rights for all. Economic control is understood as political power, where the downtrodden majority – including Muslims – are left behind.

Islamist discourse on these issues was evolutionary, and has tended to internalize issues common to the peoples of the globe irrespective of creed or race. In essence, Islamist theologies and ideologies of liberation may be more similar to those of radical Catholic priests in Latin America, but the way in which this dimension of politics is articulated, with its motifs and associated literature, makes it more of a Muslim possession. Such leaders and groups, movements and organizations, seek to challenge, reform and even overthrow the prevailing order – the *status quo*. Their agendas for change encompass a rainbow coalition of Muslim perspectives and strategies for achieving their goals. Some would appear to work in tandem, yet differ in approach or resonance. Others may result in competing pressures and divergent courses. Protest politics is also subject to rites and processes of 'sacralization' that mark out Islamist campaigns from those of others against whom they may even be competing at an internal level. One example was during the first Palestinian uprising (*intifada*) of 1987–1993. One of the most interesting aspects of this mass-based movement of Palestinian social protest and protest politics was the mobilization of every sector of Palestinian society in campaigns of civil disobedience, street protests, demonstrations and agitation. Its goals: the end of Israeli occupation, with the achievement of self-determination and independence and a community-wide withdrawal from Israel and its manifestation as military and civil occupier in the West Bank and Gaza Strip. A significant characteristic of the uprising was the rapid emergence of an Islamist dimension in internal competition with the nationalist protest organization. This new movement was called the Islamic Resistance Movement, and became known by its Arabic acronym Hamas. The leadership of Hamas was drawn from pre-existing social and political Islamist networks from throughout the Gaza Strip and the West Bank. Although Hamas in the twenty-first century is labelled primarily as a terrorist organization, when it was formed in early 1988, its leaders and supporters sought to engage in the politics of protest, demonstration and civil disobedience against the Israeli authorities. Many of their protest campaigns – such as protests to the ICRC, commercial strikes, calls for visits to the families of martyrs – mirrored those organized by nationalist elements. Yet Hamas sought to 'Islamify' such issues. One issue that had enormous impact was the brief but contentious *hijab* (headscarf) campaign spearheaded against Palestinian women in 1988. The *hijab* 'was promoted (and to a general extent became understood) as a sign of women's political commitment to the intifada...a sign of respect for the martyrs' (Hammami, 1997, p. 199). Here both Islamist and nationalist men competed, albeit briefly, to redefine the politics of protest as it pertained to women. Hamas has succeeded more generally, however, in sacralizing the protest against Israel's occupation and accompanying political divisions. In its literature, poems, graffiti, artwork and other media, the religious dimension of protest is demonstrated and designed to strike a chord with the popular masses.

Here the politics of protesting against injustice, as perpetrated through Israeli military rule in Palestinian territories, is defined by Hamas and other Palestinian Islamist groupings as a religio-political force for emancipation against foreign and non-Muslim political domination. In this respect Hamas reflects and betrays its Islamic heritage and foundations in the reformist Islamist movement of the Muslim Brotherhood founded by Hassan al-Banna in 1928. Revival of faith through societal embrace of Islamic mores and values would result in the emergence of a political system attuned to Muslim fundamentals. Such views are echoed in the stand that Hamas takes against its internal competitors for liberation – the nationalist Palestinian Liberation Organization (PLO). As its Covenant declares: 'Despite our respect for the PLO and without underestimating its role in the Arab–Israeli conflict, we cannot use secular thought for the current and future Islamic nature of Palestine. The Islamic nature of Palestine is part of our religion, and everyone who neglects his religion is bound to lose' (Hamas, 1988, article 27). Hence the protest and struggle are appropriated from nationalist monopoly.

Political culture in Muslim domains becomes subject to a new scrutiny and is found wanting by those who claim to represent authentic Islam and its fundamental tenets. Successive thinkers, leaders and ideologues have sought to turn this call for protest and action against incumbent Muslim rulers. It has been claimed that there is a disinclination within Muslim political culture to internal strife and rebellion. The civil conflict that gave rise to Islam's initial schismatic difference has traditionally been viewed as dangerous and divisive. There is plenty of evidence of medieval jurists and theologians cautioning against internal strife with figures such as al-Ghazali preferring the domination of an unjust tyrant to the unknown dangers of civil conflict. In more contemporary times, however, Islamist discourse has reflected an adjustment to this viewpoint particularly in relation to debates about the limits of tolerance in the face of injustice and authoritarianism. Islamist radicals, reformists and moderates have all looked anew at governance and leadership in their own domains, and where they have found them wanting, they have advocated change and protest. As a result, new dimensions of politics and protest have been formulated as a strategy for achieving a return to what is considered untainted and untarnished: an authentic Islam.

Schizophrenic cultures?

As a contemporary phenomenon, then, Muslim protest politics has emerged in more than one guise. A reflection on two types of Muslim locale can illustrate this point. The first lies within modern nation-state constructs in which Muslim governance, or governance by Muslims, has emerged through the forging of new states (and national identity) or movements for independence. The second set of locales are in those areas where Muslim minority populations exist. Some of these locales are traditional – such as the Philippines – while others are new – such as the Muslim minority populations of European countries such as France and the United Kingdom.

The twentieth century gave rise to new patterns of global politics, with direct effects on Muslims and their political cultures. Traditional forms of Muslim governance, such as the Ottoman Empire, were swept away and replaced with new states and the politics of change spearheaded by men in uniform. More and more of these new states and independent political orders were Muslim. Yet the ideology of change was predominantly nationalist rather than Islamist in tenor, ideology and rhetoric. Unification of the community through protest was more often nationalist than Islamist. The new states that emerged in Africa, Asia and the Middle East were fragile, uncertain structures in which Muslim-ness would feature as perhaps only one part of new national identities. The unifying function of Muslim-ness and *umma* under the Ottoman Empire was seriously undermined. Islam was not even necessarily central to the political system and was subject to the perceived ravages of the secularization of political culture. Hence the social forces that gave rise to popular rebellion, protest and movements of liberation and independence tended to the nationalist-, socialist-, Marxist-inspired models of change and revolution, and not Islam, which was increasingly understood as traditional and backward. The facade of new nationalism and nations was sufficient in terms of legitimating new states in a changed global order (Vatikiotis, 1987, pp. 37–8). Once control of the state had been forced from the hands of colonial puppets or forged from partition and conflict, new dilemmas emerged that were symbolic of the competing pressures inherent in ideologies that appeared to be incompatible. In Egypt for example, Nasser, who had seized power with the support of the Muslim Brotherhood, ignored a populist demand for a new political order based on Islamist principles and pursued the building of a new political regime that included nationalist-socialist rhetoric and the persecution of such Islamist elements. When such policies of oppression were combined with agrarian reform, nationalization and a claim to regional supremacy, the destruction of an Islamist opposition was largely ignored; but as soon as Nasser's regime turned sour, so too did Egypt's mass. In Islam they rediscovered a voice of protest and opposition denied to them by the leaders of their own states.

In Pakistan this tension was always apparent. It was made clear in the competing multiplicity of perspectives on the nature of the new state that was eventually forged from the distressing partition of India. How Islam defined the new state and those who would form the core of an opposition demonstrated the protest dimension inherent in contemporary Muslim state forms. In this context Islam was deeply symbolic of the political rather than the clerical, as the political elite of the new state sought to define itself in relation to territory and its new neighbours. In the case of Pakistan, there has always been an uneasy accommodation of these notions with certain political leaders declaring Islam the property and legitimate domain of the state. The Jamiaat al-Islami so important in the founding of the new state has nevertheless found itself the voice and representative of opposition and protest, as part of the system. Tibi refers to this contest as a primarily political one, noting that Islam has never really been absent from societal norms and values. Thus the real issue revolves around the motif of the 'repoliticisation of the sacred', which in Tibi's opinion enjoys a monopoly in the hands of 'militant political groups. Numerous political writers and pamphleteers raise the claim that Islam is not only a religion but also a *din wa dawla* (religion fused with a state order' (Tibi, 2001, p. 118). It can be contested, however, that in contemporary discourse the reclaiming of Islam for the political is also about movements and power outside the state, including opposition and protest.

The state and its elite, then, have become fair game, and despite attempts by such elites, including even those who claim to rule in the name of Islam, such as Saudi Arabia, or of post-revolutionary Iran, the flowering of a new dimension of political culture has found expression through protest and opposition. This in turn has undermined the stability of the state in Muslim domains, generating fears about a Muslim backlash. Yet the grounds for dissent are justified, for a variety of reasons. They are linked to the nature of the state in terms of an abandonment of principles considered integral to an Islamic domain. In other circumstances dissent is motivated by bare-faced perpetuation of state-led policies that are unjust and oppressive. This has been made manifest in grass-roots opposition to dynamics of politics that appear contrary to the aspiration of an Islamic ideal.

In many respects this is illustrated in the Algerian context, where the collapse of a nationalist socialist state-led project that brought revolution and independence erupted in internal protest and conflict that dissolved into a civil war between the state and the Islamist forces. When Algeria achieved independence from the French, after a century of colonial rule, in 1962, the revolutionary populist forces of the FLN (Fronte de National Liberation) seized control of the state. The state, led by President Boumedienne, initiated decades of one-party rule according to the rhetoric of popular socialism. This entailed the demise of plural parliamentary politics, with the national assembly and other institutions suspended. Only economic prosperity derived from Algeria's vast oil and gas reserves prevented a quick rather than gradual descent into growing protest and opposition among the ordinary massed ranks. By the mid- to late 1980s, however, when global recession began to bite deeply into the Algerian economy, pressures began to build. In October 1988 popular demonstrations by Algeria's majority Muslim population swept the country. Demonstrations were called by a variety of Islamist elements to protest at the economic crisis, price rises, and increasing poverty and to demand real democracy. Reform was announced by then President Chadli Benjedid. A year later a national referendum seemed to signal the end of single-party dominance; FLN dominance had paved the way for the formation of new political parties, including the Fronte Islamique du Salut (FIS), an Islamist movement promoting a political agenda in opposition to the state-ruling FLN. Their electoral victory in the provisional elections of June 1990 and the national assembly elections of December 1991 sent shock waves through the region and beyond. What mattered in the wake of the victory was that, despite opposition and protest from Muslims waged through a democratic process, the victory was denied to FIS. FIS had garnered 3 million votes and won 118 seats in the assembly election – without resort to bullying or gerrymandering – and the government responded by effectively suspending the system of democratic politics, imposing a state of emergency and mass arrests and presiding over a nightmare descent into civil war. The claim to the moral high ground and the voice of Algerian protest and dissent lay with Islamists who had not sought a violent confrontation with the state but ended up being drawn into such a confrontation anyway. Yet, in the eyes of the West, as Burgat points out, 'leaders of a previous military junta...masters of manipulating violence, managed to acquire the unlimited confidence of international financial institutions and stuff full their prisons and ballot boxes with impunity; so carefully had they established their credentials as a "buffer to fundamentalism"' (Burgat, 2003a, p. 178). Resolution of the conflict that lay in Algerian dissent and protest remains problematic and troubling.

It is clear that the transition of state to nation to national identity divested of its Muslim dimension becomes subject to contest, opposition and protest which places a premium on the resurrection of that identity. In modern Turkey this has been highlighted with increasing regularity within the fractured political system of this modern nation-state. The enforced secularization of the state and society was orchestrated at the beginning of the last century in the wake of Ataturk's modernist agenda for the new state. Islam and its symbols, including the *hijab* and even the *fez* (traditional Turkish headdress for men), were divested of meaning, emptied and prohibited. Through a military–bureaucratic alliance, successive regimes devised policies for the exclusion of Islam from the face of the modern Turkish state. Secularization of the state as part of the modern Turkish national project resulted in the replacing of one monolithic power form, the state elite, with another, the military. Indeed, the pattern of military *coup* (in 1960, 1971 and 1980) and the maintenance of the military in power in democratized modern Turkey have resulted in immense tension and protest from the masses. In the 1990s Islamists in Turkey emerged as a body, a representative voice for elements of Turkish society. Yet the Islamist message and protest were conveyed or interpreted as anti-Western and designed to bring down the secular structure of the state. By the mid-1990s Islamist parties started making electoral inroads, however, first at local municipal levels, where protest was translated into votes for Islamist parties such as the Refah (Welfare) Party, then nationally when in 1995 the Refah Party succeeded in achieving governmental power led by Necmettin Erbakan. For the secularist Kemalists the result was seismic. Alarmed at the result, and choosing to ignore the protest element on real issues of social and economic injustice, secularist and military elements worked to bring down Islamist elements. Within a year Erbakan was ousted from power. Eventually the Turkish Constitutional Court sought to ban Refah, charging it with an attempt to introduce Shari'a law in Turkey, being in receipt of funding from Islamic countries, and destroying the secular foundation and constitutional principle of the state. Yet the foundation of the revival and protest it reflected should have alerted Turkey's secular leadership, but did not. The roots of Refah lay in the urban working class and the middle class who had grown disaffected with military rule, corruption and economic crisis. For if the state was unprepared to meet the demands of the urban mass for basic education, welfare and justice, the Islamists were prepared to step into the breach, and protest was effectively translated through the electoral route. As has been argued, 'Refah used democracy as a yardstick by which to judge the failures of Turkish secularism to be truly pluralistic, to respect the rights of all its citizens, including their freedom of conscience' (Esposito and Burgat, 2003, p. 80). In failing to address the protest element motivating the shift to the Islamists, however, the state elite has perpetuated rather than resolved the problem.

Polarization of society, between the religious and the secular, has occurred over the nature of opposition and protest, which focuses on very real and genuine grievances associated with any universally recognized rights-based agenda. As such it becomes tied to apparent differences around the basic definition of national identity and the nature of the Turkish political system. Protest is not accommodated, because it is perceived as Islamist and thus inevitably anti-democratic, anti-secular, authoritarian and violent. Yet a Muslim identity is core to most citizens of the Turkish state, even if other factors such as ethnic or class-markers differ. Secularism has become almost the property of the state for all the wrong reasons.

Yet although these examples highlight the issue of Muslim protest in Muslim secular states, similar issues are revealed even in states where the ruling elite claims Islamic credentials, such as Saudi Arabia. For if the nature of power is to constrain, limit or prohibit participation, plural voices and challenge, then a protest element, even in Islamic states of a fundamentalist Wahabi legitimacy, is unsurprising. In one respect this is because the critics of the regime (for they represent more than one perspective) believe that how the state currently interprets Islam is a denial of a plural dimension and tradition of justice and protection for the oppressed that should motivate the faithful and their leaders. The clerical elite or establishment is criticized for tying itself to a hereditary elite that is perceived as betraying the principles of Islam.

Perhaps the notion that protest occurs in Saudi Arabia is unfamiliar. Yet protest as a political act, although perhaps not frequently reported, is a dynamic of political life and has the potential to fatally threaten the ruling authorities. One of the most widely reported acts of protest was the Mecca uprising of 1979. Further protest has been undertaken by Saudi Arabia's Shi'a minority and groups such as women and students. The Shi'a minority accounts for around 12–15 per cent of the population of Saudi Arabia and mostly reside in the al-Hasa province. The official orthodox Wahabi position towards the Shi'a population is hostile, reflected officially by the clerical elite. The 1979 revolution in Iran emphasized differences between Shi'a and Sunni Wahabi orthodoxy and unsettled the ruling elite in Riyadh. The Shi'a were subject to discrimination by the state, which had resulted in past protest, including the 1953 and 1956 Saudi Aramco workers' strike in which Shi'a workers were the majority. In 1956 a royal decree was issued prohibiting strike action. Following the Iranian revolution in 1979 there were reports of Shi'a protest and Saudi crackdown in the al-Hasa region, but on the occasion of the annual *Hajj* in Mecca that year, it was Sunni not Shi'a discontent that erupted against the Saudi authorities in a devastating protest. Protest and opposition erupted in a major confrontation with the state at the most holy site in Islam – Mecca. The Sunni opposition in Saudi is home-grown, and in addition to a focus on theological and religious dissent has highlighted protest around allegations of Saudi corruption and human rights abuses as well. The protestors remain hostile to the state-employed clerical establishment, accusing them of being nothing more than emasculated legitimators of Saudi rule. During the *Hajj* in November 1979, these Sunni elements took over the Grand Mosque in Mecca. Their leader, Juhayman al-Utaibi, promoted an anti-royal, anti-Western agenda. His targets were the royal family and the clerical establishment. His hundreds of supporters betrayed the depth of dissent in a kingdom where stability had hitherto been taken for granted. The siege lasted weeks, with hundreds killed and many more injured. Although lacking widespread popular support, the nature of the protest alerted the Saudi authorities to the shaky ground they occupied. Wealth sharing was not enough to buy loyalty and legitimacy.

Saudi opposition was forced underground, but continued throughout the 1980s to formulate a critique of the state that echoed growing discontent throughout the country. A well-educated and expanding stratum of young people experienced disillusionment at the lack of freedom so apparent in their political system. Economic tensions rose when oil prices and rentier revenue began to drop, leaving the rich still rich, but with a huge disparity between them and the poor. Additionally, the Afghan Arab factor figured in the landscape of opposition following the collapse of the Soviet occupation of Afghanistan and the *mujahideen* victory in 1989. It was the 1990–1 Gulf crisis following Iraq's invasion of Kuwait that gave rise to the most significant and widely reported acts of protest and opposition since the Mecca rising a decade earlier. In late 1990 a wave of protest and dissent was visible in the kingdom, and was reported by the world's media. A petition calling for reform was widely publicized, highlighting lack of freedom in areas of justice and equality. The gender equality issue was highlighted by a very public act of civil disobedience, when a small group of Saudi women broke the religiously sanctioned prohibition against driving by forming a convoy in the Saudi capital, Riyadh. Their actions outraged the ruling elite, but were a powerful demonstration of the politics of protest in a restricted political arena. The politics of protest also included others in the political spectrum, such as the restive elements of the conservative Islamist corps of Saudi Arabia. Their ire was ignited by a decision of the ruling regime to allow the stationing of foreign and Western forces on Saudi territory, leading them to question the legitimacy of the regime that was claimed in the name of Islam and its values. Such critics cast suspicion on the Islamic dimensions of the Saudi-ruled state. A letter penned by one such dissident, named Sheikh Salman al-Auda, in 1996 states the case for reform:

> Corruption has taken its roots in our society as well as in nearly all other Muslim societies with varying degrees. It has engulfed all aspects of our life, from the spiritual to the mundane. It could be a grave mistake on our part to think that such a reform can be realised with theories and intentions only. This is wishful thinking. . . . Reform will not come about until we are ready to bear hardships for the sake of our beliefs . . . We are calling for freedom of expression which allows people to express their beliefs and lets them participate in the reform process for this nation (Ummah), which is surrounded by dangers from all sides. It is an open secret that our society has become analogous to an island in the middle of a restless sea waiting to devour it. (http://www.saudhouse.com/dissidence/letter_from_salman_al_auda.htm)

Clerics like al-Auda and Sheikh Safar al-Hawali struck a chord with many rights-poor Saudis, and their message of protest was a threat to the authorities. They preached a fundamentalist slogan, but embraced the rhetoric of reform, change and protest as a vehicle for their goals. They had challenged the power on the throne and in the state pulpit throughout 1991 and 1992, when they achieved the signature and support of hundreds of clerics in demands for reform to conform to the Islamist vision. Such figures were using the power of preaching and the pulpit as a means of protest – a popular base to informal political action in a society with limited opportunities for formal public protest and debate.

The demand for reform was outlined not just in fundamentalist terms, but linked to issues of independence of certain state actors, mechanisms of accountability, greater opportunities for political participation, a crackdown on corruption and reform of public administration. In July 1992 the fundamentalists took their protest further and issued what became known as the Memorandum of Advice. Reform was top of the agenda again – reform towards a more, not less, authentic Islamic state. This meant enforcement of Islamic strictures (as interpreted by the clerics) and a demand that relationships with non-Islamic states be severed. This was tied to the demand that the clerical establishment be made independent of the al-Saud family. The government responded with condemnation coupled with denunciation by the ruling clerics. The most outspoken elements of the opposition were then subject to the full power of the security services and were considered a threat to the state. Stricter regulation of what was said in mosques was also intimated in a speech by King Fahd in 1992. Yet the regime believed the source of opposition and protest to be inspired by radical external elements designed to undermine the credibility of the al-Saud–Wahabi alliance that was the glue of the modern state. At this stage the source of internal protest was in some respects unacknowledged as just that. The government chose to root out opposition and instituted only cosmetic reforms to the political system. Opposition elements were driven out of the country, to become exiles in more liberal states, such as the UK. By 1993 the noose was tightening, and a wave of arrests of opposition/protest elements was instituted. Those who escaped prison lost their jobs, or their families were subjected to harassment, and travel restrictions were imposed on them. Sheikh Salman al-Auda and Sheikh Safar al-Hawali were both arrested and held in administrative detention. This news prompted further protest and demonstrations, yet it would be six years before the two were released. Nevertheless, the potency of their protest message had inspired others, including the radical Saudi, Osama Bin Laden. In Bin Laden's case the protest took a very bloody form, and was translated into terror of a devastating kind. Within Saudi Arabia, in the absence of meaningful reform, protest politics will continue and probably become increasingly violent.

A very real problem of Islamist and liberal opposition exists underground. It splits families, it nibbles away at the legitimacy of the ruling authorities, and prepares for change. Bin Laden, who had lost the right to Saudi citizenship and been exiled to Sudan in 1994, had championed such protest. One issue that Bin Laden has not championed, however, is that associated with the protests over women's rights in Saudi Arabia. Prejudice against women is commonplace, particularly in public arenas, including the political, from which women are excluded altogether. The privilege of citizenship does not accord them the same rights as men. Protest has been limited, but has been a powerful demonstration of a political system that leaves them devoid of a formal role and influence. Nevertheless, Saudi women are tied to the politics of the subordinate, not that of the dominant.

Minority locales and protest politics

It has been demonstrated that in contemporary times the nature of protest politics in majority Muslim domains is varied and expressed through a variety of means, including the ballot box, street protest, the mosque pulpit, and the act of preaching. Issues of protest appear to be rights- and reform-driven, although the end goal may vary. Do such patterns of politics change when we examine the politics of protest in locales where Muslims constitute a minority, and more specifically in political systems deemed liberal-democratic in nature? Are the issues around which protest takes place altered by the degree of political participation available in such societies?

Although in the West it is common to think of Muslim minorities as a modern phenomenon, tied to immigration by Muslim national groups such as the Turks to Germany, Albanians to Italy, Algerians to France, and Pakistanis to the UK, Muslim minorities have a historic presence in many African and Asian countries, such as Mali, Nigeria, the Philippines, Benin, India and China. Muslim minority politics is, therefore, a global occurrence, of which protest is one element. Western Europe enjoys a diverse Muslim minority population of around 13 million in its states, and has neighbouring states to the east with historic Muslim minorities, such as Bosnia and Albania. Diversity is the hallmark of European minority populations even within the boundary of any one state. Muslim minorities may consist of predominant national groups, but their political allegiances are varied. Political issues around which certain groups coalesce may be local, connected to rights of worship or social exclusion; national, linked to national economic or foreign policy; or international, expressed through mobilization around issues such as the global war on terrorism and the Palestinian–Israeli conflict or the Kashmir dispute. Yet it would be disingenuous to assume that even global issues are able to unite or give a monolithic dimension to Muslim opinion or protest. Such issues are dynamic and can have a changing focus. Some mobilization is focused on a critique of the state – particularly as it relates to race or immigration issues or the role of religion in public and political arenas.

Protest politics has increasingly coalesced, however, around issues related to the socio-economic conditions of Muslim minority populations, including unemployment and social exclusion. In this respect mobilization around political issues is similar to that of other immigrant communities in Europe which have also experienced discrimination and inequality. This is particularly pertinent to second-generation and young immigrants, many of whom experience real issues relating to their identity and sense of belonging. This has been translated into a reflection of a real tension between experiencing life in a majority secular culture and framework of politics and the sense of identity derived from a religious attachment to Islam. Contrary to many popular perceptions, this does not necessarily translate into Islamist radicalism, but can mean a heightened sense of political consciousness that challenges mainstream secular culture and the norms and values associated with it.

This particular point can be demonstrated by reflecting on the well-publicized disputes in France over the assertion of a Muslim right to wear Islamic dress in schools and public workplaces. The furore over a very public demonstration of religious attachment in a highly secularized society hinted at deep-seated issues within that culture. As has been highlighted, the protest undermined a particular stereotype of Muslims: in 'France, for a very long time a good Muslim was one that was not such anymore, except maybe for the pointy-tipped slippers that he sometimes wore at home at night, or his hardly British way of making tea' (Burgat, 2003b, p. 32). When young Muslim school students asserted their religious identity through a demand to be allowed to don the veil, they were perceived as being opposed to the very foundations of the French state as a secular structure emptied of any religious dimension. The protest kicked off in 1989, when three female students wore the *hijab* to school, and their principal barred them. This prompted a wave of protest by some Muslim elements, leading to a national controversy. The state was increasingly compelled to take a decision in the face of a demand that religion be accorded a place in France's public school system. By 1992 the state had ruled that the *hijab* would remain banned from the public school system. This issue reflected on dimensions of a Muslim minority presence in such states and the role of the state in mediating relations.

For in multi-cultural Europe, integration, or assimilation, may be a desired norm, but is not necessarily achieved. In Germany the mainly Turkish Muslim minority population has remained at large, at a remove from society. Until very recently they were kept at arm's length by the state and treated more as guest-workers than immigrants. Yet Germany has the most recent record of Muslim movement. The arrival of Turkish workers was prompted in the early 1960s by economic demands, and was secured through bilateral agreements between Germany and Turkey. This group is not unitary in terms of a Muslim marker, particularly given the secular nature of the Turkish state. The nature of this arrangement ensured the notion of 'guest' rather than immigrant, with significant consequences for application for citizenship. In most recent years the profile of the Muslim population in Germany was altered as a result of immigration from other areas of the globe, including Afghanistan and Africa. The Muslim community has organized itself through associations and organizations, but a major political profile has never been maintained. This could be explicable if the connection between citizenship and political rights were explored. Protest has coalesced around issues of racism and discrimination and global issues. Yet, in common with the experience of other Muslim minorities in Europe, the Muslim population of Germany has an age profile that is becoming increasingly younger. Like their counterparts in France and the UK, such people tend to fall into the unemployment and social exclusion trap, which in turn results in alienation from mainstream politics and an increased propensity to radical or protest politics. Formal representation of Muslims in European parliamentary systems remains low to non-existent. In France, for example, whereas the right wing has made significant electoral inroads, there is not one single Muslim elected representative. This can be read as symbolic of an alienation process from mainstream and formal democratic institutions, and thus serves as a warning for such norms and values, particularly in relation to the debate about plurality in democratic societies and the place of minorities within them. The manifestation of informal alternative politics made evident in protest that has a direct impact, however, is discernible if one examines localized politics among Muslim minorities in UK cities such as Birmingham and Bradford. In these places aspects of Muslim communal solidarity have translated into a political voice not just in opposition to the system (though that remains) but as part of the system as well.

Matrix between economy and protest

Economic development of the Muslim world and the economic marginalization of Muslim communities, as demonstrated above in the context of minorities in Europe, add an additional dimension to the debate about the ways in which protest as a political and economic factor is manifest. For the push in the contemporary era to a global capital-based economic system draws politically conscious Muslims into action that reflects the promotion of their norms and values. The matrix between politics and the economy is not unusual, not even as a dimension of protest politics. What is striking, perhaps, is how political and economic empowerment through such actions is perceived as a threat.

One area in which Muslim identity and protest have become apparent in the economic arena concerns the marketing and sale of Cola drinks in Muslim domains. In late 2002, amidst news of a growing boycott of American products in some Muslim countries, a Cola factory in Iran hit the headlines as a new competitor against the global Coca-Cola brand. Zam-Zam (named after the holy spring in Mecca) Cola was proving a major export hit in Muslim countries such as Saudi Arabia, where Coca-Cola enjoyed a traditional market lead. Zam-Zam has been produced as an alternative to Pepsi- and Coca-Cola since the 1979 revolution in Iran, and has always been seen as an Islamic alternative. The notion of a fizzy drink marketed and purchased as an 'Islamic substitute' to US-owned global brands such as Pepsi- and Coca-Cola chimed with a series of consumer boycotts and protests with an anti-American focus. A Saudi newspaper reported that 'sale of US products, especially soft drinks and fast food chains, was adversely affected due to a powerful boycott campaign launched in Saudi Arabia and the rest of the Arab world for perceived US support of Israel' (*Middle East Times*, 20 August 2002). In neighbouring Bahrain, consumer boycotts and public protests were linked to Muslim disquiet at continued American support for Israeli policies in the West Bank and Gaza Strip. American brand-names and fast food outlets were targeted for this boycott. Indeed, in response to the outbreak of the second Palestinian uprising in September 2000 and the Israeli reoccupation of the West Bank in the spring of 2002, Islamist leaders and clerics from across the Muslim world debated consumer boycotts of American products as a means of protesting against its support of Israeli policies. Muslim leaders and groups in Egypt, the Gulf and Pakistan issued *fatwas* urging a consumer boycott of American-produced goods as a signal of Muslim protest and support for the Palestinian resistance. The move was designed to bring pressure on global capital as a point of political protest. In Tunisia economic protest was more informal and micro-managed, and here and there groups of workers agreed to forfeit foreign-brand drinks during their work breaks, donating the money saved to Palestinian relief projects.

Boycott or the production of Islamic consumer alternatives has been an interesting dimension of the economic-political matrix of protest. Yet the extent to which it can mitigate against economic systems in their own domains and globally that are capital-based in origin and largely devoid of an Islamic character is truly questionable. The imperial and colonial project over Muslim domains in Asia, Africa and the Middle East ensured the establishment of economic and thus political relationships of dependence, indebtedness and a move from Islamic economic principles. The development of national economies and modernization, even after the apron strings with the colonial powers were cut, veered towards exclusivity in relation to either capitalism or socialism, with very little room, if any, for a truly Islamic economic system. Even in Islamic states the inevitable tie-in through the economy and investment with capital-based economies works against any perceived obligation to Islamic economic principles. Policies of modernization and development in Muslim domains have left the majority of them poorer, not richer, contributing a further indebtedness and dependence on aid, loans and foreign (mostly non-Muslim) assistance. The political importance attached to economic practices may have been lost on economists in the West, but they are not lost on Muslims who live in regions of the globe that weaken under capitalism, offering little opportunity for overcoming the development disparity or achieving 'global competitiveness'. For them there is an important connection between economic and political circumstances, in which Islam is, as they see it, deliberately excluded.

In this respect capitalism or socialism does appear to make a marginal long-term difference to Muslim status. Experiments in the developing socialist eras of the 1950s and 1960s were apparent in Muslim countries. Under these systems, as with modern development capitalism, the secular dimension of the economic project ensured the absence of meaningful Muslim discourse, influence or guidance. Indeed, under these conditions state-paid Islam only served to legitimate the political elite that advanced such policies. Any notion of a challenge from Islamic or Islamist quarters on these issues was ruthlessly suppressed by the modernizing elite, with its leaning towards the military and a secular, socialist outlook. Political dissent or protest under these regimes was outlawed, and the apparent linkage between religion and development was deliberately severed by the state.

By and large, though, the modernization and development of Muslim economies appears to have failed. Indeed, in the wake of September 11th, 2001, economic crisis within the Muslim world was cited as a factor in explaining anti-Western sentiment within Muslim communities and as a motivating factor in their protest politics. For globalization has become associated amongst many Islamists with a Western, and specifically United States of America, project that promotes a particular vision not only of an economic order but of a political and cultural one as well. This belief has major consequences for understanding and analysing Muslim protest. The evidence works in favour of the above claim. Global economic visions have enriched the Western economies to a far greater extent than those of Muslim countries. As such, Muslim protest and complaint have been recognized and legitimated not by the political elite of the countries in which they live, but by Islamist movements and leaders seeking further ammunition for their constructed critique of the West. They are also harnessed to the mobilization of protest and the creation and promotion of alternative economic structures, including boycotts and Islamic financial arrangements.

In this respect Islamists represent one strand of the anti-global movement that tends to be more commonly associated with long-haired environmental protestors than bearded Muslim ones. Muslim suspicions regarding globalization are in fact fixed in experience, rather than in the rhetoric of fanatic clerics, and this makes the significance of their protest all the more relevant. How such protest and opposition are exploited by Islamists is also important, and it is here that the fine line between real grievance and naked anti-Western antagonism is drawn. For there is real fear motivated by poverty at the heart of such protest. Such views attest to a linkage between poverty and governance or development that has been recognized in other realms – particularly those that are benighted by conflict – through economic subvention and reconstruction and development efforts. In Northern Ireland the end of a civil conflict that has endured for more than thirty years has been explicitly linked by the European Union to the funding of a major programme for peace and reconciliation that privileges economic development as a means out of violence to more peace politics and governance. Yet, as this example demonstrates, along with failures within Muslim domains such as Afghanistan and Somalia, there is no instant correlation between such a strategy and a decline in protest which can lead to violence and terrorism. Additionally, new poverty-busting and development strategies in Muslim countries must, if they are to work, Islamists would argue, be linked to political changes and Islamic economic modelling. This is problematic for international financial institutions (IFIs) and Western aid-givers if Islamic governance results in a clash with norms, rights and values which are perceived as universal but understood as Western in origin.

Islamists seek to eclipse economic models that fail to address Muslim principles and norms, irrespective of whether they are capitalist or communist. Radical thinkers, such as Sayyid Qutb, have been particularly dismissive of Western economic models, for the values that appear to attach to them ultimately undermine what is held central in Islamist discourse. The alternative, around which protest is organized, is portrayed as technologically advanced and exhibiting an Islamic core. Yet the difficulty is the extent to which such a model can survive in an increasingly interconnected global economic system. Evidence of such a difficulty can be seen in even the most cursory examination of isolated economies, such as Iran, Sudan and Afghanistan under the Taliban. These facts mitigate against the success and even the viability of upholding such economic systems as pure types. Indeed, in present-day Iran the mobilization of the population in contentious protest focuses on the weakening economy and its detachment from the international capital-based economic system. The hardliners maintain, however, that by maintaining independence from the corrupting influences of capitalism and the forces of globalization, the future of the Islamic project in Iran will be safeguarded. This adds salience to what appears to be the empty and oft-repeated government line against America as a foe supporting the forces of corruption, oppression and impoverishment throughout the Muslim world. Iran's spiritual leader, Ayatollah Khameini, declared in a sermon in the wake of September 11th, 2001, and the attacks on America that America and Britain had 'perpetrated acts that will be registered as unforgettable war crimes... with no pity for the lives of these people – children, women and old men' (Associated Press, 7 December 2001). The cause of economic woes are pinned on forces outside their grip and the alternative offered as an ideal around which protest can coalesce. Yet contrary evidence is offered by Western economists. The statistics are used to demonstrate that 'these states [Arab and other Muslim] and their peoples have benefited greatly from participation in the global economy.... Economic growth in non-Arab Muslim states averaged 4.5 percent annually during 1965–98, reaching as high as 6.8 percent in Indonesia and Malaysia. By comparison, growth averaged just 2.6 percent for the United States and 3.0 percent for all high-income countries over this period' (Marsden, 2001, p. 1.).

All that these kinds of statistics do is hide the real nature of economic instability which lies at the heart of most Muslim coun- tries, leading to food riots, demonstrations against government- imposed price rises, and eventually violence born out of sheer frustration at unresponsive governments bound by corruption. I am contending, therefore, that economic crisis in Muslim coun- tries has 'profited' Islamist groups and organizations. Through their charitable and welfare organizations they have demonstrated a capacity for assistance to the local population that rivals or out- strips that of the state. This was demonstrated in Egypt following the Cairo earthquake in 1992, when the Muslim Brotherhood stole a march on the government in terms of a rapid and effective response to victims of this natural disaster. In the West Bank and Gaza Strip, the Palestinian Authority, with its well-known reputation for cor- ruption and mismanagement, has lost popular support in the face of well-organized Islamist welfare provision and emergency assist- ance. Moreover, the non-Muslim nature of such economic systems further alienates those who suffer the most, further boosting a turn to the Islamist fold. Under the banner of Islam, protest at economic crisis is promoted and takes place throughout the Muslim world.

Creating a voice out in the wilderness

An argument that Islamism is a product of protest culture in Muslim countries does begin to gain saliency. It is the interpret- ation of the potency of this movement, and the way in which it is represented, however, that has resulted in its being understood primarily in the West as the core of a violent fanatical threat that could pull down Western civilization. In such contexts the justice of protest is lost in the confusion of a variety of political behaviours manifest in Muslim countries and by Muslim minorities in other countries. They are conflated as a representation of one and the same thing: the existential threat that is Islam. This aligns with Huntington's thesis of a clash of civilizations, where the bloody borders are drawn by Islam with the West. Any manifestation of protest is, like a voice in the wilderness, lost in the cacophony surrounding the notion that the Islamist association marks protest out as rooted in terrorism and revolution. Islam becomes the face of the threat, whether it is associated with demands for rightful self-determination or with racism in education policy acted out on Muslim minorities. Hence Islamism represents a form of political protest that is at odds with the tempo of global order. Protest is understood not as a legitimate expression, especially in those countries where such actions are criminalized and prohibited, but as part of a transnational conspiracy spearheaded by characters like Osama Bin Laden. Hence the not unnatural response of those targeted for attack to develop policies designed to undermine or destroy such threats. There are retorts that other means of meeting the threat have been explored, but the counter-response is that the menace is not unpicked with any degree of consistency or nuance that satisfies those who believe their lives are pushed into poverty and powerlessness as a result. Thus, while the threat within Islamism should be acknowledged, it must be distinguished from the politics of protest. In the same way that in the 1960s Black protest politics was eventually disaggregated, with the justice of demands acknowledged, the same should happen with Islamist protest politics. This needs to be recognized because for an increasing number of people Islamism is a dimension of their political identity, displacing other markers such as socialism, Marxism or nationalism. Yet the issues around which Islamist protest are organized are not specifically Islamic. A failure to tackle the problem without addressing the cause of the problem will be likely only to provoke more protest, not less. Islamism has offered a voice to the dispossessed and disenfranchised, those who are socially excluded or pushed to the fringes of modern society. In this respect modern society, whether in downtown Jakarta or in the shanties of Cairo, appears to have failed Muslims, who are motivated to raise their voices in protest through the megaphone of the muezzin's call from the mosque.

In conclusion, then, Islamic politics has an extensive profile and a history that is rich and diverse, and protest and opposition are a legitimate, yet under-examined dimension of it. In the contemporary period, protest politics has been firmly associated with Islamic resurgence and Islamist politics in all its varieties. Most politically active Muslims are spurred on by issues of justice, rights and the place of faith in politics and society, including economic status, in the modern world. Muslim communities are inextricably tied into the modern global tempo and are, by virtue of their human condition, moved to react to it. If the majority of Muslim populations live in countries characterized by economic crisis, poverty, spiralling inflation, high unemployment, high infant mortality and child malnutrition, and authoritarian governance, it is natural to find opposition and protest associated with a demand for change. The Caliphate may have crumbled with the decline of the Ottoman Empire, but the aspiration for governance with Islamic hues remains in the heart of many politically mobilized Muslims. They do not, however, all look backwards for a future model that is fundamentalist and violent. In this respect contemporary Islamism or political Islam represents a transnational protest movement for justice and rights for those who are denied them. The perceived threat that they represent is, it can be argued, partly explained by the failure to meet or recognize the legitimacy of such demands, particularly when they are met elsewhere.

4

THE DEMOCRACY DEBATE: INTRACTABLE PATHS?

Introduction

> No doubt, the defining concept of the 1990s is democracy. Like *Coca Cola*, democracy needs no translation to be understood everywhere. Democracy, however, is easier to say than to create.
>
> Norton, 1993, p. 206

Democratization, the promotion of liberal democracy and its relation to Islam, became the catchword of the 1990s. Throughout the 1990s Western governments spent hundreds of millions of dollars promoting democracy in Muslim domains. Yet, as political scientist Larry Diamond highlights, democracy does not come in a prefabricated package such that 'one size fits all'; nor is it something that will work when imposed wholesale by external actors. Diamond contends, in the context of the debate about post-war reconstruction in Iraq, that

> democracy is not a gift we as Americans can bestow on Iraqis – or any other people. It is an opportunity that each people must discover, grasp, and craft for themselves. All we can do is to help them establish a new national context of legality and order, of consultation and mutual respect and trust, in which such a new political and economic future can be crafted. And even that we can only do effectively in collaboration with many other international partners and institutions. (Diamond, 2003, p. 4)

Some would argue, from within the Muslim world and outside it, that the promotion of democracy was, however, a way in which the West once again used its economic and political influence not only to shape but to dominate global debates at a philosophical and political level in the ultimate service of global capitalism. The logic of this argument is that by directing and driving democratization from above, it is not difficult to discern an attempt by policy-makers in Western governments to influence political systems across the globe which fail to meet the yardstick of liberal democracy and its economic counterpart of capitalism. The fact is that surveys such as those produced by Freedom House identify a major democracy deficit in Muslim domains. Moreover, while the rest of the world moves inexorably along the path of democratization, Muslim regions, notably the Middle East, are characterized by majority Muslim countries where the prospects for democracy have been stymied. The absence of democracy and freedom has direct consequences for the majority Muslim populations of many modern states. In 2001 and 2002 the Freedom House surveys identified only one majority Muslim country that they rated as 'free'. Only eighteen countries were rated 'partly free', and twenty-eight were rated not free at all. Yet, Freedom House contended that this did not necessarily indicate a fundamental incompatibility between Islam and democracy. It pointed out that 'the majority of the world's 1.2 billion Muslims live under democratically elected governments, in countries like Bangladesh, India, Indonesia, and Turkey' (Freedom House, 2001, p. 1). The democracy deficit in Muslim countries was identified by Freedom House as attributable to 'high degrees of military influence, the persistence of monarchies and personal authoritarianism, and the influence of radical ideologies such as Baathism and jihadist Islamism. All have helped give birth to tyrannical regimes and violent movements in the region' (Freedom House, 2002, p. 1).

As the survey evidence demonstrates, the drive towards democratization in societies and states with majority Muslim populations presupposes the absence of democratic trends. Furthermore, many commentators point to an incompatibility of Muslim ideologies with accompanying notions of freedom, pluralism, participation, equality of opportunity, justice and a global economic order based on free-market economics, in explanation of the weak root of democracy in so many Muslim domains. Appreciation of this approach has informed the programme of many Western governments and international financial institutions such as the IMF and the World Bank, which have supported economic recovery programmes and debt rescheduling across the developing economies of majority Muslim domains. As a result, many Muslims interpret Western motives as a form of targeting of Muslim domains. Western-supported development programmes are interpreted by the leaders of populist Islamist movements as an anti-Islamist plot. Islamist leaders argue that Western governments use such issues as a pretext or excuse for interference in the politics and economies of Muslim countries. There is a tangible dissonance between what the West says and what Islamists hear. Many Muslims remain genuinely suspicious of Western motives in promoting democratization efforts in Muslim domains. Up to a point, this suspicion has been acknowledged. As US State Department official Richard Haass stated, 'Muslims cannot blame the United States for their lack of democracy. Still, the United States does play a large role on the global stage, and its efforts to promote democracy throughout the Muslim world have sometimes been halting and incomplete' (Haass, 2002). Take, for example, the former Soviet Muslim states of Azerbaijan and Kazakhstan, where the fall of communism led to the establishment of successor states with resurgent and developing national identities in which Islam was central. The possibilities offered by natural resources of oil for development and input into the global rather than the Soviet economy has also been apparent. It can be argued that governments of the USA and Europe, wanting to exploit such resources, only engaged in advocacy of democratization when explicitly linked to economic liberalization. Moreover such approaches were inconsistently applied across Muslim domains. Haass accepts this as a drawback of previous interventions. 'At times,' he acknowledges, 'the United States has avoided scrutinizing the internal workings of countries in the interests of ensuring a steady flow of oil, containing Soviet, Iraqi and Iranian expansionism, addressing issues related to the Arab–Israeli conflict, resisting communism in East Asia or securing basing rights for the US military' (Haass, 2002).

Identification of the 'absence of democracy' or the presence of the 'wrong kind of democracy', especially one that was locally devised rather than European in origin, informed a particular foreign policy approach by many Western governments. In this way the policy-makers relied on an academic corps to support their new policies on democratization and its import for engagement with Muslim states. Such policies and the promotion of such ideas were an extremely important dimension of the first Bush Administration, when the USA found itself engaging in conflicts as combatants or peacekeepers in states and countries with significant Muslim populations or in which Islam was a core of identity, from Iraq to Bosnia to Somalia. The war for democracy was one aspect of the *raison d'être* for new engagements and interventions. Thus, the discourse or debate against Muslim societies and their real or perceived anti-democratic tendencies became a feature of the early 1990s and a signature tune of the post-Cold War era linking the debate into other realms in relation to Islam as the new enemy and major terrorist threat. In this debate not only was exception being taken to the absence of democracy in certain regimes, but there is evidence to suggest a greater respect for sovereignty in these matters, depending on the nature of the regime engaged with. Haass remarks, 'By failing to help foster gradual paths to democratization in many of our important relations – by creating what might be called a "democratic exception" – we missed an opportunity to help these countries become more stable, more prosperous, more peaceful, and more adaptable to the stresses of the globalizing world' (Haass, 2002). Within the debate, however, Islam as both a faith and an ideology was attacked for its anti-democratic features. Such features were ascribed overwhelming importance, and other features of the faith that may have been said to display democratic tendencies were dismissed as 'ideological' and not 'real' in so far as they did not measure up to the Western yardstick that was employed in countless surveys and studies of developing democracy and democratization in the first half of the 1990s.

Furthermore, according to such criteria, there was growing evidence of a discourse within a number of Islamist movements, and especially those on the more militant and radical fringes of the political spectrum, that fundamentally rejected democracy as incompatible with the ambitions and political programmes of these groups and organizations. The compatibility of liberal-democratic concepts with Islam became a key focus of internal Muslim debate. Many leading Islamist ideologues, such Hassan al-Taurabi or Sheikh Rashid al-Ghannushi, articulated ideas that were either broadly supportive of democracy or that advocated a mixed model of representative democracy within the framework of Islamic law. Others, such as the leadership of the Islamic Salvation Front (FIS) in Algeria, rejected what they perceived as 'Western style' liberal democracy from the outset of its campaign of opposition to the rule of the FLN. FIS opposed the maintenance of so-called democratic institutions that, under the rule of the FLN, had perpetuated the iron fist of one-party rule. FIS, other Islamists and secular opponents opposed such democratic concepts in a country that had succeeded in overthrowing the mantle of French colonial authority only to find itself cloaked in a secular regime of increasingly authoritarian rule pushed into economic crisis by an anti-democratic elite. The stance of so many other Islamist movements across the globe *vis-à-vis* democracy was informed, therefore, not just by a particular interpretation of Muslim scriptures on the topic, but by the experiences of Muslims living in regimes that were largely secular and anti-democratic in nature. Antipathy to the advocacy of liberal-democratic models, then, was also informed by the less than even-handed approaches of Muslim regimes as well as Western governments.

A number of important themes have thus emerged from the debate about democratization in Muslim societies. The first theme concerns the critique and counter-critique that Islamic and Arab civilization is uniquely undemocratic and, therefore, that the Muslim world can never democratize in a meaningful manner. This debate has raged for a number of years, resting on discourse and debate generated by work such as Huntington's 'Clash of Civilizations' thesis, Kedourie's work on Muslim political culture, and political scientists like Martin Kramer who argues that Islam, in particular, 'repudiates' the contemporary features of democracy. As I have already noted, such an approach finds support for its case in the work of various Islamist ideologues who do indeed reject democracy. I shall examine their ideas and the basis for their approaches. In addition, a number of other Muslim and non-Muslim authors refute this critique of Islam and contend that there is evidence within Islamic political culture of a meaningful discourse and engagement with democracy, and that not only have such debates taken place, but that there is evidence of representation, participation and plurality in a variety of Muslim political systems past and present. Indeed, they point to an extensive debate about the relationship between democracy and Islam that emerged at the beginning of the twentieth century and re-emerged in the 1990s. In this respect Muslim discourse about democracy has been intimately connected to the debate about modernity and the impact of modernization on Muslim domains. The association of such processes with the experience of colonial domination and foreign occupation has also played its part in shaping the discourse as a response and reaction to contemporary politics throughout the twentieth century.

The impulse to actively support or engage in programmes that promote democracy, as part of global political and economic restructuring, is as strongly promoted by Western governments in the twenty-first century as it was in the twentieth century. It is important to recognize, though, that the errors and damage, in terms of a variety of relationships at a variety of levels, wrought by earlier activities is acknowledged. In part this acknowledgement stems from the fact that the majority of Muslim majority countries have failed to democratize. Moreover, Western governments have also recognized that the prejudice that accompanied previous efforts resulted in negative consequences for the democracy project. Attempts to pressure for liberalization or greater democratic change in Muslim societies have floundered and created pockets of conflict and disorder. This has been recognized as problematic by policymakers like Haass. He states: 'Yet as we make democratisation a higher priority in our dealings with the Muslim world, like medical doctors we must above all obey the Hippocratic oath and first do no harm. Unrestrained zeal to make the world better could make it worse' (Haass, 2002). If the advocates of democracy remain committed to their cause, then there is a need to examine past experiments in Muslim domains, to understand why these domains were so unreceptive to them.

In the case of Algeria, the pressures for democratic change pitted Islamists and others against a secular national government in a political confrontation that then spiralled into a bloody civil conflict in which hundreds of thousands of lives were lost, atrocities were committed by both sides in the conflict, and violence became increasingly atomized. Moreover, external actors continued to support and extend legitimacy to an authoritarian regime that waged war against its own population. These external actors, and more specifically EU states, reinforced a monopoly of power that worked against democratizing tendencies on the ground. In such a context the line between Islam and the absence of democracy was deliberately blurred. Islamists were perceived, and more importantly portrayed, in the international media and other literature as inherently anti-democratic and the enemies of pluralism and free association in Muslim domains. Yet at the same time Islamist and Muslim social and political forces across the Muslim world spearheaded the campaign to end authoritarian structures. From the outset, the problem with such campaigns was that they targeted both secular and Muslim authoritarianism, and the self-proclaimed goal was the re-establishment of 'genuine' Muslim self-rule and governance. Islamists were even prepared to resort to arms against authoritarian regimes where democratic tendencies had long been absent. Such regimes survived, not necessarily because of popular support, but because the international community appeared unwilling to support democratic change that might empower Muslim political communities, whether radical or reformist, along the way.

The international community, and in particular Western governments, argued that Muslim ambitions for self-governance, achieved by utilizing democratic mechanisms such as free elections, would result in one form of authoritarianism being replaced by another. These arguments were bolstered by the patterns of regime change that had taken place in states such as Iran, Afghanistan and Sudan. These examples, and the press coverage associated with them, went a long way in tempering the debate about Muslim engagement with the democracy agenda. In addition, there is historical evidence that states with majority Muslim populations that did try democracy, particularly in the post-independence era of the 1950s and 1960s in the Middle East, Africa and South Asia, quickly collapsed into authoritarian and anti-democratic regimes topped by nationalist one-party structures or autocratic monarchies. Such a perspective proved the culturalist argument that Islam did not embrace or exhibit democratic characteristics. Thus it was that the idea that Islam was uniquely resistant to the norms and values associated with democratization grew. As Salame stated, 'the idea of an Arab or Islamic exceptionalism . . . thus re-emerged among both Western proponents of universal democracy and established orientalists' (Salame, 1994, p. 1). The account of Islam's antipathy towards democracy, which cites it as an exception to other faith systems, engages first with particular understandings and interpretations of Islam as a modern phenomenon. Secondly, such approaches also raid Islam's history to pick out examples of anti-democratic practice as a means of proving the inherent rather than episodic or philosophical exception to the modern liberal version of democracy.

The critique: end of history

In the late 1980s and early 1990s a series of events around the world occurred that encouraged the promotion of the democratization agenda. The collapse of the former Soviet Union, the dramatic confrontations of Tiananmen Square, the fall of the Berlin Wall, the rise of democracy in Eastern Europe, and the Gulf Crisis of 1990–1 all contributed to the definite demise in some quarters of the globe of an old order or *ancien régime*. The concurrent and apparent rise of a new world order, in which the United States of America would dominate the world stage, signalled that political change in the international system was inevitable. Not only did major events occur in the former Soviet Union and Eastern Europe to tip the balance in a 'war of ideologies' that had endured for almost half a century, but a purported philosophical and ideological sea-change occurred that, as Held points out, 'not only provided a reassuring counterpart to the early preoccupation with the USA's fall from hegemony, but, in their confident and assertive tone, went some way to restore faith in the supremacy of Western values' (Held, 1996, p. 278).

One such contribution to this new-found sense of confidence and assertiveness was the work of a former US government official and academic named Francis Fukuyama. Fukuyama in his examination of the tumultuous events of 1989 came to a significant conclusion regarding their import for the future. In his assessment of events he concluded that the ideological foundations of the modern age would never be the same again. Fukuyama asserted that the bankruptcy, evidenced in the collapse of the Soviet Union, of the competing ideology of communism in a global conflict with liberal democracy that had dominated global politics, symbolized the end of history. For Fukuyama, history represented an ideological continuum in which the end of conflict based on such foundations not only represented a victory for liberal democracy but obviated the chances of further conflict on an ideological basis. Fukuyama was contending that not only had liberal-democratic values triumphed in this particular ideological war, but that with the collapse of communism no other ideological challenge would stand in the way. He declared: 'What we are witnessing is not just the end of the Cold War, or a passing of a particular period of postwar history, but the end of history as such: that is, the end point of mankind's ideological evolution and the universalization of Western liberal democracy as the final form of human government' (Fukuyama, 1989, p. 4). Fukuyama was not alone in his assessment of the new world order. The 'End of History' thesis was disseminated and debated widely. It dwelt in the realm of ideas rather than reality, yet reflected an aspiration for reality that was shared in many quarters of the US policy-making establishment. He thus noted that 'the victory of liberalism has occurred primarily in the realm of ideas or consciousness and is as yet incomplete in the real or material world' (Fukuyama, 1989, p. 4). Liberal democracy, as a superior ideological model, would be the means by which the process of 'universalization' would be achieved. Acceptance of this thesis automatically established the USA as a hegemon. Any alternative ideology – whatever its cultural, philosophical or religious roots – was increasingly unimportant to the victors of democratic capitalism and its supporters. There was a belief that the collapse of communism from within somehow signalled the concurrent validity of the universal appeal of Western liberal democracy. For the authors and architects of this new vision, the march of liberal democracy had to be advanced and supported in the national interests of those states that already championed liberal-democratic tendencies and had political systems that cherished such features. As Haass highlights, 'There is no hidden agenda. America's rationale in promoting democratisation in the Muslim world is both altruistic and self-interested. Greater democracy in Muslim majority countries is good for the people who live there. But it is also good for America' (Haass, 2002). It was inevitable, therefore, that the eyes of the democrats would fall anew on the thirty-seven or so states with Muslim majorities in Asia, Africa and the Middle East, and that they would adopt a renewed determination to assist such states on the democratic path. Such a viewpoint, summed up in many studies and publications, increasingly centred on an argument that the Muslim psyche was resistant to liberal-democratic norms and values, including concepts of liberty, human rights and the individual. Muslim history, Muslim politics and Muslim faith were cited as key components in explaining why Muslims were not democratic.

From this perspective, Islam was understood as a monolithic component in the otherwise complex and diverse historical experiences and cultures of contemporary Muslim domains. Like some complex process of distillation of a thousand petals for one drop of intense, concentrated perfume, Islam was identified as a hugely important symbol in explaining to the academic community and beyond why these societies were more resistant to the gospel of Western democratic liberalism than others. Moreover, many scholars asked why the leaders of Muslim countries did not themselves develop liberal-democratic systems. I believe that such approaches also helped some Western governments 'explain away' negative foreign policy outcomes in a series of Muslim countries across the globe that resulted in the exacerbation of authoritarian tendencies in the face of pressures from Muslims for democratic reform. Thus, the reason why hostility to Western policy initiatives on democracy was growing in great measure in states like Pakistan and Bangladesh was explained by policy-makers and diplomats who asserted that there was little wrong with the Western-advocated or supported approach, and that the problem lay with the hostile forces of Islam that condemned anything that smacked of a further invasion of the All-White, All-Great, All-Western vision of the New World Order.

In one respect their fears were hardly without foundation. In the Middle East, Islamists were citing recent histories of Western interference in state creation to demonstrate the saliency of their critique. Hence the role of the British in manipulating constitutional processes for the benefit of their own economic and strategic interest was often cited in Islamist counter-discourse on Western liberal democracy. Nor was this criticism confined to Islamist discourse; it was also evident in other discourses that constructed a critique or were suspicious of the agenda for Western liberal-democratic reform being promoted in a variety of developing societies. Democracy, an embrace of liberal-democratic values, it was believed by policy-makers, business interests and diplomats, was the way the world should head as it approached the twenty-first century. The humanitarian dimension of this project – the way in which universal principles of human rights were underpinned in a democracy – was often overlooked when the discourse was interpreted in Muslim societies. Thus, it is important to recognize that a fundamental feature of this debate was predicated on the idea that the adoption of any old democracy would not do. Democratic socialism, for example, was explicitly frowned upon, and certainly did not figure in the development models, approaches and policies formulated during long policy-making meetings at the White House, the headquarters of the World Bank in New York, or a variety of think tanks and philanthropic organizations headquartered in London, Paris or Geneva. The model had definite limits, and these limits were defined, shaped and moulded in the West. Muslim contributions to the debate were rarely aired or considered. There was a consensus in such circles that Islam was not compatible with democracy or the liberal values associated with the version that would be advocated by government aid specialists, development workers, NGO activists and diplomats. I would contend that the democratic model subsequently promoted to the heads of governments, dictators or putative democrats, indigenous NGOs and local business communities in Muslim majority countries was designed to reflect Western democracy that was linked to neo-liberal free market and anti-state intervention principles. In other words, for some major players the call for democratization did not go up simply for the sake of democratic principles. For such projects were tailored to the economic agenda for the liberalization of the global economy at a time when many Western industrialized states were emerging from severe economic recession, and technological developments appeared to break down distances, national boundaries and barriers like never before. The strictures of the model and its interpretation of economic and political values were, therefore, predetermined and writ large, with no eye to the existence of other orders or approaches that might differ. The sincerity of the liberal or neo-conservative economists was apparent in their approach. For the approach was underpinned by a notion that freedom would be obtained through this model of economic development. Moreover, some principles of Islamic economics were not incompatible with such approaches. Nevertheless, on this model, economies would develop only if they underwent radical restructuring, debts were rescheduled, loans rethought, markets liberalized and privatized, and decentralized industry taken out of the hands of the state. Welfare reform was also important, as was bringing down inflation and cutting unemployment. Economies were to be developed as outward- rather than inward-looking – the global, not the local, market was what mattered. Conditions for aid, at bilateral government-to-government or multilateral World Bank or IMF levels, were rigorously stipulated and included the demand for political liberalization. The concurrent demand for evidence of political change in the direction of increased democratic institutions, mechanisms or practices according to the liberal perspective, as we shall see, was often open to interpretation and tempered by perceived threats to Western interests at home or abroad. In terms of the model, the economic dimension took precedence, and if sacrifices had to be made, there were few in elite policy-making and administrative circles who were prepared to put political principles associated with democracy first.

Clash of civilizations

The issue of Islam and the hostility of Islamists to Western liberal democracy was, as I have already noted, identified as a major obstacle in relation to the ambitions of Western liberal democrats. It had been laid out in specific detail in Huntington's thesis of the 'clash of civilizations', that in brief argued that 'the fundamental source of conflict' in the present day and future will rest on a 'clash of civilizations that will dominate global politics' (Huntington, 1993, p. 22). Huntington, believing that identity from civilization was more important than other types of identity, argued that religion is the most important feature contributing to this new identity; 'even more than ethnicity, religion discriminates sharply and exclusively among people,' he wrote (1993, p. 27). The basis for conflict, argues Huntington, lies in the 'fault-line' between civilizations. The one particular 'fault-line' to which he gave prominence was the one he perceived to exist between Islam and the West. For Huntington, the relationship between the West and Islam was always, and always would be, based on military conflict. His definition of the fault-line is rather problematic. In naming 'Islam', one presumes he is referring to a religious system, but in naming the 'West' he is talking about a civilization. The generation of such labels is contentious, and one is left with many unanswered questions in relation to these definitions. Does the West, for example, include Russia or Australia or South Africa? Does Islam include Pakistan, Nigeria or Morocco? Whatever Huntington's assumptions, he does give further clarification of his arguments against Islam.

For him, Muslims are members of an aggressive civilization. Islam, he declares, has 'bloody borders', and violence is repeatedly cited as an indiscriminate way of life by Muslims against Serbs, Jews, Hindus, Buddhists and Catholics. This theme was developed from Huntington's earlier reflections in an article written in 1984. In 'Will more countries become democratic?' Huntington declared, 'Islam has not been hospitable to democracy...the prospects for democratic development seem low. The Islamic revival, and particularly the rise of Shi'ite fundamentalism, would seem to reduce even further the likelihood of democratic development' (1984, pp. 208, 216). The combination of violence, Islam and anti-democratic tendencies highlighted by Huntington paints a picture of the Muslim world in which Islamic civilization is portrayed as backward, static, authoritarian and vicious. Huntington views the shift to democracy, in whatever form, with a high degree of ambiguity. In addition, any attempt to engage with democratic practices, particularly by those Islamists who in the 1980s he declared were an obstacle to development along this path, must be treated with the utmost suspicion. Huntington leads one to conclude that democratization is almost a non-starter among the people of this particular civilization.

Other authors have gone a considerable way in backing Huntington up. Elie Kedourie, for example, has suggested that within the Muslim world the prospects for democracy are weak. Kedourie declares that democracy will always fail in a Muslim context.

Representative government and other features associated with democratic society and government are, writes Kedourie, 'profoundly alien to the Muslim political tradition' (1994, p. 6). Political tradition, according to Kedourie, is based on a form of 'oriental despotism' which has dominated the Muslim world for centuries. This tradition of rule, which survives to the present day, remains, argues Kedourie, hostile to any form of democratic government through popular and constitutional representation as practised so successfully in the West. For, under the conditions of rule associated with the despotic tradition of Islam, the chasm between ruler and ruled is immense. Discounting democracy as too 'ambiguous', Kedourie sets out to demonstrate that Islam could never accommodate itself to forms of representative government as they have evolved in the West. Indeed, it is clear that representative government in this context is associated with modern, forward-looking, secular and dynamic societies, and that Islam is thereby excluded from the equation. The absence of such a framework in Muslim countries implicitly means that Islam is unrepresentative in the political realm and is traditional and backward-looking to boot. Unquestionably there are elements that contribute to all sides of the debate and, by doing so, draw not just on the present but on the past as well. In respect of the past, Islam is cited as a faith system of a monotheistic type that shares much with Judaism and Christianity. Yet, in terms of a political tradition that has developed over a number of centuries, democracy remains rooted in the West rather than in Muslim domains. This gives it a cultural hue that hinders it in translation to other contexts.

From its cultural locus in the West, it is easy to understand the hostility and ambiguity of fundamentalists and other Islamists in Muslim domains to the democracy project. The import of such projects is regarded with suspicion. At a polemic level the suspicion is then linked to fear of and hostility to engagements with the West that are based on dominant and subordinate relationships. Moreover, there is a defensive posture within Muslim realms that centres on the argument that fair and just governance is part of the pattern of Muslim polity. Yet authors like Lewis highlight that elements of such a polity mitigate against liberal-democratic principles. He contends, for example, that in Islam 'in principle, at least, there is no state, but only a ruler; no court, but only a judge. There is not even a *city* with defined powers, limits, and functions, but only an assemblage of neighbourhoods, mostly defined by family, tribal, ethnic, or religious criteria, and governed by officials, usually military, appointed by the sovereign' (B. Lewis, 1993, p. 6). Such foundations imply the absence of institutions and structures under which democratic tendencies flourish. In this way Muslim institutions, according to authors like Lewis, inhibit democratic impulses that are common to Western cultural contexts. Theocracy is the form of governance that Islam reinforces. As Lewis argues, 'in principle the state was God's state, ruling over God's people; the law was God's law; the army was God's army; and the enemy, of course, was God's enemy... the history of the Islamic states is one of almost unrelieved autocracy' (Lewis, 1993, p. 6).

In addition, if Islam in general, rather than just the fundamentalists, is guilty of anti-democratic tendencies and is associated with a closer affinity to the despot than the democrat, then there is one specific group that has been given careful scrutiny. This group is scrutinized not only for its passive and unquestioning obedience to Islam, but for its actively anti-democratic and anti-secularist hatred of the West. The reason why this group warrants such close attention lies in the contention that it would abuse democratic mechanisms, such as elections to bicameral legislatures, as a means to achieving its ultimately anti-democratic goals of re-establishing Islamic state systems across the globe.

In this vein Martin Kramer's contribution to this debate has been to dismiss the claim that in the 1990s some Islamists represented the drive within Muslim society for political liberalization with some democratic features. The irony that Islamists were acting as 'champions' of democratic mechanisms rather than democratic principles was not lost on Martin Kramer. He critically questioned the claim by Islamic fundamentalists to truly embrace the values associated with this term. In Kramer's opinion the Islamic fundamentalists embraced democracy only as a short-term strategy or tactic to aid them in the establishment of Islamic states. The Islamic state system, according to Martin Kramer, is both authoritarian and inherently anti-democratic. 'Democracy', he wrote, '[its] diversity, accommodation – the fundamentalists have repudiated them all. In appealing to the masses who fill their mosques, they promise, instead, to institute a regime of Islamic law, make common cause with like-minded "brethren" everywhere, and struggle against the hegemony of the West and the existence of Israel' (Kramer, 1993, p. 41). For Martin Kramer, as for Kedourie, the attempt by others (including Islamists themselves) to impute democratic qualities to Islamic culture is the dangerous and naïve preoccupation of apologists who fail to recognize the threat implicit in all Islamist movements across the globe. Yet, how easy is it to tally this vision of Islamism in the contemporary era with the role and activities of, for example, the Lebanese Hizballah movement? For it was true that during the collapse of democracy and the brutal civil conflict that engulfed Lebanon in the second half of the 1970s and all of the 1980s, Hizballah, a Shi'ite militia of revolutionary vision engaged in a campaign to end the Israeli occupation of Lebanon, engaged in practices that were far from liberal-democratic. Hizballah was just one of many militias in a deeply divided society in which the principles of liberal democracy were abandoned in order to 'win' the civil conflict. Other militias, including the Christian-backed militias, were also responsible for terrible crimes and atrocities. Hizballah's record since the signing of the Taif Peace Accord in 1989 has, however, been significant in terms of confounding the critics. For since that time, and despite waging a campaign of resistance which was nationally supported, in the south, against Israel, Hizballah has become a fully-fledged participant in a consociational system of democracy that, if imperfect, has to all intents and purposes remained functioning. Hizballah deputies now serve all their constituents in the Lebanese parliament and have worked to promote the reconstruction of Lebanese society under a democratic framework. Indeed, Saad-Ghorayeb asserts that one of the most remarkable developments of the mid to late 1990s was the apparent abandonment by Hizballah of a previous commitment to promote revolution and the establishment of an Islamic republic along Iranian lines in Lebanon itself. As Saad-Ghorayeb contends, 'Hizbu'llah now depicts itself as a party which represents all Lebanese ... such developments ... are primarily a product of its desire for popular legitimation' (Saad-Ghorayeb, 2002, p. 84). Critics of Hizballah would contend that such activities are not truly representative of the anti-democratic and violent principles that ultimately guide the movement. Ultimately the designation of Hizballah as a terrorist organization by the US and other governments limits further discussion about those who engage only with the political project and its democratic dimensions. A decade of parliamentary accommodation has not convinced the critics.

There are many more who have added their voices to the critique of Islam as either wholly undemocratic or exhibiting undemocratic tendencies that leave it at odds with the global impulse for liberal democracy. Indeed, as other chapters in this book highlight, the debate about Islam and democracy is not abstract but part of other tensions or issues. This is the case particularly in relation to the debate about Islam and the West and the national interests and foreign policies that are elaborated within such a framework. In general, the critique against Islam grew throughout the 1990s and was given added impetus in the light of growing hostility and attacks on Western interests by Islamist radicals. The rise of terrorism, an anti-democratic action if ever there was one, only added fuel to the fire of those critics who warned that Islam and its followers could never behave in a sustained liberal-democratic fashion. Many studies of terrorism, which subsequently examined the Islamist phenomenon, started from the premiss that Islam was anti-democratic and that such bloodthirsty acts were explicable in this base and atavistic context. Such assumptions allowed little room for an examination of the nuances in the debates that were taking place under the wider remit of democracy and liberalization. As the following section highlights, such debates allowed the opportunity for a less reductive account of Islam and its response to democracy.

Fighting fire with fire?: Muslim democracy

Democracy is not a phenomenon created by secularism, a religion and society such as Islamic society can be and is democratic.

Ayatollah Bojnordi of Iran

As the quote above indicates, there are some Muslims who assert that Islam hasn't and never did shut the door in the face of democracy. An attempt to wrest the debate about definitions of democracy from West to East also recognizes the inherent and inextricable link between the Western origin of the concept, its secular roots and the economic dimension. Thus, it should be clear that one motive that Muslim intellectuals, theologians and others have when they engage in the debate about democracy is centred on undermining the Western monopoly of the concept. In this respect they are fighting fire with fire in an attempt to disprove Islam's critics and enemies. They are not, however, arguing that Islam can be moulded to some universal liberal-democratic model that condenses the essentials of secular democratic principles into a useful template for economic development in the global and capital-based world order. Nor do such thinkers and writers attempt to reduce Islam to some one-dimensional perspective that assists the West in understanding patterns of politics across the globe and within societies. How can Islam's democratic tendencies be reduced to a definition or template that explains the nature of politics among the Muslim communities of France or Germany and Oman's changing electoral system and widening of the franchise? The simple answer is, it can't. The proponents of such an approach also need to recognize the dynamic rather than static nature of the debates about democracy and Islam. Moreover, the issue of inter-pretation that has emerged in the work of many influential Islamist theologians and Muslim writers and intellectuals who have en-gaged in the debate over the last century needs attention. Thus, the Muslim debate about democracy covers a spectrum of perspec-tives, from the radical and revolutionary to the liberal and quietest. What is most pertinent of all, however, is that, contrary to the popular perception of Muslims literally turning their back on dem-ocracy, there is evidence of a substantial century-old debate about democracy and its place in the Muslim realm. In other words, democracy or its Muslim variants such as *shura* are a significant feature of Islamist and Muslim discourse in both the twentieth and the twenty-first century. Even in the nineteenth century Muslim thinkers in the Asian subcontinent generated significant debates about democracy, its apparent linkage to Western cultural norms and values, and the response to such assumptions. To contend, therefore, as Islam's critics have, that democracy is deliberately absented from Islam overlooks the debates within the Muslim world on this and related issues. Islam's alternative agenda has a democratic dimension that has been carefully examined, measured and interpreted in relation to Islam's holy scriptures and honed to political standards that ultimately aim to change political orders that are despotic, authoritarian and undemocratic. The following sections, therefore, will include the views of significant Islamist figures such as Hassan al-Banna and Sayyid Qutb of the Egyptian Muslim Brotherhood movement on the modern democracy debate.

Before such contributions are examined, however, it will be useful to outline the terms and definitions that are regularly employed by Islamists and Muslim thinkers when the issue of democracy is debated. It should be clear that this discourse is not about liberal democracy. For in Islam essential elements of liberal democracy, such as the principle of equality, are not accommo-dated. Rather, it is a discourse about elements of democracy, where principles are aligned. The Muslim debate about democracy (*democratiyya*) includes attention to and elaboration of religious conceptions of consultation (*shura*), governance (*hakimiyya*), com-munity (*umma*), legislature (*majlis*) and legislation (*shari'a*), as well as sovereignty (*seeyada al dawla*), elections (*intikabat*) and pluralism (*tawadad*). The terms above, with the exception of the word *democratiyya*, are all part of the language of Islam and are not alien constructs or unfamiliar vocabulary in the Muslim realm. The terms are all-important features of the political realms of Islam and have been interpreted by Muslims in a variety of ways and at various historical junctures. The terms, therefore, cannot be rigidly defined but represent generalized conceptions of principles or activities in this sphere of Muslim life.

The concept of *shura* is most commonly associated with the Islamist and Muslim debate about liberal democracy in the contemporary era. Indeed, it is a principle element in the response to the modern secularizing influences of the democratic philosophies of socialism and communism that can be interpreted as a general process of consultation with the people by the ruler or rulers in an Islamic context. This can be described as a Muslim approximation of democracy (*sans* the equality principle) that is given a dictionary definition of 'government by the whole people of a country, especially through representatives whom they elect'. If one takes the example of the Islamic Republic of Iran since 1979 and measures it against such a definition, one discovers a system of regular elections by the whole people of the country (including women and its ethnic and religious minorities such as the Kurds and Jews) of representatives to a legislature where laws are debated and promulgated with the subsequent approval of a Supreme Council of Religious Clerics. According to article 62, section 1, of the 1992 Constitution, 'The Islamic Consultative Assembly is constituted by the representatives of the people elected directly and by secret ballot.' Such aspirations were thwarted, however, by the centralized and theocratic grip extended by Ayatollah Khomeini as he established the new republic. Yet in the decade following his death, the 'second republic' in Iran has been characterized by a growing movement for democracy that reflects many dimensions, including the clerical class, of Iranian society. The movement for democratization represents an institutional as well as a populist Iranian demand for greater representation and democratic governance. The protests and demands for greater democracy have come from students, women, workers, teachers and merchants. Leading clerics such as Hassan Tabatibi Qumi, Hussein-Ali Montazeri and Muhammad Sadiq Ruhani have supported the democratic agenda. Moreover, demand for democratic reform has echoed in the institutions of government, and in particular the *majlis*. Iranian parliamentarians have ended up in dispute with the Guardian Council and the President over demands for democratic reform of the constitution and electoral laws. The principle of *shura* remains intrinsic to the majority of debates about governance in Muslim domains and is a key feature of new dimensions of liberalization of governance. The increasing attachment to this principle by Muslims belies the traditional assumption that Muslim governance tends towards the authoritarian rather than the consultative.

Governance is also extensively debated in the modern context. Furthermore, historical reference points of Islamic governance are constantly cited by proponents and critics alike. For many interpreters the history of Islam is littered with examples of the abuse of rule by individual men in the name of Islam. Often in direct contrast to the known examples of governance set or believed to have been set by the Prophet Mohammad and his immediate successors, the rightly guided Caliphs, are one apparent historical episode after another where men who ruled in the name of Islam behaved like despots and failed to rule in a just manner. Indeed, there are those who abused the system of governance and the institutions of Islam that were at their disposal and failed their people. One such example is Mohammad Ali, the Pasha of Egypt, who, Kedourie asserts, 'set about destroying all centres of power in the country which might threaten his unfettered rule or pretend to some independence of action, indeed it was the Pasha himself who assassinated his rivals with no apparent conscience' (Kedourie, 1992, p. 27).

Nevertheless, even in the earliest historical episodes of Islam, issues of governance between the ruler and the ruled were recognized as important. If a ruler were considered unjust or ignorant of the people in whose name he claimed to rule under the banner of Islam, then in principle he would be held accountable. Indeed, this was the fate of the third Caliph, Uthman, who lost his life in the face of demands that his rule be just and take account of the calls, demands and debates among his followers as to the nature of the state and its influence or governance over people's lives. His clannish and nepotistic tendencies were undoubtedly frowned upon, and 'a movement of unrest in Medina, supported by soldiers from Egypt, led to Uthman's murder in 656. This opened the first period of civil war in the community' (Hourani, 1991, p. 25). Some historical and contemporary examples do illustrate the 'despotic' tendency in governance and the demand for blind obedience to authority. On the other side of the fence, however, are historical and contemporary episodes of rebellion by the people against unjust rule and authoritarian governance and defence of representative rule in Islam. While in the West it is believed that it is the French and the Russians who have an uncommon appetite for rebellion and revolution, there are rich pickings to be had from the history of Islam. One need only stop and think of the nature of Aisha'a rebellion that is extensively discussed in chapter 5, or the example of the Muslim movements of Egypt that played such an important role in ending both colonial domination and the rule of a corrupt and unjust monarch. Yet, when these past and present demands for better, more open governance are demanded by Muslims from across the globe, they are regarded with deep suspicion because the end goal is governance under an Islamic rather than a liberal-democratic framework.

The role of the *majlis* in any Muslim society varies in importance and size. Traditionally the *majlis* has acted as an organizational principle for collective decision making and legislation as it relates to the law. This mode of organization of public life follows from the Qur'anic tenet that believers should consult amongst themselves on matters relating to leadership and rule of mutual affairs in any Muslim society. In theory, then, the *majlis* acts as a consultative body in service of the ruled as well as the ruler. The establishment of a *majlis* and the role of a *majlis* in any given Muslim society can be important in terms of acting as a check on the role of the ruler in Muslim societies. In Kuwait in the early twentieth century, for example, the merchant class demanded the establishment of a *majlis* to represent and balance their interests against those of an increasingly autonomous ruler. Other examples of *majlis* structures with a legislative function carried out by elected representatives can be found across the Muslim world, including Iran and Pakistan, where successive constitutions have enshrined an important relationship between principles of democracy and Islam. In the Muslim state of Pakistan the principle of parliamentary democracy, through the *majlis* framework, was constitutionally enshrined. There was, therefore, constitutional provision for a federal legislature (*majlis al-shura*) within a bicameral assembly and senate structure. The national assembly elects 217 members and the senate 87. There is provision for universal suffrage. Parliamentary life was suspended following the *coup* orchestrated by Pervez Musharaff in 1999. In October 2002 Musharaff allowed elections. The results confirmed a support for Islamist elements particularly near the border with Afghanistan. Citizens participated in a poll for both the national and provincial assemblies, yet irrespective of the outcome, Musharaf, backed by the military, remains in political control of the state. He can still dissolve parliament and retains ultimate authority.

Sovereignty is an extremely important canon in the discourse of democracy and is given particular resonance and importance in the Muslim context. This is because in contemporary liberal-democratic theory sovereignty (authority to exercise power) rests with the people. In this respect sovereignty as the authority to rule is hence explicitly linked to the notion of representation and accountability in the modern age. The French Republic established in 1789 embodied such principles of sovereignty and representation of the people by the people, ending the divine rule of unaccountable kings and the supporting institution of the French aristocracy. Such conceptions of sovereignty in respect of liberal democracy in particular are problematic in the Muslim context. For in Islam sovereignty is ultimately divine and rests with Allah, and not the people. In such a context, where divine and holy authority is the ultimate arbiter and power, there is an assumption that representation as it is commonly understood in the liberal-democratic tradition is absent, and that the people are not the masters of their own fate but are instead tied in blind obedience to the sovereignty of God and his laws. Such organizing values for society present Muslim and Islamist thinkers with a significant challenge. Such a challenge has not been insurmountable, and not every Muslim thinker has chosen to engage with this particular topic. Nevertheless, for Islam's critics this is the ultimate rebuff in assessing whether the faith's credentials are compatible with liberal democracy.

In outlining such terms, the aim here is not to hold up some ideal alternative to the model of liberal democracy, but to point to broad points of commonality or principles that are shared between the advocates of Islam and those of liberal democracy. In addition, the drawbacks associated with particular Islamist principles, particularly in relation to issues of plurality and equality, highlight the imperfect models that they advocate. In practice, once again, there are examples of Muslim 'democratic' constructs excluding women and others where women are included. Moreover, with debates more globally about democracy and gender, does inclusion in Muslim schemes guarantee a more inclusive attitude to the role of women in the political life of a state? Even Western liberal-democratic systems are resistant to equality and inclusiveness.

Now that some basic terms and concepts have been outlined, it is important to return to the internal debate and discourse that has engaged Islamists and Muslim thinkers for over a century. The nature of such discussions can generally be identified with two main strands of thought or approaches: the modernists and the traditionalists. These include diverse opinions and interpretations that transcend the schismatic boundary between Sunni and Shi'a, as well as differences between, for example, Hanbali or Shafi.

In addition, as I have already noted, this debate is durable in relation to both time and geography, often surfacing as Muslim societies and their leaders engage in the political evolution demanded by the dynamic nature of global politics in the twenty-first century. Indeed, the transnational dimension of such a debate or discourse should not be ignored. While it is true that some arguments about Islam and democracy have had a specific or local character, other debates and the work of other thinkers have transcended the boundaries of the modern nation-state and influenced political actors in a wide variety of contexts.

One such thinker is Egyptian Islamist Hassan al-Banna, founder of the Muslim Brotherhood and ideologue of the reformist movement in contemporary Islam. Hassan al-Banna's ideas in relation to democracy and Islam were not only of importance in Egypt but permeated throughout the Middle East and afield to Asia and parts of Africa and Europe. Indeed, by the end of the twentieth century, al-Banna's ideas, which he had developed in the 1920s and 1930s, lived on and were not only available in print form across the Muslim world but also accessible through the Internet portals associated with the Muslim Brotherhood movement which he founded in 1928. Dissemination of ideas has always been an important feature of the contemporary debate about Islam and democracy, and the use of such techniques to spread the word is not unusual.

Many of al-Banna's ideas on democracy have been examined and analysed by Ahmed Moussalli, who regards al-Banna as representative of neither a conservative nor a revolutionary political Islam. Instead, Mousalli describes al-Banna's contribution to the debate as exhibiting a 'readiness to compromise, both practically and theoretically and relegates ultimate earthly authority to the community' (Moussalli, 1999, p. 108). It is apparent, then, that al-Banna, a student of the modernist trend, yet inspired by a desire to hasten the resurrection of an Islamic state, largely opts for a middle ground in his explanation of the relationship between Islam and democracy. The difficulty for al-Banna lies in abstracting the democratic from the secular context in which it is constructed in the West and making it part of a politics of self-preservation in an era of colonial dominance. This approach demands that Muslim utopian discourse embrace values associated with democracy that are common in Islam. In addition, he offers a pragmatic agenda that recognizes the limitations under which Muslims are currently constrained to operate. In sum, this is an extremely difficult task. It comes as no surprise, therefore, that the vehicle that al-Banna employs to avoid a compromise between Islam and the secular tendencies of the liberal-democratic model is *shura*. Thus, al-Banna advocates *shura* as a means of putting power and accountability back into the hands of the people and discourages authoritarian tendencies in rulers. Such an approach regulates the relationship between the ruler and the ruled, and casts a watchful eye over the issue of sovereignty which remains with Allah and not the people, irrespective of their individual status or power. Hence, for al-Banna the democratic process (*shura*) can be perceived as a safety mechanism ensuring that sovereignty remains inviolate and protected from those with political ambitions for power that tend towards the despotic or autocratic. In addition, al-Banna reveals, according to Moussalli, 'no problem with Western-style constitutional rule, because in accordance with Islam it maintains personal freedom, upholds *shura*, postulates people's authority over government, specifies the responsibilities and accountability of rulers before their people, and delineates the responsibilities of the executive, the legislative and the judiciary' (Moussalli, 1999, p. 124).

Does this mean, in other words, that there is little doubt that al-Banna is a Muslim democrat who believes that democratic mechanisms and institutions can protect Islam and serve the interests of its people? It is apparent that his problem with liberal democracy stems from its abuse in the name of colonial and imperial interests, secular strategies of reform or change, and the monopoly that he believes those in the West claim. From al-Banna's work emerged a perspective on democracy that made sense to subjugated Muslims and was a viable vehicle for their empowerment. Indeed, democracy could serve as a tool for the liberation of Muslims across the globe. It would meet the oppressive challenge of colonialism and Western hegemonic domination head on, and it employed terms of reference that were not only modern but relevant to those who opposed the Muslim project for resurgence and regeneration. In theory, then, there is evidence to suggest democratic thinking in al-Banna's ideas and programmes, but only as a means for Islamization of the state as a more appropriate model of Muslim rule. In practice, there is limited evidence that the Muslim Brotherhood has participated in electoral systems with democratic pretensions, and the internal structure of the organization itself is sorely lacking in liberal-democratic mechanisms. It is the absence of such mechanisms that characterize so many contemporary Muslim political parties that contest and offer candidates for election to institutions that offer the best hope for political liberalization in Muslim domains. In this respect, importance is attached to the internal character and organization of the Muslim Brotherhood in Egypt, the Muslim Brotherhood in Jordan, Hizballah in Lebanon, FIS in Algeria and Jamiaat al-Islami. Similarly, the Hamas movement in the West Bank and Gaza Strip engages in its own rejection of internal liberal-democratic tendencies, partly rejects its function in the Palestinian arena and criticizes its nationalist opponents in the PLO for anti-democratic tendencies. It has always regarded PLO calls for democracy as a ruse to consolidate nationalist power. Reflecting on the issue of democracy and reform, Hamas leader Ismail Abu Shanab asserts, 'our conception of the reform and the election is something different from the Palestinian Authority. Arafat thinks that the election means that he will stay as president...We suggest that elections are the best way of reform...we don't have real representatives. If there are elections to the Palestine National Council then in this sense we can get real representatives' (Abu Shanab, 2002). Hamas leaders have always faced a difficult task in reconciling their rejection of democracy as a Western secular idea with popular pressure to represent the Palestinian street. Their own democratic credentials are left wanting.

Elsewhere, there are cases where the Muslim Brotherhood and its offshoot organizations have refused to engage with the democratic process for reasons based on important principles related to other aspects of Islam. Where the Muslim Brotherhood has engaged in the democratic process, through elections, such as in Jordan, it has initially met with some considerable success. Such success, however, normally encourages the ruling elite to perceive the Muslim Brotherhood as a significant threat, and means are usually devised to restrict its influence among the popular masses. In Jordan in 1989 King Hussein attempted, through relatively free elections, to co-opt the Islamists into the system that they had previously been critical of. By co-opting the Brotherhood into the system, through democratic election, the leader of the regime was able to provoke fissures and tensions across the Islamist movement as a whole and ultimately to undermine the electoral weight of the Brotherhood in subsequent polls. In addition, despite the mantle of democratization, the Jordanian regime pursued an anti-Islamist campaign throughout the 1990s, resulting in arrests and show trials in military courts of Islamist opposition members who criticized the nature of the political system in Jordan. As one such figure, Islamist parliamentarian Laith Shubailat, asked in the wake of his arrest, trial in military court, death sentence and subsequent amnesty from the king: 'Who shook the regime? Was it Laith Shubailat, Laith Shubailat's trial or the farce of the military court's procedure?'

(FBIS, 1992, p. 4). In Jordan the Islamist movement and its political organizations, including the Islamic Action Front, have been incorporated into and become a part of the democratic experiment, with mixed results in terms of a mediating role between society and the ruling elite.

In Egypt, the birthplace of the Muslim Brotherhood movement, an engagement with democratic practices such as elections has met with mixed success, largely as a result of the heavy-handed, state-based anti-Islamist policies of the 1960s and also under the Mubarak government of the 1990s. In addition, systems that have democratized in countries with majority Muslim populations have at the same time engaged in campaigns that identify Islamists of all hues as enemies of democracy and the liberalizing projects that such states are undertaking. In Tunisia, for example, the moderate pro-democratic and anti-violent al-Nadha movement has been targeted by the leaders of the regime. The leadership of al-Nadha, including Sheikh Rashid al-Ghannushi, has consistently outlined an ideological position that embraces democratic values that are relevant to Islam and a path that advocates change in tune with the popular masses. Al-Nadha represents the modernist liberal wing of Islamism and a culturalist approach to the modern Tunisian context in relation to Islam and democracy. Islamist theorist Sheikh al-Ghannushi has consistently and actively promoted Islamism as a democratic and pluralist construct. Al-Ghannushi is a product of his time; there can be little doubt that his views have been shaped by growing up under French colonial rule, being educated in Cairo and Damascus, and spending his working life in France, Tunisia and in exile in London. He was imprisoned by the Tunisian authorities for his leading role in Islamist revivalist groups and his treatises on a variety of issues, including democracy. Ben Ali's regime, however, viewed such commitments with immense distrust, believing Tunisia's Islamists to be a significant threat to the opening of society in the furtherance of democracy. In response to the perceived threat, the regime arrested its leaders, closed down its publications, prohibited the formation of political parties in its name, forced its prominent intellectuals into exile and harassed its supporters. From the Islamist perspective of al-Nadha, a so-called democratizing regime had employed most undemocratic means and inhibited people's freedom of worship. As al-Ghannushi has asserted, 'the Islamic trend demands political change with the objective of setting up Islamic democratic and consultative institutions instead of existing dictatorial and secularist ones' (al-Ghannushi, 2001, p. 115).

From this perspective, a non-violent engagement with democratic theory and practice had brought the wrath of a secular liberalizing regime on the heads of modernist Islamists in the Maghreb. The issue that the response of the Tunisian regime raises in relation to the programme and activities of movements across the Muslim world like the moderate al-Nadha relates to the cynicism and distrust which has been levied against Islam's connection and discourse on democracy. In Tunisia, the experiences of neighbouring Algeria clouded experiments with the opening of the political system to allow a greater role for Islamists and was combined with a global hostility to Islamists and their presumed rejection of democratic values. In Algeria the outward dismissal in radical Islamist circles of the democratic mechanisms used to promote political and economic liberalization and the ensuing conflict and violence established significant obstacles for those in the Islamist spectrum who sought alternative routes. Under such conditions it is difficult to place the terms commonly associated with the liberal-democratic model, such as pluralism, liberty, freedom and human rights, in a perspective which enhances one's understanding of the debate. Instead, what emerges is a very fuzzy picture which is neither black nor white but instead exhibits hues of grey across the Muslim globe. Islamist movements of the radical variety denounce the liberal-democratic model as a culturalist conspiracy to further harness the global economy to the hegemonic control of the USA and transnational companies who want a homogenized global order built on liberal-democratic values. In Pakistan a military leader declares a *coup* against, albeit, weak democratic forces in the name of Islamization, and in France the state orders the removal of the *hijab* in the name of secular democratic freedoms. Yet the engagement with the discourse of democracy with Islamists from across the globe continues.

Rejectionists

There is, then, evidence of an antipathy to liberal-democratic discourse as promoted by the West within some Islamist circles. Often such rejection is linked to a hostility to the West in general and an accompanying vision of conflict that pitches the adherents of Islam against the West. The departure point for the generation of such views often lies in a response to the lived or historically constructed colonial experience and the sense of subjugation of

Muslim majority populations to the economic forces of the free-market economy and accompanying notions of secularism and democracy. This rejectionist discourse was initially limited to the intellectual and theological elite of some resurgence movements which were evident particularly, though not exclusively, in the Middle East. In this context democracy was rejected not because of the core principles associated with it, but because of the political model to which it appeared to be inextricably tied. For in the contemporary era some Islamist interpretations of democracy are founded on an acknowledgement that democracy implies acceptance of secularism. This begs the question of the extent to which believing Muslims can accept the relegation of Islam to the private sphere. Many would argue that what makes democracy possible in the modern era is the declining importance of religion as a public and political institution. For a state that places faith at its centre cannot be democratic. Thus there is a tendency to conflate democracy and secularism and leave them inextricably tied together. When Islamists oppose secularism, they automatically reject democracy because democracy is assumed to be a secular phenomenon with any religious dimension emptied from it. Indeed, as Muqtedar Khan asserts, one aspect of this issue relates to ownership of the concept. For Islamists who reject secularism and, therefore, democracy reject their own stake in the discourse and 'falsely allow the modern West ownership... They reject democracy only because they reject the West. The large number of Muslims who came out to vote in the Presidential elections in the US and those Muslims who vote in hundreds of millions in Pakistan, Bangladesh, Iran, Malaysia, Indonesia, Turkey, Egypt and elsewhere testify to their comfort with democracy' (Khan, 2001, p. 2). Do interpretations of Islam that empty the faith of its democratic credentials undermine some of the most important principles? For the most part there is little room for accommodation between liberal democracy and democracy as interpreted by Islamists. In truth there is a sharp distinction between one and the other, and evidence of an unwillingness to recognize that democracy Muslim style may be little more than theocracy in disguise is apparent.

Of course, there are those who will argue that such an interpretation is correct and that in fact Islam is fundamentally anti-democratic. They pursue, for example, the rigid interpretation of a thinker like Sayyid Qutb, who contended that democracy, if it equalled popular sovereignty, was at odds with the sovereignty of Allah that lies at the heart of the Islamic faith. Qutb himself acknowledges the importance of consultation (*shura*) in the abode of Islam (*dar al-Islam*) and the Islamic state, but this is not the same as democracy itself. In his influential text entitled *The Milestones*, Qutb advocates consultation as the path out of societal disorder and ignorance (*jahiliyya*) and promotes an Islamic state as the alternative. He further describes such a society as a place where 'the shari'ah is the authority and God's limits are observed and where all the Muslims administer the affairs of the state with mutual consultation' (Qutb, 1978, p. 221). In sum, Qutb obviously believes that the whole of the Muslim community has a stake in its own affairs of governance, and there is little evidence here of an acceptance of diktat from on high. This is not the same, however, as advocating liberal democracy and popular sovereignty through an enfranchised mass. Is it possible to argue that a country that regularly holds free elections to a variety of political posts is undemocratic and does not exhibit minimal democratic characteristics? Moreover, there will always be anti-democratic elements in political movements, including those within the Islamist spectrum. Yet many Muslim commentators argue that this should not be tantamount to declaring that Islam, the faith of more than a billion adherents across the globe, is anti-democratic. Muslim and Islamist interpretations of democracy exist throughout the globe, sometimes reflecting an easy accommodation of principles and sometimes creating more political instability than stability.

In Indonesia, the largest Muslim country in the world, the experiment with democracy that gripped the country in the late 1990s and early twenty-first century has had important Islamist overtones within the essentially secular structures of the state. In Indonesia Islam is a unique and indigenous expression of faith that acknowledges local culture and tradition alongside the modernist manifestation of nationalism and secularism. Indonesia's post-colonial experiences have not created an environment in which democracy has prospered, but it would be completely inappropriate to conflate the absence of democracy with the presence of Islam in the Indonesian context. The absence of democracy in Indonesia has much more to do with the nature of the state, the role of the military in politics, and the imprint of Sukarno's rule than with modernist or traditional Islamism Indonesian style. The democratization process in Indonesia has thrown up many dimensions of an Islamist input, including an array of Muslim and Islamist parties that have freely engaged in the electoral process. Muslim parties have been a constituent element of post-independent Indonesia even under the authoritarian *pancasila* facade for democracy promoted by Sukarno. In addition, the rocky transition from authoritarian to more democratic rule has not necessarily been chiefly because of the negative impact of Islamist forces on this process. Muslim leaders, including Abdulrahman Wahid, have publicly supported the democratic process, including the advance of the principle of popular sovereignty. In this context, then, Islam cannot be said to act as the biggest impediment to a more democratic culture, nor as a restraint on it, as political systems are compelled to change by the transient expectations of society.

In conclusion, there is evidence that the religious fundamentals of Islam are incompatible with modern secular liberal democracy. Moreover, the majority of modern-day Muslim societies are characterized by authoritarianism and an intolerance for pluralism and principles of popular sovereignty and equality. Principles of *shura* manifest in relationships between ruler and ruled in modern-day states are highly restricted and are not inclusive of all in a society. Tyranny under the guise of Islam has coloured such interactions. Opponents have been denounced as apostate and a threat to Muslim order. Yet Muslims across the globe have demonstrated their support and attachment to democratization projects whether they be in the Middle East, South Asia or Africa. For many of these Muslims have recognized that democratic revolution may be the only way to deliver them from the hands of the dictators and despots that rule their states.

Many of these projects have also been addressed by the radicals for whom the principles of secular liberal democracy are repudiated. They call on the Muslim community to overthrow tyranny (especially of the Western-supported variety) and institute Islamic governance. Such calls have resonated powerfully in urban shanties, among the poor and the underprivileged in a variety of Muslim societies across the globe. They have sustained believers and given an alternative dimension to the modern political spectrum previously dominated by nationalists, socialists and Communists. Such calls bear little resemblance to the liberal evolutionary reformist agenda for democracy and the principles that underpin it that are so dearly cherished in the West.

The radicals perceive liberal democracy as an impediment to their project. Nevertheless, there are those among them who recognize that democratic mechanisms present them with an opportunity to go some way in overturning authoritarian rule. This is where the dilemma for democrats arises. As authoritarian regimes purge their own societies of the Islamist threat by imprisoning thousands and further eroding freedoms for the majority in the name of state security, how can Western governments stand aside? If Muslim leaders like Hassan al-Turabi declare that 'The ideal, of course, is democratic Islam. Islam shuns absolute government, absolute authority, dynastic authority, individual authority', are democratic states obliged to intervene on the side of the Islamists? (al-Turabi, 1998, p. 16). In Algeria the democratization process was suspended partly as a result of pressure by Western states to prevent an Islamist electoral landslide. Yet the military-backed grip of the state elite in the wake of the suspension of elections plunged the country into civil conflict. Western misgiving was apparent in statements by US officials: 'We are suspect of those who would use the democratic process to come to power, only to destroy that very process in order to retain power and political dominance. While we believe in the principle of "one person, one vote," we do not support "one person, one vote, one time"' (Djerejian, 1993). Reconciling Muslim and Western aspirations for democracy, therefore, has proved almost impossible, for two reasons. First, contemporary Islamism exhibits both authoritarian and progressive, democratic and anti-democratic, populist and authoritarian characteristics, oftentimes within the same movement or organization. The reformist agenda fundamental to most modern Islamist movements is a threat to the prevailing hegemonic qualities of Muslim majority states. Such states, however, are for the most part responsible for denying democracy to its citizens. Secondly, the internationalization of liberal democracy must be questioned in a variety of contexts, including Muslim ones. The salience of such a project is tied to processes of globalization that have significant and oftentimes negative consequences for developing domains. Moreover, the difficulty of finding 'torch-bearers' for liberal democracy is common in as many non-Muslim as Muslim domains. In this respect political pluralism as a fundamental element of liberal democracy encounters many difficulties across a variety of domains. Islamism remains a challenge to the architects of the new liberal democracy project, and will remain so for the foreseeable future.

5

BRINGING DOWN
THE BARRICADE:
THE GENDER DEBATE

Introduction

Women – their status, rights and responsibilities and their place in modern Muslim societies – have become a major motif of Islamic politics across the globe. Indeed, one of the most popular images of Islam in the modern age is the veiled Muslim woman. The Muslim media use women as a motif, a modern form of communicating an image of Islam that is shared and part of an aspiration of empowerment for many Muslim populations across the globe. Globally the media have also been responsible for perpetuating an image of Islam in which women are a symbol of Muslim repression, lack of rights, violence, constraint and a lack of freedom. In the Western media the Muslim woman is a symbol of all that is unwelcome in Islam. This image is part of a cultural antipathy to Islam that dominated the romantic era of orientalist writing, art and culture in the late nineteenth century. Orientalist accounts of Muslim women chiefly portrayed them as concubines of the harem and secluded from public life. This image has endured.

The debate about women and Islam reflects, to a great extent, issues of modernization, tradition, Islamic resurgence, political power and internal conflict in contemporary Muslim domains. This process highlights an issue that has come to the fore in the realm of Islamic politics. The issue focuses on the rationale for a process that, after placing women on the margins of society, economy and politics, has now made them so central in the battle between Islamists and secularists, Islam and the West, the rights agenda of universal or specific norms and values.

Irrespective of the general or specific guidance contained in the holy texts of Islam, including the Qur'an and the hadith, the discourse surrounding women and Islam has many strands, including the politics of sexuality, legal rights and status, political participation, employment rights in developing countries, power relations between men and women, the role and function of the family as a social and political unit, the politics of the body and dress in the global age. Authors such as Tucker assert, that 'there is actually little agreement on what the central texts of the religion have to say about gender. The Qur'an ... is rather vague or so all-encompassing on most gender questions as to offer only very general guidance on the subject' (Tucker, 1993, p. ix). Nevertheless, through the motif of women, many debates that animate developing and developed societies can be facilitated from Muslim perspectives on the issue of women. For Islamists in particular, Muslim women serve as a particularly important symbol of their growing influence over society and politics. As they challenge the secular agenda of the nation-state, whether in Mubarak's Egypt or Mitterrand's France, the battlefield is often one centred on the place, role or rights of women in society. Exploitation is a noun, therefore, that in relation to this debate needs careful analysis and reflection.

Faith and gender

Debate within Muslim domains, then, frequently focuses on faith in relation to gender issues. Contemporary discourse on the rights of women in relation to marriage, polygamy, inheritance and dress (including the veil, or *hijab*) is largely monolithic and rigid. Few Muslim scholars of the modern age have argued for a radical reinterpretation of Muslim doctrines that have evolved over many centuries. Yet such issues are as open to explication as others. L. Ahmed (1992), for example, has argued that there is no blueprint in Islam in relation to faith and gender. Instead, she contends that a variety of roles fashioned as much by history, class, culture and economy as by the faith of Islam itself can be discovered in Muslim discourse on the topic. For example, it is commonly assumed that Islamic law promotes precedence for the man, not the woman, in relation to marriage and family life, yet in Indonesia the example of the Minangkabau Muslims flies in the face of this assumption. For the Minangkabau Muslims of Indonesia, with strong traditions of matrilineal norms, 'marriage does not necessarily mean the subordination of women to male authority. In Minangkabau Islam is thought to strengthen the bonds of marriage and to advocate complementarity in the roles of husband and wife' (Whalley, 1998, p. 233). In this context Islam reflects the maintenance of matrilineal relations. Such examples, however, are more the exception than the rule.

The immutability of Islam in a modern, forward-looking age is held as a negative factor tying women to outdated and old-fashioned practices and ways of life that clash with secularizing norms associated with the globalization process. Islamists and fundamentalists argue that renewed interest and adherence to the faith of Islam have contributed positively to the self-perception that Muslim women have in such societies. Islam and political Islam in particular, the Islamists contend, has been a vehicle for liberation from the shackles of colonial economic and political exploitation. Islam, they argue, has allowed women to recover their dignity, and their denigration and objectification is counterbalanced. Such arguments may be difficult to understand in the context of Afghanistan, where the Taliban's literalist approach to the fundamentalist tenets of Islam gave rise to a regime that radically eradicated the rights and responsibilities of Muslim women. One Afghan women's organization detailed Taliban restrictions as follows:

1   Complete ban on women's work outside the home, which also applies to female teachers, engineers and most professionals. Only a few female doctors and nurses are allowed to work in some hospitals in Kabul.
2   Complete ban on women's activity outside the home unless accompanied by a *mahram* (close male relative such as a father, brother or husband).
3   Ban on women dealing with male shopkeepers.
4   Ban on women being treated by male doctors.
5   Ban on women studying at schools, universities or any other educational institution. (Taliban have converted girls' schools into religious seminaries.)
6   Requirement that women wear a long veil (*burqa*), which covers them from head to toe.
7   Whipping, beating and verbal abuse of women not clothed in accordance with Taliban rules, or of women unaccompanied by a *mahram*.
8   Whipping of women in public for having non-covered ankles.

9   Public stoning of women accused of having sex outside marriage. (A number of lovers are stoned to death under this rule.)

10 Ban on the use of cosmetics. (Many women with painted nails have had fingers cut off.)

11 Ban on women talking or shaking hands with non-*mahram* males.

12 Ban on women laughing loudly. (No stranger should hear a woman's voice.)

13 Ban on women wearing high heel shoes, which would produce sound while walking. (A man must not hear a woman's footsteps.)

14 Ban on women riding in a taxi without a *mahram*.

15 Ban on women's presence in radio, television or public gatherings of any kind.

16 Ban on women playing sports or entering a sport centre or club.

17 Ban on women riding bicycles or motorcycles, even with their *mahram*s.

18 Ban on women's wearing brightly coloured clothes. In Taliban terms, these are 'sexually attracting colours'.

19 Ban on women gathering for festive occasions such as the Eids, or for any recreational purpose.

20 Ban on women washing clothes next to rivers or in a public place.

21 Modification of all place names including the word 'women'. For example, 'women's garden' has been renamed 'spring garden'.

22 Ban on women appearing on the balconies of their apartments or houses.

23 Compulsory painting of all windows, so women cannot be seen from outside their homes.

24 Ban on male tailors taking women's measurements or sewing women's clothes.

25 Ban on female public baths.

26 Ban on males and females travelling on the same bus. Public buses have now been designated 'males only' (or 'females only').

27 Ban on flared (wide) trouser-legs, even under a *burqa*.

28 Ban on the photographing or filming of women.

29 Ban on women's pictures printed in newspapers and books, or hung on the walls of houses and shops. (*http://rawa.fancymarketing. net/rules.htm*)

Clearly the rights of women under Taliban-interpreted Muslim rule were limited. The ideological impulses behind such interpretations are not difficult to discern. Yet, quite simply, the task here is to acknowledge the depth and diversity of discourse about faith and gender that reflects on the lives of Muslim women across the globe. The resurgence of Islam across Muslim domains has had an important impact on women's lives. Islam does embrace particular attitudes towards women, and in the contemporary era these attitudes have been utilized to portray a certain image of women that has been dominated by the conservative Islamists.

Significant others

Islam has a lot to say about women. The Qur'an and other religious tracts and texts address the rights, roles, behaviour and ideal of women of faith. In the contemporary era the issue of women remains pertinent to Muslim discourse. As leading theologian Sheikh Yusuf Qaradawi acknowledges, however, attention to this issue 'tend[s] to go to extremes when dealing with social and intellectual issues. We are rarely guided to the "middle" which represents one of the general and most prominent features of Islamic theology and commandments. This is strikingly clear in this issue as well as all other issues related to contemporary Muslim women' (Qaradawi, 2003). Moreover, contemporary discourse also focuses on dimensions of equality that have dominated debates in other contexts about women's rights in the modern age. Women are significant others in the matrix of faith and rights. The historical context, however, matters. Moreover, it is important to understand the context in which the issue of women was addressed by the founder and supporters of the new faith system.

In seventh-century Arabia women were part of social arrangements determined by the tribe. They endured a highly restricted role, governed by patriarchal diktat. It has been argued that in many respects the new faith of Islam, its Prophet and his followers promoted a radical vision in relation to the rights and roles of women in society. The veracity of such assertions need not be viewed with modern-day cynicism if the rigid conservative context in which this new faith and its prophet burst upon the scene, radicalizing other aspects of political, social and economic life, is taken into account. For at this time women were largely held to be the property of men – truly enslaved and traded as any other commodity, such as dates or camels, might have been. Women were *persona non grata* in the tight political networks of tribe and clan that governed the norms and values of this society. Women did not enjoy any rights; even the right to life was disregarded. Female infanticide was not uncommon at that time. Patriarchal patterns placed a natural premium on males, and females were regarded as little more than an inconvenient drain on tribal finances and collective wealth. This was the context – the pre-Islamic period – referred to as *jahiliyya* (ignorance), to which the Prophet Mohammad introduced an alternative way of life. As Jawad declares, with 'the advent of Islam, the position of women was radically redefined' (Jawad, 1998, p. 4).

What is apparent is that although the Prophet Mohammad accorded men a position of dominance in the new faith, the appeal specifically to women as individuals, rather than as chattels, was apparent from the outset. For not only did the Qur'an outline a new perspective on issues related to women, but the Prophet himself engaged in relationships with women that, in some senses, broke the conventions of the time. The women who played such an important part in his life and that of the new faith were exceptional characters. A large number of verses (sura) in the Qur'an deal with women and issues affecting them. These verses proclaim on marriage, divorce, education, polygamy, inheritance, child rearing, menstruation, discipline against disobedient women, adultery and relations with men. The nature of the proclamations in the Qur'an is sometimes clear but at other times ambiguous. The issue of women's dress, for example, is referred to in the following verses: 'And say to believing women, that they cast down their eyes and guard their private parts, and reveal not their adornment save such as is outward; and let them cast their veils over their bosoms, and not reveal their adornment save to their husbands' (Sura XXIV: 30). What is pertinent here is whether the verses are a commandment to be taken literally, whether the verses are open to interpretation, or whether the commandment demands compulsion against women who interpret the verses differently or are compelled by circumstance to adapt. In short, Afshar claims that the majority of the verses of the Qur'an do not contain verses that 'contain explicitly or implicitly all the divine commandments' (Afshar, 1998, p. 2). The specificity of the debates on each of these issues will be examined later in this chapter. What is important in the general context is the amount of attention that the holy texts of Islam and its theologians pay to issues that either directly or indirectly affect women. In this respect, then, women were visible from the earliest inception of the faith system. Jawad, for example, identifies many verses in the Qur'an that attest not only to the status of women elevated from tribal slaves to distinct individuals, but as equal to men. She goes on to assert that 'Islam also changed the mentality of both men and women and created a new relationship between them based on respect and mutual understanding; taking care of the woman and respecting her were also emphasised' (Jawad, 1998, p. 6).

The Qur'an and other holy texts makes women visible by outlining a position and role for them in the community. Islamic law also addresses the position of women in relation to men with respect to issues such as divorce, inheritance, as mothers of children and as widows. The following verses from the Qur'an illustrate these issues: 'Divorce must be pronounced twice and then (a woman) must be retained in honour or released in kindness. And it is not lawful for you that ye take from women aught of that which ye have given them' (Sura of the Cow, verse 229). On inheritance the Qur'an declares: 'Unto the men (of the family) belongeth a share of that which parents and near kindred leave, and unto the women a share of that which parents and near kindred leave, whether it be little or much – a legal share' (Sura of Women, verse 7).

Other texts, such as the hadith, also go a long way to illustrate the importance attached to the role that women played in establishing the new religion and partnering the Prophet Mohammad and his followers in their difficult endeavours. Mernissi even believes that the 'Prophet's interactions with women, his intimate quarrels with his wives, his behaviour with the women he loved, are the basis for many legal features of the Muslim family structure' (Mernissi, 1983, p. 54). Certainly the women who featured prominently in his life, such as Khadija his first wife, Fatima his daughter and Aisha his third wife, were eminent figures in their own right. The extent to which they are cited by the theologians as role models for Muslim women is, however, debatable.

It is important, though, to look at these women and the roles they played, because they have become an increasingly cited point of reference for a variety of Muslim women engaged in a renaissance of the faith in the closing decades of the last century. Khajida was a widowed businesswoman in the Arabian town of Medina. She was older than her husband Mohammad by some fifteen years, and at the time of her marriage enjoyed considerable influence in her own right. Contemporary chroniclers highlight her importance. Ibn Hisham's biography of the Prophet is cited by Mernissi as important in not only illustrating the role of women like Khadija but in counteracting modern-day fundamentalist Islamist discourse that argues that the Medinan state never accorded women an important public role. Qaradawi, in discussing the issue of gender segregation, also cites examples from the Medinan period, where it is apparent that gender was no barrier to public life. Qaradawi states:

Women used to attend the Jamaa prayers and the Friday prayers in the Mosque of the Prophet. The Prophet encouraged them to take their places in the rows behind the men... Women also attended the prayers of the two feasts and participated in this big Islamic festival that included the young and old, men and women, out in the open, praising God out loud.... Women attended lessons of knowledge, given by the Prophet, with men. They asked about issues related to their religion that many women today would be embarrassed to ask. (Qaradawi, 2003).

It has been contended by authors like Mernissi that Khadija was a key element of support in the founding years of the faith. While Khadija is admired for her resolute steadfastness and independence, the discourse and controversy surrounding the woman referred to as the 'Prophet of Islam's favourite wife and companion', Aisha, is remarkable for both its bitterness as a symbol of political contestation and its inspirational empowerment for Muslim women themselves.

Aisha's role in the establishment of the religion and the power struggles subsequent to the death of the Prophet is viewed from two diametrically opposite positions. Traditionally Aisha, who was married to the Prophet from a young age and was his third wife, has been viewed by Islam's historians and clergy as a dangerous and controversial example of the threat to the faith posed by women. What was it that compelled great scholars to take such a hostile stance against this one woman? One view is that she symbolizes the rights of women in early Muslim history. Those who make the claim against women's rights, particularly in realms of politics and on the battlefield, cite Aisha's role in the struggle for succession as an example of the chaos and internal disorder that such women promoted. Chaos and disorder are considered a threat to Islam, particularly during the early decades of its establishment in a political and tribal environment that was often inhospitable to the new faith. Moreover, it was Aisha who went to the battlefield in a challenge for the leadership that resulted in the first major schism within the religion. There is evidence to suggest that such bold action was not universally respected at the time, and further historical accounts that cite this incident do so to admonish Muslim women who believe that they have a case for wider participation in politics and society. According to Zuhur, however, '[t]hose who have supported women's activism in political life (including several of the female Islamists) hold that Aisha was justified in her political activities because of her status as the Prophet's wife, her intelligence, her concern for the *umma*, the Muslim community' (Zuhur, 1992, p. 37).

For Islamist women and Muslim women seeking a greater role in the political life of the community, Aisha is not the only personality who is cited. Indeed, as Afshar highlights, in the case of post-revolutionary Iran, the commonly held hostility to a figure such as Aisha has naturally led to the upholding of other figures, such as Fatima the daughter of the Prophet, as a popular symbol of womanhood (Afshar, 1998). Fatima represents a dedication to public and political life based on the principles of Islam that emphasize education, harmony and community spirit based on mutual respect. Remarks from Iranian President Khamenei highlight the importance the regime attached to her: 'The Leader [Khamenei], who like the Founder of the Islamic Republic Late Imam Khomeini, traces his descent to Hazrat Fatima (SA), described the Prophet's daughter as a sparkling star whose service to Islam and her great faith in the Almighty Creator provide the greatest example of feminine virtue' (Khameini, 1994). Fatima remains a revered figure throughout Muslim domains, and is promoted in a positive light. Not only was Fatima perceived as a symbol by Muslim women themselves, but in states such as Iran the Khameini-led government employed Fatima as a symbol of their authority and legitimacy. Moreover, the publications of the Women's Society of the Islamic Revolution of Iran (WSIRI) variously portrayed Fatima as a model or ideal that is 'never passive and subordinated, knows her identity as a Muslim, and takes initiative in learning and participating in society as an independent person, not merely as an assistant to a man' (Nakanishi, 1998, p. 87).

Irrespective of the way in which Fatima is employed as an 'ideal' type, she reflects the historical lineage that is important to the role of women in Islam. Along with the other women cited, and the obvious importance the Prophet himself accorded to women, there is plenty of evidence to suggest, contrary to many modern-day fundamentalist critiques, that women were and should remain significant others in the faith. Their role is expansive, not limited. The Qur'an was a means of empowerment in a variety of realms that had been closed or restricted in the pre-Islamic era. Yet pre-Islamic patriarchal norms were never eradicated, and remained dominant. Many Muslims argue that early Islam reflects a positive model for women of the faith who wish to engage more fully in aspects of the contemporary revival that many male interpreters and theologians have declared that tradition bans them from. Does early Islam illustrate that while the domestic role of women was appreciated and honoured, women, particularly those of the elite or core that surrounded the Prophet, played important roles in the establishment of the faith through political and other means? These women were independent individuals, with their own conscious-ness and identity. To portray the women of early Islam as secluded harem-dwellers of the Arabian desert and concubines of a polyg-amous Prophet is not accurate. Yet, many of Islam's detractors and elements of Islam's patriarchal clergy have interpreted the roles and activities of these women in just this way. Said al-Ghazali, a twentieth-century Egyptian thinker, is quoted by Afshar as declar-ing that Aisha was 'sent "to put them [Muslims] on their guard any time there appeared among them a tendency to blindly imitate other nations by claiming political rights for women...The memory of Aisha should be pondered more than ever in our day"' (Afshar, 1998, p. 10). Increasingly, however, Muslim women are claiming political territory for themselves and resurrecting and reclaiming their history and those of their sisters in early Islam. Their importance in this process lies in the space and opportunity that this presents for Muslim women across the globe to discover their own history. They can utilize this knowledge as a tool for their own empowerment and growth. Feeling part of a historical and religious tradition, rather than marginalized from it, creates a cap-acity for challenge and change. That challenge and change are reflected in other areas that affect Muslim women.

Legal rights and obligations

Many modern discourses on rights focus on the issue of equality. Yet, as a concept, it is difficult to find a definitive definition. In some respects it is easier to recognize inequality than equality. Inequality leads to injustice and hinders development in a society. Sometime legislative structures, like that of apartheid, formalize difference, and at other times local norms and customs result in unequal treatment of people. Debates about equality have had a particular focus on women. Many critiques of Islam in the contemporary era concentrate on the lack of equality between men and women that the faith system perpetuates. There is no doubt that in Muslim majority domains and Muslim states women do not enjoy the same rights to legal protection, education, welfare, health and liberties as men. Such norms are reinforced by elements of the clerical classes. Egyptian cleric Sheikh al-Sharawi's views on equal-ity reinforce the point that men and women are different and as such should be accorded different rights:

[M]an is characterised by decisiveness. And the meaning of decisiveness: that the capacity of reason is what controls his actions, and capacity of emotion is almost non-existent. Women will be exposed to situations that require emotion before reason, and man will be exposed to situations which require reason before emotion...So let us leave women to her kind, and let us leave the matter of her work to necessity. (Karam, 1998, pp. 180, 182)

Women and men are regarded as equal only in worship and spiritual adherence to the faith, but difference is attributed to capacity and ability that allows for discrimination. Equality of spiritual adherence is recognized in the following sura:

Men and women who have surrendered, believing men and believing women, obedient men and obedient women, truthful men and truthful women, enduring men and enduring women, humble men and humble women...It is not for any believer, man or woman, when God and His Messenger have decreed a matter, to have the choice in the affair. (Sura XXXIII: 35).

Muslim feminists blame male jurists rather than the texts of the faith for perpetuating inequality between the sexes. Assorted systems in Muslim domains are regarded as responsible for processes whereby local customs and cultural attitudes influence Islamic life. Issues of rights and equality matter in the contemporary context, because they impact on the status, participation and role of women in Muslim domains. Islam's critics ask why, if the Qur'an guarantees rights of women to education, safety, peace and justice, the majority of these women are not treated with equality with respect to these rights in Muslim domains. Moreover, it has been recognized that these aspects of endemic inequality are actively holding back Muslim domains from achieving their economic, social and political potential. As a UNDP report on Arab human development notes:

The status of women is also considered a major set-back in the Arab world, as they do not fully participate economically and politically. Their participation in these realms is the lowest in the world in quantitative terms...There are approximately 65 million illiterate adults in the region, most of whom are women. One of every two Arab women is illiterate, and in some countries women are denied the right to vote. Compared to 13 per cent in Latin America, women occupy 3.5 per cent of all seats in Arab parliaments. (UNDP, 2002, p. 27).

Every society is regulated by certain rules and regulations that are subsequently codified by the state into law. The source of the law, in Islam, is the Qur'an and other holy texts. Muslims must obey the law or suffer the consequences as decreed by the courts. Without crime there is no punishment, and without Islamic law there are no rights for Muslim women. In early Islam, important rights were bestowed on Muslim women – rights not previously enjoyed – and the abuse of such rights could be resolved by recourse to the justice of the courts. In theory this approach is simple. In practice, the rights that are supposedly accorded by Islam to law may be interpreted by the theologians and the state differently, and they will shape their approach according to time and context. In addition, women's awareness and demands in respect of issues such as divorce and custody have highlighted an inequality of esteem between men and women who bring their cases and claims to the court. Indeed, it is the debate about rights relative to those enjoyed by men that many Muslim women and their advocates have focused on.

In order to debate the saliency of such arguments and critiques, it is important to give a broad outline of the legal rights granted to women according to Islamic law. Broad themes, rather than specific interpretations, will be offered, as it is often the issue of interpretation known as Islamic jurisprudence that has led to charges of patriarchy and bias against the rights of women as ordained by their religion. In her book *The Rights of Women in Islam: An Authentic Approach*, Haifa Jawad outlines eight fundamental rights that she argues Muslim women are entitled to. The eight areas of rights include what Jawad refers to firstly as independent ownership – including personal wealth and property. Secondly she believes that women should have freedom in decision making in the choice of marriage, which is also identified as a fundamental right, as is the decision to terminate an 'unsuccessful' union between the sexes. Thirdly, the basic right of a woman to education is outlined, and the various sources in the holy texts, including the Qur'an and *Sunna*, attesting to this factor are numerous. Not only do the holy texts outline this issue, but the role of learned Muslim women and their contribution to the Muslim community (*umma*) remain both a historical and a contemporary theme in Islam. As Jawad adds, '[t]he Prophet moreover encouraged education for both males and females...He made it clear that seeking knowledge was a matter of religious duty binding upon every Muslim man and woman' (Jawad, 1998, p. 9). Examples of recognition of this principle of Islam can be found throughout Muslim domains and wherever

Muslim communities are found in number. In Lebanon, for example, the Shi'a community in Tyre, through the local institution of the Imam Sadr Foundation, undertakes an obligation to provide education for young girls and young women. The value of such women and their contribution to society is regarded with pride and as a premium for the development of a society ravaged for so many years by bitter and bloody civil war. The definition of what constitutes an education, its content and where an education may be received, however, remain the privilege of the male religious elite. Thus, although education is honoured, the right to knowledge has been constrained by men and has historically discriminated against women in favour, once again, of men. Control over a Muslim woman's right to education figured in the resistance of India's Muslim elite during the British colonial era. Elements of the male Muslim elite were hostile to the public education of Muslim women, as advocated by the ruling authorities. Indeed, there was evidence of a firm intent to ensure that control (and ultimately power) in relation to this issue stayed in the hands of Muslim men and not the state. Indeed, as Jalal notes, 'Confining women's education to household chores and religious teaching insulated them from corrupting influences...Muslim women fed on religious scriptures and household wisdom rarely, if ever, staked a claim for a role in public affairs' (Jalal, 1991, p. 81).

The fourth basic right that is identified relates to the issue of identity and, therefore, a concept of being an individual rather than an appendage of a man or his chattel. According to Muslim convention, women are not obliged, upon marriage, to take the name of the husband and his family. According to Islamic law, then, a woman is not compelled to relinquish this particular aspect of her identity. A name is an important signifier of identity and individuality in any context, but no doubt acquires an added potency in cultures and societies that are usually patriarchal in respect of power relations. In the case of marriage, which is often arranged by male members of a family, the maintenance of one's own identity through possession of one's own name promotes a concept of individuality that was considered progressive and feminist in Western societies that came to such adaptations in a relatively belated fashion. Even in the twenty-first century it is still uncommon for Western women to retain their own name upon marriage. This argument is countered by the assertion that Muslim women, even if they do retain their own name on marriage, are still named after their father's family and not their mother's. As such distinctions of this sort are superficial, Muslim identity remains gendered in a way that privileges men.

The fifth right that Jawad identifies Islam as bestowing on women is controversially linked to what she refers to as 'sexual pleasure' within the boundary of lawful marriage (Jawad, 1998, p. 9). Jawad does not address the topic of sexual pleasure outside the boundaries of marriage. Within the boundaries of marriage, the right to mutually satisfying sexual pleasure in the course of reproduction is certainly outlined in various *hadiths* attributed to the Prophet Mohammad. Yet, stepping outside the boundaries of such arrangements instantly devalues the rights of women far more than those of men. In addition, an opposing view, which is aired by Fatima Mernissi, postulates that even within marriage women are perceived as a sexual threat over which men must assert their control. Coming from an almost opposite pole from Jawad, Mernissi, commenting on sexual relationships between husband and wife, argues that, for a woman, pleasure can never be derived from a relationship predicated on inequality (the husband commands and the wife obeys). With particular attention to al-Ghazali's pronouncements, Mernissi presents evidence that suggests that women in marriage do not have the right to sexual pleasure and that the faith and traditions associated with it actively hinder attainment of such a goal. Mernissi even declares that '[t]he conjugal unit presents an even graver danger than ephemeral sexual embrace; erotic love has the potential to grow into something much more encompassing, much more total. It can evolve into an emotional bond giving a man the plenitude that "only God is supposed to give"' (Mernissi, 1983, p. 114). Such a statement stands in stark contrast to the sexual rights that Jawad believes married Muslim women are entitled to.

It is hard to determine where common ground might be generated in such a debate. Are there such radical differences because of the way that Islam is interpreted? The answer may lie not so much in the realm of jurisprudence as in the difference between a theoretical right that Jawad identifies and an acculturated patriarchal reality that Mernissi is describing in relation to male–female dynamics in the modern day. For there is little doubt that Mernissi's study acknowledges the blurred boundaries between Islamic doctrine, local folklore and traditions and the selective adoption of certain hadiths and suras from the Koran that meet the specific patriarchal agenda of clerics such as al-Ghazali. Al-Ghazali is not alone in sharing this perception of women, even within marriage, as a sexual threat. In Iran, as the Shi'ite clergy generated

new debates under the heel of Reza Shah's modernizing programmes, the theme of women and the sexual threat they presented
to men was aired by prominent clerics such as Ayatollah
Motahari (Moghissi, 1994, p. 64). Sexual pleasure becomes a
vehicle for debating the sexual threat that women are perceived
as representing.

Sixthly, the right to inheritance, for example, that was considered
a revolutionary concept in seventh-century Arabia is diminished in
a context where a Muslim woman's independence is restricted by
the threat she is perceived to pose to male society. Nevertheless, the
right to inheritance is evident in the Qur'an and, unlike other
rights, has been less open to serious manipulation through the
male-dominated tradition of clerical interpretation. Violation, however, is notable: 'very often in reality the culture of specific Muslim
countries subject women to social pressure to renounce their shares
to the immediate male members of the family' (Jawad, 1998, p. 10).
The private domain often leaves Muslim women under pressure
and the sole control of men, whether they are husbands or male
relatives such as a father or a brother. As Tucker remarks, 'Not
surprisingly, male relatives at times attempted to defraud a woman
of her rightful inheritance from a husband or father, hoping no
doubt to avoid fragmentation of family property. In such cases,
however, women were quick to resort to the court to invoke their
rights as legal heirs and to call upon the judge to restore their
property (Tucker, 1993, p. 204). In Tunisia, where there is evidence
of some of the most liberal personal status laws in the Arab world,
human rights organizations have still focused campaigns on
women's rights, including inheritance issues, 'circulating petition[s] that declare support for women's equal access to work,
education, civil and political rights, divorce, guardianship of children after the husband's death and the enhancement of the inheritance rights of single female offspring' (Hatem, 1993, p. 36). This
kind of campaign has often been part of a reaction to the increasingly prominent place of Islamist discourse in public debate about
such rights.

A seventh legal right that Muslim women are considered entitled
to relates, according to Jawad, to 'election and nomination to political offices and participation in public affairs. Islam encourages
women to be active politically and to be involved in decision-
making' (Jawad, 1998, p. 10). While it may be true that women in
early Islam, particularly those of the elite that surrounded the
Prophet Mohammad, enjoyed certain political and public positions,
the same cannot be said of women in modern Muslim societies.

Indeed, Muslim women constitute some of the globe's most politically disempowered. Women have attempted to assert their rights
in this realm where reactionary attitudes dominate. Rarely do Islamist parties that contest elections include women candidates at
the poll. In Muslim countries the franchise is not always extended
to women. Such reactionary views can prevail even in Muslim
societies undertaking a process of political liberalization whereby
the base for political participation for a country's citizens is
broadened. The motive behind such liberalization is usually economic, but as the case of Jordan highlights, women tend to become
victims of the process rather than winners.

The process of political liberalization in Jordan is well documented, and there is no doubt that the early reforms of the late
1980s and early 1990s introduced by its late monarch, King Hussein, promoted certain freedoms and rights in the public and political realm that Jordanians had not enjoyed for many decades
(Milton-Edwards and Hinchcliffe, 2000, pp. 165–7). Yet the first
full and free elections ever to be staged in Jordan, in 1989, were
disastrous in terms of an expansion or exhibition of women's
political rights and representation in the Jordanian political system.
Not one single woman was elected. In addition, the campaigning
for the election revealed the staunch opposition of Jordan's Islamist
forces to women candidates such as Toujan Faisal. Faisal's candi-
dacy was openly criticized by Islamist elements in Jordan, who
sought legal measures to stop her from asserting her rights. The
female electorate in Jordan is also constrained by a societal context
that places a political premium on tribal patriarchal patterns of
social order. Under such circumstances, and despite the pretence
at an opening of the political arena, are women voters in Jordan
always to be influenced by their husband, father or brother when it
comes to decisions at the ballot box? Support for the participation
of women in politics has been slow in coming. In the general
election of 2003, however, not only did the Islamic Action Front
support its first woman candidate, declaring 'this came in line with
our belief that women have an important role to play in our life',
but of the 776 candidates, fifty-four were women, and the state also
allocated six seats in the legislature exclusively for women. However, important legislative changes concerning the rights of women
in divorce and penalties for honour killings have been consistently
rejected by Islamist and conservative parliamentarians.

It is difficult to cite examples of many Muslim domains where
women enjoy the same political rights, positions of political power
or access to public positions, in posts such as the judiciary, as their

male counterparts. The Islamic Republic of Iran is one place where a close approximation to these kinds of participation is found. This is not to say that many Muslim women are not politicized or political actors. Rather, the formal political realms have still not opened up in a more equitable fashion. Less formal arenas of politics are where the majority of politically active Muslim women are to be found. In the rare cases where Muslim women have succeeded in formal political arenas – such as Benazir Bhutto, who became leader of Pakistan – the fall from grace has been inevitable and accompanied by the crowing of reactionary Muslim clerics, who remain hostile to any role for women in the political or public arena.

Such lack of respect for women as political equals is more than apparent, and remains largely at odds with Jawad's view that the eighth right of Muslim women is one of respect from their male counterparts. Thus, although she declares that 'Islam regards women to be equal to men as human beings; hence it emphasises mutual understanding and respect between the two sexes', there is evidence to suggest that if such rights represent the authentic roots of the faith, then they have often been abandoned in the contemporary era (Jawad, 1998, p. 11). Nor do such rights figure strongly in the agenda of the contemporary revivalist movements, whose leaders claim to advocate a return to the 'fundamentals of the faith' and a true interpretation of the Medinan model.

Here the issue rests once again on a perception of what Islam offers, and not the reality as it is currently interpreted or framed by the male-dominated clerical establishment of Islam. So long as interpretation remains a male-dominated undertaking, there is a real fear that women will remain on the margins. Yet there is a case to be made for the right of women to interpret Islam. There is a historical precedent; furthermore, feminists such as Ezzat contend that

> public jurists and political position require special competence in both men and women. They remain at the end the full occupation of a minority of people and among them some women are definitely eligible. . . . It is my conclusion that only few women can practically manage both the responsibilities of family and jurisdiction at a time. If they have the capability or can gain it they have full choice – even a responsibility – to participate on these political levels in a Muslim society. (Ezzat, n.d., p. 2)

Jawad believes the faith system, including its holy texts, have an important message of empowerment for women. In this respect

Jawad and other Muslim feminists remain on the margins of a male-driven tradition of interpretation based on more orthodox approaches. In this respect the divisions within the spectrum of political Islam are exposed, and it is difficult to draw a firm conclusion as regards whether the subjugation of women is an inherent aspect of Islam or the result of a misinterpretation. One can draw a number of conclusions from any large, complex religious text. But clearly, some interpretations are better supported than others. In recent years the saliency of alternative approaches to the male-dominated shaping of the agenda, as they relate to rights, is increasing.

Many Christian apologists argue that the Gospel and the rest of the New Testament represent a liberation for women from the traditions and practices of the time. None the less, we are stuck dealing with some rather tricky passages which clearly subordinate the wife to the husband. This is not the same as restricting the role of women in public life, but these passages have been used to argue for a generally submissive role for women in public as well as private life. Those who would restrict women's roles in public life are aided by some passages in Paul's later writings that forbid women from teaching men. Now, many Christians reject that as an actual tenet, but they do so by arguing that Paul's real point was that issues of personal rights do not supersede the importance of spreading the Gospel. The same is said of Christ's admonition to the slave to return to his master. Some want to conclude (few Christians nowadays, of course) that Christ considered slavery permissible. Most Christians want to conclude that his point was that one's personal situation, no matter how unjust, is not so important as one's witness. Indeed, there is a raging debate within parts of the Christian community in the USA as to whether the freedoms and access to the political process that women enjoy in the USA are in fact biblically supported.

Lack of rights

In the summer of 2001 a television documentary programme broadcast in the UK on the Taliban regime in Afghanistan set out to highlight the injustice of Islamic law as interpreted by the ruling regime in Kabul. The Taliban regime claimed to rule Afghanistan according to their interpretation of Islamic law. As such, Afghanistan had become an Islamic state governed by a consultative council (*majlis al-shura*) consisting of clergy. Under the edicts of the Taliban government, the rights of Muslim women in Afghanistan were severely restricted. As the documentary-maker, a British woman of Afghan descent, highlighted, on the Taliban's interpretation of Islamic law, women no longer enjoyed the right to education; they were prevented from employment, compelled to veiling and complete covering outside the home, and did not have the right to be in public without a male relative. Public execution of women for 'crimes' of adultery were also portrayed in the film, highlighting the extent to which the Taliban had taken authoritarian and ruthless control over women and their fate in Afghanistan.

To label the so-called literalist interpretation of the Taliban as representative of Islamist responses to the issues of women and their rights in the modern era, would, however, be disingenuous. Islamist positions on the rights of women cannot be reduced or condensed as rigid in this respect. In the case of the Taliban, leading Pakistani clerics had already questioned the Taliban's actions against women and girls, with one doubting 'their [Taliban's] ability to interpret [Islamic law] in keeping with the objectives of progress and prosperity in a Muslim country' (Matinuddin, 1999, p. 40). The position of the Taliban leadership *vis-à-vis* this issue contrasted strongly with the views of radical Sudanese cleric Shekh Hassan al-Turabi. Described as 'the leading and most powerful fundamentalist thinker of the contemporary Islamic movement', his views on women offer an alternative perspective to one that is regularly portrayed in contemporary images of Muslim women in the Western media (Moussalli, 1999, p. 90). Al-Turabi proves to be a rare exception to the legal order prescribed by men and subject to male judicial authority in many Muslim societies.

Other documentaries and articles on Islam have focused on the injustices meted out to Muslim women at the hands of Islamic courts in Bangladesh, Iran, Pakistan, Egypt and Saudi Arabia. Women are portrayed veiled, vulnerable and suffering at the hands of a system of justice which interprets Islamic law in such a way as to constrain and repress them. Irrespective of whether a state is Islamic or secular, personal status laws are often based on Islamic law in Muslim societies across the globe. Thus, while Egypt became a secular republic with the *coup* led by Gamal Abdel Nasser in 1952, in the realm of personal status law – relating to divorce, custody issues, inheritance, etc. – the Egyptian legal system has traditionally leant heavily on principles of Islamic law. While aspects of the law surrounding personal status issues in Egypt have been amended and altered, the fundamental principles remain the same. Thus there is a widespread perception among women that such laws are biased against them and that the legal system relating to these issues is also dominated by male legal professionals. Such a perception has created a culture of awe and fear of the legal route for recourse to perceived injustices with respect to the rights of women. An inherent contradiction thus emerges: the legal system, even if it grants women particular or specific rights, is not utilized to this end, because women are afraid to pursue their claims to justice and are aware of the inherent biases of the system in favour of men. As Karam points out in relation to divorce Egyptian Shari'a style, '[a] blatant inequality exists between men and women when it comes to divorce. Husbands need give no explanation for their divorce, whereas women have recourse to a variety of conditions, some of which are difficult to prove in court' (Karam, 1998, p. 148).

This reality contrasts strongly with the Islamist discourse of al-Turabi, who argues that Muslim women are victims of Qur'anic misinterpretation. Al-Turabi believes that in Islam women have 'complete independence ... If the Qur'an postulates her complete religious freedom, so it stands to reason she is also free in other aspects of life – in society and state ... She has equal rights in public life' (Moussalli, 1999, p. 92). For al-Turabi the question once again boils down to interpretation of an authentic Islamic construct according to the Qur'an and the Prophet Mohammad. In this re-spect he presents radical credentials even within Islamist circles. Such radical credentials strike a sympathetic chord with Muslim feminists and Islamist Muslim women, who are also in the position of often challenging common orthodoxy *vis-à-vis* women and pro-moting new ways of interpreting the authentic rights bestowed on women via their faith.

Thus, for many Muslim women their religion has acted as an important shelter and protector of their rights. For them, Islam provides honour, dignity and strength within the faith, society and the family. In the present day this interaction with a rights-based discourse on women and Islam has been an important theme in many academic works. Jawad, for example, while acknowledg-ing that equality (in the eyes of the law) may never be achieved, also attacks the men of faith who fail to respect the message both explicit and implicit in the Medinan model. Indeed, Jawad blames 'misogynistic interpretations of Islam' for its decline, and argues for an emphasis not on the fundamentalist terms of reference but on the 'Islam of Aisha, Khadija, Fatima and Umm Salama: all well-known

Muslim figures and excellent role models for interpretation' (Jawad, 1998, p. 98).

In the era of Islamic resurgence, many nominally Muslim women have returned to active expression and adherence to their faith as a new means of independence. This return to the faith has been facilitated by the Islamic movement itself, particularly the conservative and radical elements who have campaigned to bring women back to the Muslim faith. In fact, conservative regimes in the Gulf have provided the money for Islamic dress for thousands of women in Egypt, have facilitated segregated education from primary to tertiary levels, and funded the thousands of books, leaflets, magazines and articles written by Islamists for women. For these women, wearing the veil is an act of empowerment that means they can remain in the workplace with respect and move freely in public male-dominated space.

The conservative Islamist view of women is, however, contested, from those within the religion and outside it. As Eickleman and Piscatori remind us, 'The regime, established religious authorities, and counter regime Islamists all claim to be the defender of family integrity and of the role and rights of women in an Islamic society. In so doing, each makes the ideas of family and women pivotal to contemporary Muslim politics' (Eickelman and Piscatori, 1996, p. 99). Haleh Afshar takes this issue further, focusing in the Iranian context on the price that the state must pay for making women the 'emblem of Islamification'. Women in Iran feel increasingly confident about articulating a rights-driven agenda in this environment, and, according to Afshar, 'they want to dictate what the Islam that their veiled presence upholds is all about: it is something to aspire to and something that accommodates their needs ... At the same time Iranian women have begun reconstructing a multi-faceted Islam which is increasingly delivering what elsewhere could have been called feminist demands' (Afshar, 1998, p. 215). Nevertheless, the important point here is that, particularly in states where political control is in the hands of the clerical establishment or driven by clerical voices, Islam acts as a framework in which the ways in which women can contribute to society are shaped or altered. This does not mean, however, that Muslim women in Islamic or Muslim states are disbarred from particular roles in the ways that we commonly assume; there are Muslim women soldiers and resistance fighters, engineers, doctors, lawyers and scientists working in societies and contributing to the development of their communities. The boundary between patriarchal attitudes and Islam is frequently blurred, largely resulting in Islam being identified as the chief culprit.

Thus, the claimed authenticity of the conservatives is challenged. This challenge, however, has been marginal historically, and in the present day represents a minority and marginal view within Muslim domains. Nevertheless, the contributions of women to the debate about state-sponsored Islamization, particularly in countries like Bangladesh, have illustrated or brought to the fore its highly selective process with respect to women. The strategic deployment of the 'woman question' in Bangladesh has been critical in local politics, nationalist rhetoric and the international context. Siddiqi points out that 'Gender issues manifest most transparently the contradictions in state and developmentalist discourses as Bangladesh's march to modernity clashes overtly with its desire to be part of a Muslim brotherhood' (Siddiqi, 1998, p. 223).

Islamic modernists at the turn of the century emphasized the need for reform within Islam and a new interpretation of women's rights and roles. The modernists have seen 'reform on women's issues as centrally important to the reform of society as a whole, and ... includes women's participation in the public sector (politics and work)' (Stowasser, 1993, p. 14). For modernists the education, welfare and health of women remain central to a positive regeneration of Islam that empowers them in the contemporary era and withstands the scrutiny of the West. Women who wear the veil to work as a means of empowerment represent this limited modernist trend.

To veil or not to veil? That is the question

The debates, controversies, legislation, campaigns, images, literature, media and conflict generated over this issue of Muslim women and the veil (*hijab*) is quite astounding. The veil is a profound symbol of Muslim identity, a marker of faith and symbol of piety wherever in the world its wearer may be. The veil is more than a cultural costume. It has assumed immense political overtones for much of the latter part of the twentieth century. The veil is associated with a battle for control over Muslim women and their public identity. Along with the veil, we encounter *chadour, burqa*, harem and seclusion. Political battles over Muslim women's dress, however, were even an issue in earlier decades of the twentieth century, and once again came to symbolize larger battles between competing ideologies of secularism and Islam. Islamists have increasingly used the issue of women's dress as a vehicle to articulate arguments and criticisms of Western engagement over the issue of women's freedom and sexual exploitation. Islamists have been especially hostile to Western-influenced feminist agendas and have sought many paths to take control and dominate debate about women and their dress. This has led to campaigns forcibly compelling women to dress according to Islamic mores and values as interpreted by modern-day Islamist leaders and their male followers. Such campaigns have left women in fear of their lives because they have resisted compliance and been isolated by a political and religious community unable to challenge the strictures of Islamist bully-boys. Veiling has become a means of asserting a Muslim cultural identity, a resistance to Western values, a challenge to occupation authorities, a taunt to secular political authorities, a means of controlling the space to which women have a right, protecting their honour and chastity, and an expression of power in a milieu where men may find themselves politically or economically disempowered.

Such issues can be scrutinized in the Egyptian context. For many centuries now Egypt has been a Muslim country, but in the 1970s, as we know, a revival of Islam was evident in the country. The revivalism covered a variety of issues, but was also perceived as a politically based challenge to the pre-existing state of secular nationalist political rule presided over by President Sadat and then President Mubarak. The Islamists agitated for political reform of the system that would institute Islamic rule in Egypt and bring an end to the secular nationalist political system of the present era.

Islam is perceived as significant in the lives of women in Egypt and regarding the question of women's issues. The revival of Islam has incorporated the issue of women into its agenda and has organized a number of campaigns around the role of women in contemporary Egyptian life. One issue affecting women, which has assumed disproportionate importance, has been the veil. The veil – wearing a headscarf (*hijab*) to cover the hair and shoulders, and Islamic modes of dress including the *chadour* (long loose-fitting black coat) – and the politics surrounding this issue have been contentious in Egypt for a variety of reasons. Many Egyptian women stopped wearing the veil as they discovered the freedoms associated with Western ideological approaches – feminism, nationalism, socialism, etc. The veil was a symbol of many things that many believed were associated with the way that Islam affected their lives. The veil was considered by some to represent the domestic seclusion and segregation of women that Islam demands. Others believed the veil was symbolic of the patriarchal authority which Islam supports, denying equality to women in all aspects of their lives. For a vast majority of Egyptian women, however, the veil (worn in a variety of ways) was not political in either nationalist, feminist or Islamic form.

For Islamists, however, the wearing of the veil was a political issue. They argued that women who did not wear the veil were symbolic of a society and state that had lost Islam, was obsessed with Western consumerism, the sexual exploitation of women and a decline in moral standards and modesty that Islam has tradition- ally required. The Islamists were determined that women should wear the veil again. The campaign was first conducted on univer- sity campuses in Egypt, where Islamists pressured women students to wear Islamic dress. By the 1980s more and more Egyptian women were wearing the *hijab* and other forms of Islamic dress, but as Eickelman and Piscatori argue, such decisions, particularly among the lower middle classes, were also about 'conveying the social message that a woman could hold a job in the government bureaucracy or in a bank without abandoning her roles of wife and mother. Wearing hijab showed respect for the boundaries of a well-ordered, moral society without inhibiting social change' (Eickelman and Piscatori, 1996, p. 91). The decision by women to wear or not wear the veil has become important, politicized and used by Islamists and their opponents to measure the moral, social and religious climate of Egyptian society. The words of Fatima, a seventy-year-old widow from Cairo, sums up this complex debate:

> Why have young girls started to cover themselves in this new type of veil and dress like old women? I think this is just a trend, a fashion like any other.... However, I do not think this new veiling is a religious duty. A woman's modest conduct is more important than what she wears... Although I have this opinion about the new veil being a trend which is not an essential part of Islam, I am not against what it stands for if it means society is becoming more concerned with morality and turning against some of the modern ways and western values which started to take hold. (Watson, 1994, p. 151)

As Fatima's words highlight, each woman who becomes drawn into this issue in Egypt is 'caught between worlds' in the sense of facing conflicting pressures and what Watson refers to as 'compet- ing cultural values, traditions and personal aspirations... In this respect, the adoption of an identifiable Islamic form of dress can be regarded as a "sign of the times" which entails the assertion of independence, separate identity and a rejection of Western cultural imperialism' (Watson, 1994, p. 151). Thus, although the debate about Islam, the veil and Egyptian women may at first glance appear to distinguish this from other debates about women and politics in the Third World, there is a strong connection if we accept the logic of Watson's argument. Islamic dress, then, represents the reassertion of indigenous identities in opposition to the colonial experience, the impact of secularization, Westernization, the importation of Western-inspired ideologies which have been judged by the Islamists as having failed in Egypt, the Coca-Cola culture, the liberalization of social and moral values according to a Western agenda, belly-dancers and pop music. Indeed, in Egypt, the Islamists targeted the country's most famous belly-dancers and won many of them over. These women, previously symbols of Western sexual exploitation, decadence and degradation, now appear at public rallies on behalf of the Islamists, declaring their new-found liberation in Islam and Islamic dress. Such declarations have proved difficult for many Egyptian women to resist, but the voluntary adoption of such dress has been on their own terms. It is the forced imposition of the *hijab*, which has occurred in many parts of Egypt, that so many women fear, once again representing the assertion of patriarchal values as much as a religious way of life.

Outside the religion secular Arab critics of Islam have bemoaned the position of the religion on women. Writers like Mernissi have argued against the image of Islam which the male adherents of the religion promote. They point to the important role which women have played in society and politics and criticize the Islamists' objectification of women as a sexual threat. Such critics argue that Islam is holding women back, that if fundamentalists had their way, women would be further enslaved by Islam and their literal interpretations of seventh-century scriptures. Secular critics also identify the state as a chief culprit in aiding and abetting the Islamists in their task. By failing to take the initiative on family and civil law, the state allows the Islamists to win the argument, and the state-paid clergy play their part in reinforcing the enslavement of women. Few examples exist in the region where the state has taken the initiative and used the law to change women's status for the better. The former People's Democratic Republic of Yemen (PDRY) is a rare exception, where, as Molyneux claims, 'the transformations in the structures and practices of law which were brought about...had far-reaching implications for women...the changes that were introduced can be recognised as important without exaggerating their overall impact or their contribution to "women's emancipation"' (Molyneux, 1991, p. 266).

Muslim women's movements and Islamist feminists

Although it is acknowledged that in formal realms of politics many Muslim women in Muslim societies are denied a participatory role, there is growing evidence that in the last two decades of the twentieth century Muslim women in a large number of Muslim states, from the former Soviet republic of Tajikistan to Indonesia and Iran, have become involved in political advocacy and debates not only about their roles in society but about larger political issues such as democratization and economic development. For many of these women the conduit through which they have engaged in this form of activism, advocacy and emancipation has been political Islam and the movements associated with it, including radical movements such as FIS in Algeria and moderate reform movements such as Jamia'a Islamiyya in India.

The role of women in such movements was initially viewed with some suspicion and hostility by Western feminists, who argued that such women were actually being politically exploited by the male Muslim elite of such organizations and movements. They were being used, it was argued, as a symbol of revivalist domination and patriarchal control in societies which should have evolved beyond such social structures. Such feminists declared that the fundamentalist revival which in Islamic circles dominated the closing decades of the twentieth century in a bloody and violent blaze was an assault on the basic rights enjoyed by women across the world. In addition, the Islamist movements of the Middle East, South and South-East Asia, Africa and the former Soviet republics were repeatedly associated with a full-scale offensive against the hard-won role and rights associated with indigenous yet secular women's movements which had grown up in many post-revolutionary and post-colonial Muslim societies. In other words, the battle-lines between fundamentalist Islam and secular feminism were firmly drawn, and a fight was on for the hearts and minds of Muslim women in general. The fight has been long and bloody. It has often created unnecessary chasms between women and bound them to descriptions and distinctions which were often rendered meaningless in reality. Indeed, there is plenty of support for the argument that with respect to this issue the revival of Islam and political Islam in particular has altered the political dynamic between men and women in many societies where a large Muslim community is present. In this respect, therefore, there is plenty of evidence to refute Roy's assertions that 'basically, the influence of Islamism is more superficial than it seems' or that 're-Islamization has in no way changed the rules of the political or economic game' (Roy, 1994, p. 26). For urban Egyptian women such a statement would appear to be trite and ignorant of the politics that is played out in their lives on a daily basis. For Egyptian author Nawal el-Saadawi, whose novels have been interpreted by a hostile Muslim clergy as an attack on Islam and who have used the Egyptian court system to divorce her from her husband, re-Islamization in Egypt, initiated by Islamists and benignly supported by the Mubarak regime, has changed the political game and the game of rights in every way conceivable.

The emergence of a Muslim feminist and Islamist feminist trend, then, has occurred under the wing of Islamism and the political and social gains reaped by its various campaigns in the 1980s and 1990s. And it is true that the deliberate strategy of involving women in Islamist campaigns around issues such as education, welfare and of course veiling often ran in contradiction to campaigns in which secular women in Muslim societies had been involved for many years previously. All too often the specific campaign or issue became a symbol of wider struggles and conflicts in society, such as the veiling campaign which took place and was organized by the Palestinian Islamist movement Hamas during the Palestinian uprising of 1987–1993. In this context Palestinian feminists and women activists found themselves in a battle with the leadership of an Islamist organization for the Palestinian street and the freedom to walk it as one chose.

Although Islamic movements had been part of the fabric of Palestinian society since the 1920s and 1930s, it was during the Palestinian uprising of 1987–1993 that a large-scale movement emerged with enough popular support and logistical strength to challenge the Palestinian nationalist movement, and the PLO in particular, in claiming sole and legitimate representation of the people. Hamas undertook a variety of campaigns and strategies that were designed to undermine and discredit Palestinian secular nationalism and entrench a programme of re-Islamization of every sector of Palestinian society, from the squalid refugee camps of the Gaza Strip to the urban-based merchants and entrepreneurs of Nablus and Ramallah on the West Bank. The Hamas leadership directed a campaign aimed at discrediting the important role of

Palestinian women in secular-based political and social organizations in representing their rights and their call for greater freedoms
under the remit of nation building. From this position the campaign
took a more ominous and dangerous turn in 1989, when the Hamas
leadership commanded its supporters to turn their stones from the
Israeli army of occupation and the illegal presence of Israeli settlers
and target their own women instead. The women without veils
became the target of the Islamists. Such women were accused of
disrespecting Islam and the goals of the uprising – as defined by
Hamas. Although the nationalist leadership eventually responded
to the campaign and condemned it as unpatriotic, this move came
too late. As Hammami points out, 'the *hijab* campaign was the
turning point in redirecting the focus of the intifada... the campaign took up the moralism of the discourse of the intifada while
quietly subverting it. Moral discourse was moblilized against
women,' and it took a long time for women to emerge from the
climate of fear which Hamas activists and supporters so effectively
created in Gaza (Hammami, 1997, p. 203). The question that the
Hamas *hijab* campaign raises is: what should men and women play
in addressing the wider issues of feminism and liberation in
modern muslim societies.

For the women of such organizations and their counterparts in
countries like Iran and Turkey, the answer is simple. Women are at
the heart of such issues and are generating debates about the
important role that Muslim women must play in achieving emancipation along the path of Islam and the re-Islamization of societies
affected by the spread of secularism and Western consumer life-
styles. In Iran such women have increasingly formed a core in
rethinking Islamist feminism and the frameworks in which emancipation can be achieved. They have used the radical transformation of their society under the rule of Ayatollahs as a means to
achieve greater freedoms in education and public roles through
state-endorsed legislation and policies. The women involved in
Iranian-based Islamist feminist organizations may be conservative,
radical, reformist or emancipatory in their approaches. They cannot
be said to represent a monolithic approach to their own or other
issues as they are interpreted through an Islamist prism. Like their
secular counterparts, Islamist feminists engage with a variety of
approaches and views based around issues of jurisprudence and
interpretation of the Qur'an and other holy texts. In addition, some
of these women are reclaiming the role of women in Islam and
encouraging women to preach and form study and discussion
groups across Muslim domains. Networks of activist Muslim

women also exist to promote a greater role for women in Muslim society, often including public arenas such as the workplace or local political forums and legislatures. In Turkey, for example, since the 1980s women have played an important role in leading *hijab* and education campaigns against state policies and legislation. Turkish women have become prominently involved in Islamist campaigns and have taken their place on the public stage in respect of these issues. Such feminists, whether Muslim or Islamist, have taken on the state as the enemy in their debates, battles and discourses. The state is criticized by these women, by and large, because of its secularist or pro-Western tendencies, which result in policies or a society in which women do not enjoy respect or the rights which they believe they are accorded in Islam. For some of these women, therefore, involvement in an Islamist movement provides the only opportunity to resist the state and its authoritarian and anti-democratic tendencies. In the previous chapter on democracy I explained that the relationship between Islam and democracy is a problematic, though not mutually exclusive, one. Whatever form of democracy may arise in an Islamic state, it will be constrained by religious judgements of the ruling elite. So, is democracy a necessary condition for women's rights, such that if an Islamic state rejects democracy, it must also reject women's rights? Or even if it accepts democracy in some form, will women's rights always be constrained in some way? Islamism becomes a vehicle for the expression of anti-state discontent, and this is particularly true of Muslim feminists as opposed to Islamist feminists.

An example of one such woman is the respected Muslim feminist Zaynab al-Ghazali from Egypt, who is a popular anti-secularist ideologue and role model for many Muslim women. Although initially attracted to the nascent secular feminist movement in Egypt, al-Ghazali quickly moved into the Islamist fold, and from the 1940s became a public and high-profile advocate of the Islamic alternative. A fierce critic of Nasser and other secularist politicians, al-Ghazali established her anti-secularist credentials and headed campaigns and study groups which brought more Muslim women under the Islamist wing in Egypt. Thus, as Karam somewhat acerbically notes, 'al-Ghazali's basic tenets regarding the role that Muslim women should occupy is a secular feminists' nightmare', and the duties of Muslim women are clearly determined according to the faith of Islam and not modern secular legislation (Karam, 1998, p. 209). Although al-Ghazali was imprisoned, tortured and targeted as an enemy of the Egyptian state under the leadership of Gamal Abdel Nasser, her call for the empowerment of women within Islamist movements has never wavered, and she has consistently campaigned and organized Egyptian women for this task. To distinguish between Muslim and Islamist elements in al-Ghazali's feminism is difficult, for she has been both one and the same thing in her extensive history of involvement. Thus, in many respects she represents the inherent difficulties associated with such labels and their usefulness in distinguishing between strategies and actions in generating movements for change, reform and radical revolution in the contemporary Muslim world. Suffice to say that while fifty years ago women like al-Ghazali would have been few and far between, today many others have joined her ranks. They have joined for a variety of political and other reasons, although they are all united by a desire to give their own voice, as women, to the debates and discussions which rage in their societies, including those that directly impact on the lives of Muslim women irrespective of class or location.

In conclusion, for the most part, the debate about women and Islam remains unresolved, with neither side able, to date, to claim victory. Given the discussion regarding Islam's attitude toward women, one might even ask whether anyone on either side really knows what victory would consist of. What remains important is the path that women themselves choose in relation to Islam, rather than the route that men are currently claiming for them. There is certainly evidence of growing consciousness among Muslim women in relation to these issues. They are increasingly rights-aware, and when this is coupled with the flourishing role they play in the labour force, they contribute to the manifestation of new agendas which are less male-centric in relation to the faith and what it offers, as well as what it obliges men and women to do. The Islamist revival of the late 1970s has had both a positive and a negative effect on the emancipation agenda. Women in Muslim societies have become increasingly active as adjuncts to their male counterparts in radical Islamist and mainstream Islamist movements. In Iran women were the symbol of the revolution and remain the symbol of its future. Muslim women empowered by the clergy have now gained the courage to further their independence agendas without being continually tied to official discourse of either the conservative or the reform-minded clergy. In Saudi Arabia, however, the rights of women have not improved with the ascent of the Wahabi-influenced al-Saud family. Nor have the immense economic riches derived from oil resulted in a liberalizing or emancipation agenda for Saudi women. To date they do not enjoy the same rights as other Muslim women in the region, and have far more in common with their sisters in Afghanistan than with those in Lebanon or Morocco. The rentier economy of Saudi Arabia has been utilized by the ruling al-Saud family to further limit the opportunities for women outside the home. Their potential contribution to the labour market is effectively offset by the employment of a large migrant work-force as a substitute for any contribution Saudi women might have made themselves. This contrasts with Turkey, where Muslim women play an active role in the national economy and many other aspects of public, political and cultural life. Islam, then, in relation to women has the potential to both liberate and enslave. When it enslaves, however, it is largely as a result of patriarchal traditions and the male-dominated practice of jurisprudence. When it empowers, it is largely because Muslim women and Islamist women have used opportunities created within the faith to forge ahead with new positions on the issues that mean so much to them.

6

GUN BARREL POLITICS: ISLAM AND POLITICAL VIOLENCE

Introduction

On the evening of 10 May 2000, in the Israeli-occupied area of south Lebanon, just weeks before the collapse of the South Lebanon Army (SLA) and the rapid departure of the Israel Defence Forces (IDF), back over the border to Israel, Islamic armed elements attacked an SLA position known as W132 near Ru'aysh and Rashaf. Under the cover of darkness, Hizballah armed elements crept up to attack an SLA position. Caught unawares, a minor battle subsequently unfolded, including the firing of machine guns and mortars in retaliation. Israeli support was subsequently dispatched in the form of two Cobra helicopters sent from their positions closer to their own border. The major outcome was that the SLA abandoned position W132 on the strategic ridge that it had occupied for more than a decade. This was the beginning of the end of the SLA. Furthermore, Israel's occupation of south Lebanon was being expedited by the successful attack tactics of Hizballah.

The following day in a hospital car park in Sidon in south Lebanon, a rendezvous took place with a man who would facilitate a meeting with Sheikh Qa'ouk, the commander of Hizballah's southern battalion and on Israel's most wanted list. Elaborate precautions were taken before the meeting. Wary of Israeli attempts to assassinate him, Sheikh Qa'ouk took scrupulous precautions to ensure that radio or mobile devices that might assist an

Israeli-guided missile were removed. During the meeting, Sheikh Qa'ouk spoke of Hizballah's attacks on Israeli targets, including the major action of the night before. During the course of the interview, Sheikh Qa'ouk made it clear that he considered Israel's occupation an internationally recognized illegal act, and that Hizballah, on behalf of the entire Lebanese nation, had the right to resist. He remarked that Hizballah national resistance forces would do nothing to ease Israel's exit from Lebanon and everything to promote a collapse of confidence among Israel's proxy SLA forces. He declared, 'we consider it [the SLA] the same as Israel' (Qa'ouk, 2000).

Some ten days later, as Israeli forces left, the SLA collapsed, and its soldiers fled the border for Israel, Hizballah spearheaded the drive back into the former Israeli-controlled area (ICA) and their flags fluttered from every former military position held by either the IDF or the SLA. The news of Hizballah's takeover, the images of victory speeches by Hizballah Secretary-General Hassan Nasrallah and the sight of Israel back over most of the old border with Lebanon assumed an immediate iconic status of what Islamists could achieve in the face of a previously implacable enemy. Hizballah's well-organized media wing went into a frenzy, ensuring that its television channel, publications and other media outlets throughout the globe carried the story of 'Islam's victory against the Zionist occupier of Lebanon'. Hassan Nasrallah declared at the victory rally in the town of Bint Jubail, however, that Hizballah's efforts were part of a national resistance effort, and that the liberated land would not form the territory of some new Hizballahstan, but that the Lebanese state would remain responsible for security in the whole country. In the Lebanese capital, the country's Christian president, Emile Lahoud, emphasized the role Hizballah had played on behalf of the entire nation in helping to expel a force of occupation. During liberation addresses he praised 'the unity between the army, the resistance, the population, the opposition and the loyalists; all worked together as one,' and noted that in areas of national interest, Hizballah, 'whose leadership has a high sense of responsibility, will co-operate with the peace-keepers and the Lebanese government' (*Daily Star*, May 2000).

Further evidence of the national sentiments in Hizballah's campaign against Israeli occupation in south Lebanon was apparent in the summer of 2000, when Lahoud became the first Lebanese president to receive Hassan Nasrallah formally at the Baabda Palace. Their press statements that day cemented the bond between the two forces in Lebanese society. In this context Hizballah were not perceived as terrorists but as elements of a national resistance struggle. For Israel and much of the international community, Hizballah is a terrorist organization that has been responsible for bombings, attacks and kidnappings against Israelis and other Western nationals. Hizballah was accused of holding as many as five Israelis hostage. Hizballah was demanding that Israel release fifteen Lebanese detained in Israel's jails. Hizballah continues to launch attacks on Israeli military forces and other targets in Israel's sovereign territory. Israel accuses Hizballah of aiding and abetting terrorist elements in Palestinian refugee camps in the West Bank. Such perceptions juxtaposed against one another demonstrate the blurred boundaries that are drawn in relation to Islam and violence in the contemporary era.

This chapter will reflect the complexities of this issue as it has been shaped throughout the late twentieth and early twenty-first century and its impact on contemporary political discourse. The purpose of this chapter is manifold, and aims to broaden the understanding of how Islam and violence, and in particular political violence and terrorism, have come to dominate much analysis of the religion across the boundaries of state, community and ethnic group. In the contemporary era transnational Islam is understood by many actors in the West as representing the potential for terrorism in its most modern guise. Indeed, political violence or terrorism has come to dominate the lexicon of the religion as a whole. Political violence or terror is promoted as a primary signifier in the way Islam is portrayed not only in the West but in many Muslim domains as well. The second aim of this chapter is to argue that the construction of this view of Islam is diametrically at odds with the real relationship between faith and *jihad* (striving) that continues to be important to the majority of Muslims across the globe. Finally, I will review the catalogue of violence that has been perpetrated in the name of Islam. I will also examine the socio-economic context of such acts, particularly in relation to ongoing conflicts and wars that have gripped the contemporary world since the fall of the Berlin Wall. Moreover, the extent to which the 'War on Terrorism', announced by the Bush Administration in the wake of al-Qaeda's attacks on America, is understood as targeting Muslim domains will be examined. This is because in the 'War on Terrorism' common perceptions of conflict and peace in the post-Cold War era have failed, and conventional military options have not been enough to bring an end to the climate of fear that has prevailed in the contemporary global order in the aftermath of the terror attacks in the USA.

Epic conflict

In Western capitals, opinion regarding Hizballah was unchanged by its resistance capacities and its self-claimed victory over Israel. In the eyes of US and other governments, Hizballah remained a designated terrorist organization and enemy of the 'free world'. Hizballah's campaign to liberate Lebanese territory from the illegality of foreign occupation, which in turn ended in the internal displacement of thousands of people, and the death of many, was not relevant and did nothing to dispel the firmly held opinion that this brand of Islamic radicalism posed a major threat to Western interests in the Middle East. Indeed, a US State Department summary on terrorism reported that 'Hizballah continued to pose the most potential threat to US interests in Lebanon' (US State Department, 2000, p. 2). In addition, Lebanon was identified as a location or breeding ground for the forces of Islamic terrorism. The infamous al-Qaeda organization led by Afghanistan-based Saudi exile Osama Bin Laden was believed to have trained in Lebanon. Moreover, with Hizballah so intimately tied to both its Syrian and Iranian sponsors, the linkages to governments like that of the USA were obvious.

Although the US terror report admitted that Hizballah had not actually attacked any US targets in Lebanon since 1991, it said that 'it continued to pose a significant terrorist threat to US interests globally from its base in Lebanon' (USSD, 2000, p. 2). Such statements added further clarity, if it were needed, to the fact that within the West and other parts of the globe this particular manifestation of Islam was viewed with suspicion in relation to its violent history. This reflects a growing belief that terrorism in its modern form has become increasingly Islamic in character. For if the decades of the 1960s and 1970s were associated with the radical leftist terror of the Bader Meinhof and the Popular Front for the Liberation of Palestine (PFLP), in the 1980s, 1990s and first years of the twenty-first century, Islam became the primary locus of such associations. For it appeared that Islam – the monotheistic faith system of millions – was inspiring acts of terror against innocent tourists, from Luxor to Yemen and the tropical idylls of South-East Asia. It was in the name of Islam that Osama Bin Laden waged his war. It was Islam that was inspiring a seemingly endless sacrifice of life by Palestinian suicide bombers who were encouraged to believe that by becoming martyrs they would be promised eternal life in paradise. It was active adherents of Islam who boarded planes on

September 11, 2001, and perpetrated one of the worst acts of terrorism in the modern age. More than 3,000 people died in these attacks on America. This act of terror in the name of Islam altered global perceptions of Islam and influenced dimensions of security and politics, as well as economy.

Why, then, had such acts of political, religious and religio-nationalist motivated violence occurred? Were such acts a reflection of the brutal cultures of violence that characterized Muslim domains in the contemporary era? Why had Muslims turned to terrorism? Throughout the twentieth century it had been the fate of countless Muslim millions to endure life under brutish political overlords. In Muslim majority countries such as Iran and Indonesia, rulers, whether colonial overlords or post-independent presidents or shahs, promoted a raft of policies designed to give Islam nothing more than symbolic importance in the political arena. In such states Islam was considered symbolic of the past, and as Islamists were imprisoned and the wearing of Islamic dress was prohibited by law, the forces of aggressive secularism were in evidence. Islam was deliberately pushed to the margins as the forces of modernization and secularization were experienced throughout a number of Muslim domains. Moreover, an argument that Muslims were attracted to the tyranny of violence manifest in terrorism grew and was given credence by the increasing number of attacks on Western targets. Yet it wasn't just the West that was targeted, for within the Muslim fold others, including women, were equally terrorized but far less able to defend themselves. There was a fear that episodes of tyranny and violence documented in Islam's history were resurgent again. Islam's past as tolerant, culturally vibrant and economically viable appears to have been lost to the notion that the expansion of Islam means endless war and conflict. Bernard Lewis addresses this point in an article entitled 'What went wrong?' Drawing on Islam's past, he contrasts it with its present and finds much in the present wanting. In the present day the forces of modernization have resulted in major social, political and economic changes that have undermined the authority of Islam and its rulers from within. A new generation of Muslims has grown up in societies characterized by authoritarian rule and economic crisis. Legions of university-educated Muslims find themselves unemployed, increasingly embittered and feeling embattled against regimes that deny them freedoms and meaningful opportunities for political participation. Lewis contends that Muslims must look to their own societies rather than constantly blaming the West for their predicaments. As he remarks:

impulse was strong enough, and motivation lay in the desire to wrest the Holy Land back from Muslim rule. Jerusalem, the most holy spot in Christendom, had been lost to the Caliph Umar around AD 638. Umar, a surviving companion of the Prophet, had treated the city and its place in the Christian heart with respect. Unlike his Persian predecessor, he had not ransacked the city on the eve of victory; instead, in a public reception with the Christian patriarch Sophronius, Umar pledged to provide full protection and religious rights to all the inhabitants of the city. The Church of the Holy Sepulchre would be respected and venerated and would not be damaged, destroyed or commandeered for Muslim worship. This pledge was then sealed with a treaty between Umar and the patriarch. The history of the Crusades, however, has resulted in literatures that foster the growth of hostility to, and suspicion of, Islam in the bosom of Judeo-Christian Europe, which have never truly disappeared. In many modern Islamist literatures, the motif of the Crusades is also repeatedly cited as a reason for hostility to, and suspicion of, the West. A mutual antagonism has been established around a historical episode of conflict and violence that resonates to the present, though it is fair to say that today it is the West that is more frequently portrayed by Islam's radical and terrorist elements as the 'Crusader threat'. The 'Crusader' prefix dominates much discourse. On the second anniversary of the al-Qaeda 9/11 attacks, the deputy leader Ayman al-Zahrawi declared, 'Know Muslims, the Crusaders and the Jews cannot take our countries except by the treason of lackey leaders and their supporters among the rulers' Ulema who have sold out the lands of Islam to its enemies. So hasten with all that you possess – the weapon of knowledge – so that the call may reach every group in the Muslim world community.' In this way the radicals rewrite the history of the West. It is the 'Crusaders' and the 'Zionists' whom movements like Hamas and Islamic Jihad berate for the woes of the Palestinian people. The articles of the Hamas Covenant are littered with references to the 'Crusaders' and the portent of that historic episode for the present. As article 35 declares:

> The Islamic Resistance Movement views seriously the defeat of the Crusaders at the hands of Salah ed-Din al-Ayyubi and the rescuing of Palestine from their hands . . . The Movement draws lessons and examples from all this. The present Zionist onslaught has also been preceded by Crusading raids from the West . . . Just as the Moslems faced those raids and planned fighting and defeating them, they should be able to confront the Zionist invasion and defeat it.

For Sayyid Qutb, Hizballah, Egyptian Gama Islamiyyah, al-Qaeda and many others in the contemporary radical fold, the era of the Crusades resonates with heavy-laden parallels to the present. There is a redemptive quality to the Muslim defeat of the Crusader states that is represented by contemporary radicals as a positive emblem for downtrodden Muslims whom they believe labour under the heel of the West. Saladin epitomizes liberation through *jihad* as ordained by Allah. From this perspective the parallels are easily drawn: Jerusalem lost, Western forces stationed across Muslim domains, and subjugation. The Crusades are emblematic and are woven into countless discourses. Both nationalists and Islamists have depicted their causes and their leaders as the new jihadists and Saladins. The legacy of the Crusades, including the ultimate victory against the West by the jihadist forces, remains an important force in many Muslim domains.

The way in which these historical events have been recorded, internalized into the history of Muslim and Western nations and used to form the fabric of a relationship with each other was, for so long, unquestioned. Indeed, the extent to which those fears were examined in their entirety is questionable even in the present day, and debate about such fears has been very much a recent and marginal phenomenon. As a result, the fear of Islam, for example, lies stronger in the heart of many ordinary Europeans than fear of wars and conflicts closer to home. Thus even the bitter and decades-old sectarian conflict in Northern Ireland, with its bitter religious overtones of hatred (along with class and ethnic permutations), is nothing compared to fear of Islam. As a Belfast taxi-driver once told me, 'Now it may be bad here but you wouldn't catch me hanging out with them Hamas boys. They could teach Ian Paisley a thing or two about religion.' These words came before the paramilitary ceasefires of 1994. Before then, taxi-drivers like the one who spoke to me risked random sectarian assassination on a daily basis. His fear of Islam, an Islam that was familiar to him only from representations in the media and other dimensions of culture, was far greater. In the wake of the terror wrought in America on September 11, 2001, that climate of fear has increased tenfold and has been expressed in a variety of ways. For example, one influential voice in American media and military circles declared that Muslim violence

is not the result of creative instability, but of the atrophy of a civilization... Destruction is the only thing of which they remain capable, and destruction is their true god... They are not fighting for a just peace, but for their peace – and even if they attained that peace, they

would desire another. They are, in every sense, lost souls, the irre-
deemable. Their savagery is not a result of the failure of any peace
process, but a reaction to their own personal failures and to the
failures of their entire way of life. (R. Peters, 2001, p. 15)

For Peters, there is an obvious willingness to see Islam as the
inherent source of a destructive power. He echoes the view that
the modernity project remains the antithesis of Islam.

The violent impulse is explained as a reaction. Islam is singled
out as an exception to the rule associated with the positive embrace
of the modernity project exhibited in all other domains across the
globe. In such literatures Islam and Muslims are accused of
rejecting the new global agenda authored and shaped in the West.
Islam, according to Fukuyama, 'is the only cultural system that
seems regularly to produce people like Osama bin Laden or the
Taliban who reject modernity lock, stock and barrel' (Fukuyama,
2001, p. 22). While Fukuyama recognizes that not every Muslim
will behave like a Bin Laden, he still levels an accusation that
support for Muslim violence is widespread. Indeed, he suggests
that 'perhaps the hatred is born out of a resentment of western
success and Muslim failure' (ibid.). In these ways the common view
of the West in Islamist discourses is one of subjugation and domination, and Islam is associated with backwardness and violence. It is
portrayed in the media and by many writers as a series of negatives
associated with bombs, anti-Westernism, kidnappings, blood,
guns, war, *mujahideen*, images of self-flagellating Shi'as commemor-
ating *ashura*, and terror as the lifeless bodies of infant children are
recovered from the wreckage caused by suicide bombers. Muslims,
as one author contends, don't care what it takes; 'in Islam's war
against the West and the struggle to build Islamic states at home,
the end justifies the means... radical political Islam placed atop
these societies in the Middle East has created a combustible mixture' (Miller, 1993, p. 33). Miller is not alone in making such statements; indeed, her work reflects a dominant trend that has been
apparent and influential in policy-making circles in many states. As
such it is worth spending a little time reflecting on it. Miller begins
by stating, 'in Islam's war against the West', a major assertion with
significant strategic, political, economic and military ramifications
for oil-dependent states in the West. Islam, the faith of nearly one
billion adherents, the majority of whom reside in countries outside
the Middle East, are engaged in a 'war against the West'. This war
is not conventional in the sense of pitting similarly trained armies
against each other on the battlefield, but has far more sinister

ramifications. For Islam's war against the West is represented primarily as a war of extreme terrorism – the kind of terrorism that was behind the attacks in the USA on September 11, 2001, in which the magnitude of civilian loss may never truly be felt and reflected in a fundamental reordering of the international system and politics. George Joffe, on the other hands, explains such violence as far from representative of Muslims. Moreover, he argues:

> [M]any people who engage in violence within the context of political Islam, do so because they believe there is no other way in which their opposition and their protest can be effectively expressed. They also do so in part because of an ideology that encourages them to do so, the concept of Jihad, or Holy War, although this is very often misunderstood both by those who practise it and by those who observe it ... It should be borne in mind however that not all people who believe in the Islamic ordering of society consider that this kind of violent approach is correct. (Joffe, n.d.).

In this war, the faith of Islam is led by fanatical demagogues who are beyond reason and morals. These demagogues are determined, according to Miller, 'to struggle to build Islamic states at home', and of course the fear is that such states will embody ideas and norms that do not conform to those of the West and become a threat. There is a fear of the kind of ideological politics that was supposed to evaporate with the end of the Cold War. What does this fear communicate about the nature of Western political discourse and the resurgence of a faith as ideological in the contemporary era? While there is some truth in the Hobbesian viewpoint that everyone needs an enemy, authors such as Joffe are concerned that all Muslims, rather than just those who embrace terror, have been identified as the enemy.

Despite Fukuyama's early prognosis of the end of history, Islam's ideological impulse goes a long way to disprove the comforting notion that US victory in the Cold War implied an ideological collapse that would engulf the world throughout the 1990s. Yet, as many have argued, including Islam's secular Muslim critics, the ideological alternative that Islamists offer is devastatingly simple, and does actually provide succour to those who are desperately oppressed and abandoned by the states that should be there to serve them. It is, as the secularists admit, difficult to counter an ideological spectrum that is as wide as that within contemporary Islamism but that ultimately shares the same vision that 'Islam is the solution'. Does Miller acknowledge the depth of Islamist discourse? Her perspective indubitably places 'radical political Islam atop these societies in the Middle East', and, as such represents them as the most potent force in these societies. Empirically, of course, the reality is a little different. Radical Islam is not 'atop' the political systems of most Muslim majority states across the globe. Muslim majority Brunei, Malaysia, Indonesia, Pakistan, Syria, Iraq, Mali, Chad and Burkino-Faso are not societies dominated by radical Islam. Even in the eighteen states of the Middle East, including Algeria, Bahrain, Egypt, Iran, Iraq, Jordan, Kuwait, Lebanon, Libya, Morocco, Oman, Qatar, Saudi Arabia, Sudan, Tunisia, Turkey, the United Arab Emirates and Yemen, it would be difficult to argue, despite destabilizing radical elements in Egypt and Algeria, that 'radical political Islam [is] placed atop these societies'. Only in states like Iran, Sudan and Afghanistan have radical Islamist elements seized power and taken charge at the top. Radical political Islamic organizations and expressions of ideologies are certainly a part of such societies, sometimes assuming more importance than others. Conservatism rather than radicalism is the more likely characteristic of such societies, which in turn is translated into illiberal and authoritarian rule.

Nevertheless, the import of a statement like Miller's lies in the empowering value of violence that some extremist radical elements have employed. In this context, as I will discuss later in the chapter, such values have as much, if not more, to do with the discourse of power and violence than some inherently Muslim character traits that inspire Muslims to kill in the name of Islam. Even in terms of violence, the contentious issue at the heart of many contemporary societies in which Muslims form the majority is that violence is often the main symbol of power for both state and non-state actors. The extent to which the twists and turns of this particular aspect of the debate about political violence in Muslim societies occurs is formidable. It introduces perplexing complexities in contexts such as Afghanistan or Egypt where the rhetoric of 'good versus evil' dominates. To date, the desire to make sense of events that induce fear and uncertainty has been informed by an image that meets the need for soundbite-sized explanations, but fails to push forward and eliminate the causes of terrorism in the name of Islam.

Jihad mania

The belief that Islam commands its followers to engage in acts of violence, as a doctrine of faith, is most strongly associated with the concept of *jihad*. The literal definition of *jihad* (the word is derived from *juhd*) is 'To make substantial effort'. *Jihad* itself has been defined in the *Arabic Dictionary* as 'To make the utmost effort to attain something beloved or to save oneself from something disliked'. Yet, in the latter part of the twentieth century, not only did the term *jihad* enter common usage in the English language, but it was generally construed to mean a 'holy war'. Throughout the 1980s and 1990s, a variety of media outlets proclaimed that Muslims were engaged in a *jihad*. *Jihad* was often understood as involving a war against the West, Western targets or Western interests. Islamic scholars, however, have agreed that *jihad* in Islamic terms means 'To fight in the path of Allah or anything aiding this course'. The subject of *jihad* is discussed with particular emphasis and in considerable detail in the Qur'an. It is expressed in numerous verses. The verses explain in detail the clear objective and benefit of *jihad*. The status of the *mujahid* (one committed to an act of *jihad*) is honoured. By the 1990s the debate about *jihad* reached new heights, and the threat of *jihad* assumed global proportions as emphasized by Osama Bin Laden's al-Qaeda network.

Jihad has been interpreted very differently according to historical circumstance and context by the millions of Muslims who observe and promote their faith. As Lawrence points out, 'Jihad is a multivalent category of reference within the Islamic symbol system. It is not limited to holy war, nor is it decisive to the Qur'an if one considers all the themes and counter themes of ... the book' (Lawrence, 1998, p. 146). This view contrasts with that of Daniel Pipes, who, while recognizing two variant categories of *jihad* in the past, declares that 'Today, jihad is the world's foremost source of terrorism, inspiring a worldwide campaign of violence by self-proclaimed jihadist groups ... a leading source of conflict for 14 centuries, causing untold human suffering ... violent jihad will probably continue until it is crushed by a superior military force' (Pipes, 2002). Pipes contends that Lawrence's assertions regarding *jihad* make him an apologist. The perspective offered within Western academia differs, but also reflects the currency of the vision in the West that *jihad* is the sixth pillar of Islam and as such a fundamental element of the faith that all adherents should observe and conform to. Such views fail to take account of the development of the doctrine and its place within the belief system. Such an account needs to begin with an understanding of what is referred to as the classical doctrine of *jihad*.

The classical doctrine of *jihad* is found in copious verses or *sura* of the Qur'an and hadith. Scholars of the four legal schools of thought

– Hanafi, Maliki, Shafi and Hanbali – address this important issue. Under the terms of the classical doctrine there are, broadly speaking, two types of *jihad* against the unbelievers. Thus, the *jihad* becomes a form of proselytizing, a way of establishing the faith among people who enjoy belief systems that are not guided by the hand of Islam, Christianity or Judaism. The first type is based on taking the initiative. The second is defensive – a means by which the faith and its adherents are protected from tyranny and injustice inflicted upon them by others in their own community or by outsiders.

The first form, of offensive *jihad*, is referred to as *jihad* by the sword (*jihad bis saif*). There are a variety of conditions that must be respected and adhered to before such a form of striving is undertaken. Adherents of Islam may not launch a *jihad* of this type if they have not already offered Islam in other forms and ways. Indeed, an invitation to the faith must always be offered freely and peacefully to the infidel (the one without God). Rejection is countenanced, and so long as payment in the form of *jizyah* (poll tax) is forthcoming from the individual or community, they are free to live under the protection of the Islamic community. Violence is permitted, however, if they fail to submit. The type of *jihad* recommended here may be carried out by a vanguard on behalf of the Muslim population as a whole. According to scholars of classical Islam, during the time of the Prophet Mohammad and his immediate successors, *jihad* by the sword as a means of proselytizing predominated as the influence of the religion united the disparate tribes of south Arabia and spread further into the hinterlands of the Middle East.

The obligation of Islam's adherents to spread the word of the new faith was an impulse that drove the initial expansion of Islam beyond the dust-dry borders of Arabia. This *jihad* resulted in the rapid expansion not only of a new belief system but of accompanying social, legal, economic, military and political structures that undermined the increasingly tentative grasp of Byzantine rulers of the Near East. The *jihad* created a new system that transformed the lives of many ordinary people. The historian Francis Peters contends that this was often for the better, not the worse: 'The conquests destroyed little: what they did suppress were imperial rivalries and sectarian bloodletting among the newly subjected population. The Muslims tolerated Christianity, but they disestablished it... The reduction in Christian status was merely judicial; it was unaccompanied by either systematic persecution or a bloodlust' (F. E. Peters, 1994, p. 79). Neglect of this duty to the faith system had inevitable consequences. The inevitable nature of these consequences is addressed in the second form of *jihad* – defensive *jihad*, which outlines the obligations of Muslims when they find their own societies (and, in fact, those of others) ridden with a system of rule that perpetrates injustice, abandons peace and enforces the rule of the despot on the many.

The defensive *jihad* may be outlined in the following way. *Jihad* becomes a compulsory obligation (*fard ayn*) when the community of believers (*umma*) finds itself under attack or when Muslim territory falls into the political or theocratic control of a foreign power. Defence is also an obligation if a foreign or infidel power takes Muslims prisoner. Other matters pertaining to the defensive *jihad* relate to issues such as hostage taking of women, and when a Muslim ruler orders Muslims into battle to protect their independence and sovereignty. The import of the compulsory defensive *jihad* is that every person contributes to the protection of the faith and its adherents – with a number of exceptions, including children, the insane, slaves, women, the ill and the handicapped, etc. Yet, under specific circumstances, even women, slaves and debtors may fight the *jihad* as a defensive act. The *jihad* is the obligation of everyone, but falls in the first place on the shoulders of the community that finds itself under attack. Nevertheless, all Muslims are obliged to support it where necessary. The famous medieval Muslim jurist Ibn Tayymiya, writing on defensive *jihad*, declares: 'The first obligation after *Iman* is the repulsion of the enemy aggressor who assaults the religion and the worldly affairs' (Azzam, 1996, p. 4). Such words reveal the sentiments of many nations, past and present, and others of faith who will only turn to the battlefield when all else has failed. In modern terms, this form of *jihad* can be interpreted as similar to the right of nations to defend themselves in the face of attack or an impingement of sovereignty by an outside power. All nations in the modern age have the right to defend themselves in the face of attack and injustice. If the Muslim community (*umma*) is equivalent to a nation, then it has the right to defend and protect its citizens from external threat and to employ force under such conditions.

In addition, the classical doctrine of *jihad* contains specific rules or conditions about such issues as methods of warfare, enemy persons, enemy property, fleeing from the battlefield, assistance to unbelievers, trade with the enemy, captives and prisoners or war, safe conduct, ceasefire (*hodna*) and armistice, and the end of *jihad*. All these issues are covered by classical scholars with recourse to the Qur'an and hadith, which shed light on these complicated issues. In summary, the classical doctrine of *jihad* embraces what Donner refers to as 'a relatively rich discussion on many issues relating to war, its limitation and its justification... this juristic tradition on war grew out of a combination of original Islamic values and of traditions stretching back into the distant pre-Islamic past, and it was likely subjected to continuous reshaping' (Donner, 1991, p. 57). The rules of war and battle, then, have just as vigorously shaped the discourse of *jihad* as they have that of the just war concept that is still employed in the West to justify the moral stance taken on the global stage.

Modernist doctrine of jihad

As a result of the discussion and reshaping of the doctrine of *jihad*, there emerged in nineteenth-century India what is referred to as a modernist doctrine of *jihad*. Shaped through *ijtihad* (interpretation) and the historical circumstances in which India's Muslims found themselves, a new body of work emerged that would later filter through to the Middle East and modernist thinkers like Mohammad Abduh in Egypt. Many scholars see the modernist, so-called defensive doctrine of *jihad* as originating with the Indian Muslim scholar Sayyid Ahmad Khan, who promoted a vision of Islam that was contemporaneous with the modern age and the challenges it presented – including the most significant challenge at that time, Britain's rule of India. For British rule, with its important economic, political, technical and cultural impulses, was associated with a secular system with a zeal for imperial rule in India. As a reformer, Ahmad Khan saw the challenge as proving that Islam was not an obstacle to Western rationalism or technical superiority. Through interpretation there was a way to highlight the relevance and applicability of Muslim thought, particularly in relation to the concept of *jihad* as a defensive action. Through *ijtihad* Ahmad Khan and others went a considerable way to achieving his goal. As Peters argues, 'not only did they assert that *jihad* was essentially defensive but they also limited this to its defence against religious oppression impairing the pillars of Islam... thereby excluding from it all other kinds of political oppression. Thus they introduced a separation between the religious and political spheres, an obvious innovation with regard to a religion that claims to dominate all domains of human activity' (R. Peters, 1984, p. 125). Thus, for the modernist followers of Sayyid Ahmad Khan, such as Mohammad Abduh, the act of *jihad* became essentially defensive, a duty upon all Muslims in the face of foreign aggression and usurpation from outside the Muslim community. Here the linkage made by thinkers such as Abduh and later Rashid Rida with this modernist doctrine of *jihad* and the colonial experience in Egypt is not difficult to discern. Yet this doctrine was not embraced by a new generation of Muslim radicals who arose in the Muslim world from the 1950s onwards.

Fundamentalist *jihad*

The predominant contemporary doctrine of *jihad* is that associated with the *salafi* fundamentalists, including figures such as Osama Bin Laden, Mawdudi, Hassan al-Banna, Sayyid Qutb and Abdullah Azzam. The fundamentalist doctrine owes much to the classical view of *jihad*, predicated as it is on both the aggressive and the defensive function of *jihad*. The fundamentalists encourage the propagation of Islam through *jihad*. As Sayyid Qutb declares, in direct criticism of the modernists, 'this group of thinkers, that is a product of the sorry state of the present Muslim generation, has nothing but the label of Islam and has laid down its spiritual and rational arms in defeat. They say, "Islam has prescribed only defensive war"!... Islam does not force people to accept its belief... What it wants is to abolish those oppressive political systems under which people are prevented from expressing their freedom to choose whatever beliefs they want' (Qutb, 1978, p. 100). The echoes of classical thinking are strong, and are reflected in the way the classical doctrine has been embraced by contemporary Islamists and incorporated in a modern approach, with language that is striking in an era of global instability and a historical experience of Western colonialism. The language of the fundamentalist *jihad* doctrine draws a battle line between Islam and the rest of the world. The discourse is revolutionary in character and stresses the urgency of effecting change in a global order that is perceived as both anti-Muslim and pro-secular. Indeed, it is the religious dimension or tension that is most apparent in this approach. This is reflected in the statements and activities of organizations such as Hamas. In its attack against Israel it has adopted suicide attacks, and its leaders have declared a *jihad*. Indeed, the rhetoric of a battle of wider proportions is apparent in a Hamas statement from 1998: 'What is taking place in the Holy Land is not just a battle for the Palestinian people alone. It is a battle for the future of the entire

Umma (Muslim community). It is a battle against foreign arrogance – against colonial hegemony over our world' (Hamas, 1998). For fundamentalist thinkers, the urgency of *jihad* cannot be overestimated, and the parlous state of the religion is attributed to past fear of *jihad* and its denigration, by the modernists, to a purely defensive role in Muslim society. Abdullah Azzam, an Afghan Arab leader of Palestinian origin and a man whom Bin Laden 'revered as his leader', urged his brethren to take up the struggle: '*Jihad* and emigration to *jihad*,' he declared:

> have a deep-rooted role that cannot be separated from the constitution of the religion. A religion that does not have *jihad* cannot become established in any land, nor can it strengthen its frame.... So, everyone not performing *jihad* today is forsaking a duty, just like one who eats during the days of Ramadan without excuse, or the rich person who withholds *zakat* from his wealth. Nay, the state of a person who abandons *jihad* is more severe. (Azzam, 1996, pp. 17–18)

The process advocated by the fundamentalists is tantamount to placing the obligation of *jihad* alongside the other obligations of the faith, almost creating a sixth pillar of faith, certainly outlining *jihad* (offensive, defensive, by peaceful or other means) as a core practice of the faith of Islam and vital for its proper regeneration in the modern age. Illustration of this point is found once again in Azzam:

> Establishment of the Muslim community on an area of land is a necessity, as vital as water and air. This homeland will not come about without an organised Islamic movement that perseveres consciously and realistically upon *jihad*, and that regards fighting as a decisive factor and as a protective wrapping. (Azzam, 1996, p. 23)

The fundamentalist doctrine of *jihad* meets the modern era head on, and rests on the principal assumption that the goal and duty of adherents to Islam is to establish a world of Islam (*dar al-Islam*) through the defeat of the world of war (*dar al-harb*) – the resurrection of the Caliphate can be achieved only through a proactive and vigorous promotion of *jihad*. This discourse, however, inhibits inquiry and activity associated with the greater meaning and interpretation of *jihad* and distorts its spiritual core. Eqbal Ahmad asserts that the fundamentalist interpretation is a disservice to believers.

> Without a hint of doubt, contemporary Muslim ideologues and militants have reduced the rich associations of *jihad* to the single

meaning of engagement in warfare, entirely divested of its conditions and rules. Thus the war against a Marxist government in
Afghanistan and its Soviet ally became the most famous *jihad* of the
20th century even though it was armed and financed by the United
States, a non-Muslim superpower. Today, such activities as terrorism, sectarian strife, and the killings of innocent people are claimed
as holy warfare. This reductionism is by no means unique to the
Muslim world. (Ahmad, 1999, p. 1)

Sayyid Qutb and a theology of terror?

If it is accepted that not all Islamists are radicals, and that not even
all radicals are terrorists, it gives us a clearer perspective when
examining those thinkers who have been identified as formulating
a 'radical' ideology with emphasis on Political Islam with a capital
P. One such ideologue who is commonly cited is the Egyptian
theorist and activist Sayyid Qutb. In 1966, after spending ten
years in prison, Qutb was executed by the Egyptian authorities.
He is regarded within Islamist circles as a martyr. His radical
philosophy has inspired many radical groups, including Egyptian,
Palestinian, Lebanese and Afghan organizations such as Gama
Islamiyya, Islamic Jihad (Shiqaqi faction). Qutb was a prolific
author, writing during a turbulent period in Egypt's history characterized by revolutionary change: a radical transformation from a
traditional political order to a new dawn in Arab nationalist and
secular politics. Qutb became a major ideologue of the late twentieth century, as Ayubi notes, 'Qutbian discourse...tends to influence people's thought and action in a psychologically tense way
that creates in the individual not the ability to reconstruct reality
but rather the dream of breaking with that reality' (Ayubi, 1991,
p. 141). Qutb, echoing Mawdudi's concept of *jahiliyya*, viewed
modern-day Egyptian society under Nasser in the same way. His
notion of *jahiliyya*, however, was inherently linked to the concept of
jihad. From Qutb's perspective, *jihad* was a method of release from
pagan rule, the key to the door of a true Islamic society. He called
for liberation: 'We should remove ourselves from all influences of
the *jahiliyya* in which we live and from which we derive benefits
...Our aim is first to change ourselves so that we may later change
the society.' He goes on to say: 'All that is around us is *jahiliyya*.
People's imaginings, their beliefs, customs and traditions, the
sources of their culture, their art and literature, their laws and

statutes, much even of what we take to be Islamic culture, Islamic authorities, Islamic philosophy, Islamic thought: all this too is of the making of this *jahiliyya'* (Qutb, 1978, p. 57).

Qutb's call reflected a change in the philosophy of political Islam. As Kedourie remarks, for Qutb it is Muslim rulers, above all, who are 'infected with the spirit of idolatry, who are responsible for much of the evil. They are apostates from whose deadly clutch Muslim society has to be saved' (Kedourie, 1992, pp. 332–3). Qutb (unlike Egyptian reformist and Islamist leader Hassan al-Banna, who argued for gradual change from within and the reform of society through preaching and education) called for complete disengagement from the prevailing political order and for that order's dissolution. Following Qutb's logic this is the only option open to Muslims who recognize domination of the *jahilli* system of rule (non-Muslim) over their lives. Change, according to Qutb, has a radical appearance, and is best achieved through struggle or striving: 'The truth of the faith,' he argues, 'is not fully established until struggle is undertaken on its behalf among the people. A struggle against their unwillingness and their resistance, a struggle to remove them from this state [*jahiliyya*] to that of Islam and truth. A struggle by word of mouth, by propagation, by exposition, by refuting the false and baseless... A struggle physically to remove obstacles from the path of right guidance when it is infested by brute force and open violence' (Qutb, 1978, p. 60).

Qutb's call for liberation from all forms of political rule proved inspirational – calling on Muslims to throw off unjust, secular, corrupt rule. Indeed, a return to the faith and the 'straight path' makes this act of liberation an obligation for any true Muslim living under tyranny. Tyranny, for Qutb, comes in many shapes and forms – including contemporary Arab nation-states, so-called Islamic governments such as that of Saudi Arabia, and Western states such as the United States of America. As Qutb himself put it, 'There is only one way to reach God; all other ways do not lead to Him. This is my straight path. Then follow it and do not follow other ways which will scatter you from his path. For human life there is only one true system and that is Islam, all other systems are *jahiliyya'* (Qutb, 1978, p. 60). There are many interpretations of Qutb's perspective and assessment of contemporary society and the parlous state in which Muslims find themselves. Sivan argues that Qutb's message contained a 'violence of tone and urgency... to his fellow Muslims who were tempted and even brainwashed by Western ideas' (Sivan, 1985, p. 24). Qutb is viewed as a rejectionist, a radical out of step with the global tempo. His mission, argues Sivan, 'is a total rejection of modernity – since modernity represents the negation of God's sovereignty in all fields of life and the relegation of religion to the dustbin of history' (ibid., p. 27). Sivan concludes that Qutb was clearly putting violence at the top of the liberation agenda.

There are many who have interpreted Qutb's philosophy as fundamentally violent – the new Islamic order should be established through the sword, through the violent acts of a vanguard (Islamic Jihad) clearing the path for the liberation of the whole of society, the overthrow of tyranny, secularism and modernity. Some, though, contend that Qutb himself was more circumspect, neither ruling out violence nor actively advocating it. What is certain is that the call to *jihad* was taken in its broadest sense. *Jihad* meant striving and liberation of the soul of the individual through education, a return to the faith, and disengagement where possible from a state system and political authority that encourages popular rather than divine sovereignty, permissiveness between the sexes, un-Islamic economic and business practices, and so on. And it is true that Qutb, while in prison, did eventually sanction military preparations in the name of Islam. But, as Sivan admits, 'he still believed in long-term education as well – the distinction between both courses of action remained for him essentially pragmatic not philosophical' (Sivan, 1985, p. 90).

Qutb's vision of the future, however, was shaped by a utopian image of the past, based on the early Medinan state of the Prophet Mohammad and the first four Caliphs. Qutb was a traditionalist, and berated those Islamists such as al-Afghani and Abduh who attempted to modernize Islam. While Qutb initially rejected *jihad* as armed struggle, his own experiences at the hands of the Egyptian state authorities 'radicalized' him, and he subsequently criticized the religious establishment for its role in legitimating Nasser's rule. The radical agenda that eventually characterized Qutb, his hostility to the West (especially colonialists and Americans), and the fear of tyranny from within became the starting point for many radical groups. As Esposito points out, Qutb's influence (along with that of others) on radical groups who engaged in acts of violence and terrorism is apparent: 'Ideologically, Islamic militants are heavily indebted to Sayyid Qutb and Mawlana Mawdudi. They interpret their call for an Islamic revolution and *jihad* quite literally. Force and violence are accepted as part of their liberation struggle' (Esposito, 1984, p. 216).

Qutb's influence

As Esposito demonstrates, Qutb's ideology or world view remains relevant to radical Islamist groups active in the Muslim world today. It is important to remember, however, that this manifestation of political Islam *à la* Qutb and the radicals accounts for only one small part of the current manifestation of political Islam. Nevertheless, the Qutbian discourse has been identified as a major feature of the thinking of radical groups such as *Takfir wa Hijra* (Redemption and Flight) which was responsible for the assassination of President Sadat of Egypt in October 1981. In addition, Qutbian discourse has been retained by radical thinkers like Egyptian Abdel Salam Farag, described by Kedourie as promoting the 'logical culmination of Qutb's doctrine' (Kedourie, 1992, p. 333). The fundamentalist doctrine of *jihad* has been embraced by a number of Islamic groups in the contemporary era, including al-Qaeda. Thus al-Qaeda and other jihadist groups such as Islamic Jihad, Hizballah and Jihad al-Islami are purveyors of a fundamentalist doctrine of *jihad* that in the 1990s resulted in a violent battle between the self-appointed vanguard of Islam and the *jahilli* world in which they then found themselves located. If one agrees with Eqbal Ahmad, then it is apparent that the fundamentalists have distorted the concept of *jihad* in fulfilment of an ambition for political power, through terrorism rather than spiritual freedom in a modern age. Indeed, power – a desire and ambition for it and a perception of loss of it – is reflected in the discourse on this theme. What is questionable here is whether the call to arms is truly in the name of humanity or freedom or rather to satisfy the short-term ambitions of a cohort of radicals with a desire to change the prevailing order by whatever means possible. In this respect, the ambitions of Islamists such as Osama Bin Laden are no different from those of other extreme, radically motivated religious leaders of other faiths. There are some important similarities between these religiously inspired extremist elements, militias and terrorists. The secularizing tendencies of many modern states are rejected wholesale by such elements, and sacred violence becomes a means for achieving change. Such elements are inherently conservative in their attitudes towards women. They seek an order where faith enjoys a greater public place and space. They betray a fundamental rejection of modernity that is not prevalent in mainstream views of Islam or other faiths. In India, for example, violent politics has engulfed the political and power agenda of the fundamentalist

Hindu movement, bringing a new dimension to this faith system. Terrorism stalks the margins of many ideological movements, and in this respect Islam is no different. The real difference lies in the charge that it is more than a few radical fanatics who represent the face of terrorism in Islam.

The suicide or homicide bombers?

If the peoples of the Middle East continue on their present path, the suicide bomber may become a metaphor for the whole region, and there will be no escape from a downward spiral of hate and spite, rage and self-pity, poverty and oppression, culminating sooner or later in yet another alien domination.

B. Lewis, 2002

What price is there for martyrdom operations? No price can be offered that will compensate for a lack of dignity and freedom. It's a sacrifice and fight for liberty and this is the only price for the martyrs.

Mahmoud Zahar, September 2002

Mohammed Atta committed an act of terrorism against civilians working in an office block in New York. Amrozi Nurhaysim, convicted of plotting and organizing the Bali bombing of October 2002 that killed more than 200 civilians, when sentenced to death by the Indonesian courts, declared, 'I'll be happy to die a martyr. After me, there will be a million more Amrozis.' A suicide bomber blows up the UN headquarters in Baghdad, killing its civilian staff. A Chechen suicide bomber detonates explosives outside a Russian hospital. In Jerusalem and other Israeli cities, riding the bus or eating in a restaurant is like playing Russian roulette with the suicide bombers of Hamas, Islamic Jihad and the al-Aqsa Brigades. In Palestinian towns and cities, suicide bombers enjoy cult status. Twenty-first-century terrorism appears to be shaped and defined by Muslim suicide bombers, and in their wake a carnage and seemingly endless list of victims. The Islamists, of course, vehemently deny that such acts are either suicide or terrorism. As Hamas leader Ismail Abu Shanab declared, 'suicide is forbidden in Islam, as it is in any faith. Life is sacred... Those who sacrifice themselves in the name of Islam and the liberation of Palestine are martyrs. They undertake the *jihad* for freedom and justice' (Abu Shanab, 2002). Abu Shanab was assassinated by Israeli forces in August 2003, following a spiral of suicide bombings and targeted assassinations. Speaking after Abu Shanab's death, Hamas head Sheikh Yassin asserted, 'The Movement that offers its leaders as martyrs will gain thousands of new supporters and the Zionist entity will experience an unprecedented ordeal' (Yassin, 2003). Martyrdom in the service of Islam is considered not only a duty but an honour, with the promise of a paradise with flowing rivers of wine and beautiful virgins. This discourse regards violence or military action as sacred and ordained, so one assumes that the activist or perpetrator of such a deed is compelled into violent action as a profession of faith, that to accept the faith, one must engage in acts of violence that are divinely inspired.

Indeed, it is apparent that martyrdom rather than suicide is how these Islamist actors understand their actions. The Qur'an expressly forbids the deliberate act of ending one's life. According to the martyr-seekers, however, it does recognize that sacrifice of life in the name of the faith is not prohibited. A verse of the Qur'an declares, 'So let them fight in the way of God who sell the present life for the world to come; and whosoever fights in the way of God and is slain, or conquers, We shall bring him a mighty wage' (Sura IV: 75). This is the interpretation of the Qur'an that has been resurrected and interpreted as a means by which to compel pious people to embrace a fight that they believe they are obliged to embrace.

In addition, some historians argue that there has been a tradition of suicide attacks in Islam, which by definition is a religion of violence and disorder. In an attempt to explain the apparent attraction to suicide in the name of the faith, the historical example of the Assassins and the 'Old Man of the Mountain' is raised as evidence of a predilection for this kind of terror. The Assassins were a small group within a Shi'ite sect of Islam (known as the Ismailis) which in the eleventh century attracted an even smaller band of young men to a man named Hasan as-Sabah (the 'Old Man of the Mountains'). Hasan encouraged his tiny group of followers to embrace violence as part of a power struggle within Islam. He encouraged assassination and the willing loss of life in its pursuit during a period of intense upheaval in the Muslim domain. The historical interpretation of motive and method is here not founded on an extensive surviving literature or documents produced by the Assassins and as-Sabah himself. Instead, the history of this small sect is derived from accounts written long after the events and in the context of explaining either the Crusades or the domination of the Seljuk Turks in the Middle East. Thus, the historical accounts, although they are readily cited by modern historians as evidence, cannot be said to explain adequately why Muslims engage in suicide terror campaigns. Nevertheless, evidence of the inextricable and historical relationship (that is inclusive of the Assassins) between Islam and terrorism is drawn by authors like Rapoport, who ascribes different characteristics to those he then terms 'religious terrorists'.

In drawing a major distinction between the secular and the religious, one that is easily read as a distinction by extension between the West and Islam, this viewpoint is extended to reflect that 'holy terror' is the product of 'radically different value systems, mechanisms of legitimisation and justification, concepts of morality, and a Manichean world view' (Hoffman, 1995, p. 272). To elaborate on Hoffman's perspective, Islam represents a belief system that reflects a radically 'different value system', and conducts politics down the barrel of a gun instead of via the plural forums of democracy. From such a perspective, then, Islam is increasingly defined by the terrorists. Suicide bombing is just one way in which the expression of radical difference is made manifest to a civilization typified by the freedom-loving West. This contrasts with the research of Robert A. Pape, who contends that the 'presumed connection between suicide terrorism and Islamic fundamentalism is wrongheaded, and it may be encouraging domestic and foreign policies that are likely to worsen America's situation' (Pape, 2003). Pape studied more than 188 suicide incidents throughout the 1980s and 1990s and concluded:

> There is little connection between suicide terrorism and Islamic fundamentalism, or any religion for that matter...Rather, what nearly all suicide terrorist campaigns have in common is a specific secular and strategic goal: to compel liberal democracies to withdraw military forces from territory that the terrorists consider to be their homeland. Religion is rarely the root cause, although it is often used as a tool by terrorist organizations in recruiting and in other efforts in service of the broader strategic objective. (Pape, 2003)

Yet for Hoffman religion matters; moreover, the points of commonality between faiths and cultures are absent from such explanations. Instead, the zealous orders of fanatic Muslim leaders are seen to be unquestioningly obeyed by submissive followers who strap explosives to their bodies in the knowledge that they will perish and, more importantly, that their enemies will also die. In terms of morality, then, the moral impulse is so at odds with the world that Islam is construed by these authors as a belief system that devalues and twists the right to life. This is one way in which the impulse to martyrdom is explained in the modern age. But such accounts overlook the complex political emergencies that actually characterize the conflicts that engage Islamists in a variety of ways the world over. Thus conflicts as complex processes that grip societies in which Muslims find themselves are not fully factored into the equation as a way in which the desire to end violence can be calculated and addressed. Accepting this explanation means that a certain fatalism enters the politics of global and regional conflicts in the twenty-first century. Pape offers an alternative route; declaring military options and concessions redundant, he asserts, 'In the end, the best approach for the states under fire is probably to focus on their own domestic security while doing what they can to see that the least militant forces on the terrorists' side build a viable state of their own' (Pape, 2003).

Martyrdom-seekers have thus become a disturbing phenomenon of, for example, the Israeli–Palestinian conflict in the late 1990s and early twenty-first century. Until that time, suicide attacks had been a limited phenomenon in Islamist terms – employed in a limited fashion, but with devastating consequences, in Lebanon in the early 1980s. In one respect the suicide attacks, or self-termed martyrdom operations, launched by groups like Hamas and Islamic Jihad in the late 1990s introduced an important moral dimension into the debate within Muslim domains in terms of means and ends in war. For if the means to wage war was by blowing up children in pizza parlours or teenagers in discos, there was a fear that the cause was corrupted in ways that the Muslim tradition on just war explicitly prohibited. For Islamic doctrine explicitly rules out the harming of innocents or civilians, even under the conditions of war or *jihad*. It was in the arena of the Israeli–Palestinian conflict that Palestinian Islamists embarked on this strategy of terror in 1994, a strategy that has now come to define Palestinian Islamism in the present era. The impulse to suicide operations in this context is linked to a contemporary battle that has engulfed the area for the best part of a century.

The conflict is multi-dimensional and has been engendered in the hearts of ordinary Israelis and Palestinians with the most devastating consequences for both sides. It has traditionally been described, from a variety of perspectives, as entailing a recourse to political violence, including terrorism, by both state and non-state actors. Political violence or terrorism has characterized the mutual antagonisms and the competing demands of the Israeli and Palestinian peoples. The linkage is made explicit in an interview with a putative suicide bomber: 'Our main objective is to satisfy God's will by undertaking *jihad* . . . the other is to regain the Palestinians' stolen land and dignity' (Barr, 2001, p. 5). This is a battle in which there appear to be no limits to the violence that is perpetrated, and where the so-called ordinary rules of war (including just war) do not apply. Meeting the challenge posed by young people willing to sacrifice an 'earthly' existence for the promise of paradise has confounded military and strategic experts who are used to more conventional approaches to conflict and terrorism. Furthermore, as the conflict between Israel and the Palestinians spiralled during the second *intifada*, the secular nationalist Fatah movement established armed elements – the al-Aqsa Martyrs Brigades – that committed the same sort of suicide bombings as those associated with such Muslim fundamentalist groups as Hamas and Palestinian Islamic Jihad. By 2002 and 2003, the al-Aqsa group of nationalists and Hamas and Islamic Jihad were also known to be co-operating in planning operations against Israel. The dynamic of the conflict and its association with seemingly intractable violence of all kinds limits the possibility of eliminating any one dimension unless the environment of conflict is changed to one of justice and peace that satisfies all sides. Suicide terrorism is no longer an Islamist phenomenon. It is not within the scope of this chapter to explore this debate fully. Suffice it to say that societies that have perpetrated great acts of violence against each other, including those with Muslim populations, are able to recover from the context of conflict where this form of 'politics by other means' is common currency. Justice, truth and national reconciliation have, however, to replace conflict and inequality if the saliency of violence is to be brought into question. In the Israeli–Palestinian context Pape advocates the following: 'Israel, for example, would be well advised to abandon the territory it holds on the West Bank but to go ahead with building the immense wall, 20 feet high and 20 feet wide, to physically separate it from the Palestinian population. This would create real security for Israel and leave the West Bank for a true Palestinian state' (Pape, 2003). Such solutions are specific to the context and do not go far in addressing the elimination of violence in other Muslim domains. For such domains are often characterized by internal conflicts that in turn have engaged important external actors. External actors may be important regionally or internationally, yet their engagement alters conflict and attempts at its resolution.

Islamist violence: conflict and resistance

While the end of the Cold War may have signalled an end to the meta-conflict that defined it, in its wake a variety of smaller, ethno-national conflicts erupted. The decline of the Soviet menace meant that the citizens of Western states enjoyed a new sense of security, but this was not always the case in other domains. Throughout the 1990s and into the twenty-first century, Muslims frequently found themselves in countries where conflict character-ized their daily existence and left them powerless and without rights. In 1994 Gurr and Harff identified more than fifty-seven 'serious and emerging ethno-political conflicts'. Almost half of the conflicts identified were in countries with either majority Muslim or significantly large Muslim minority populations. The causes of conflict in those countries, however, were not necessarily seen as religious in nature. In Bosnia, for example, Gurr and Harff did not categorize the ethnic cleansing of Bosnian Muslims by Serbs as religiously motivated, but rather as ethno-national in origin. Simi-larly, in Lebanon, a country engulfed by civil conflict from 1975 to 1990, the conflict was ascribed a communal rather than a religious character (Gurr and Harff, 1994, pp. 160–6).

The citing of these examples is not intended to preclude the possibility that religious factors account for the nature of conflict in these states or communities. Rather, it is to reflect on the kinds of distinctions about modern conflicts and their religious dimensions that need to be made. There is a difference, for example, between the religious dimensions of conflict in Afghanistan and Chechnya. In Afghanistan fundamentalist Islamism has been but one dimen-sion of a conflict that has benighted the country. As Rashid high-lights, 'Before 11 September all the signs were there that Afghanistan had become a major threat to international and re-gional stability. The drought, the civil war, the mass migrations, drug trafficking, the hard line espoused by the Taliban leaders and the increase in terrorist groups operating from the country should have alerted Western powers that a crisis was at hand' (Rashid, 2001, p. xii). Even Taliban state rule was but one dimension of modern Islamism in that country. In Chechnya Russian opposition to secessionist demands by this Caucasus republic have undoubt-edly established an Islamist dimension that is both internal and external in influence. The Islamization of secessionist or independ-ence struggles is not unique to Chechnya and the Russian state, but is a feature of other such conflicts in locales such as the Philippines and Indonesia. Is such a realization the same as saying that Islam inspires terror, violence and conflict? What is pertinent is the fact that many millions of Muslims find themselves the victims of conflict, state oppression and tyranny in regimes and between regimes that are in turn supported by Western states of the free world. This in turn leads to the oft-quoted charge against the West of double standards by Islamist and other critiques. This state of affairs is a source of rage for many Islamist ideologues, leaders and clergy. It is they who seek to explain a perceived discrimination and double standard applied by what they describe as a hegemonic West that they believe acts as an entity hostile to Islam and its Muslim followers. As the spiritual head of Hizballah, Sheikh Fadlallah, contends, 'When we demand compensation for the victims of Israel's occupation [in Lebanon] the UN and America turns its (sic) back. But the US continues to support Israel even when its victims litter the streets' (Fadlallah, 2000). Contemporary fact and fiction collide to reinforce such views, allowing them to become common currency in certain quarters of the Muslim world. And so the mutual antipathy grows.

The problems that characterize Muslim domains are often blamed on the West by leaders unwilling to hold themselves accountable to their people. Islamists also exploit this issue by claiming that Western states support regimes (including Muslim-ruled ones) that terrorize and subjugate Muslim peoples. In the case of Bosnia, some Islamist elements blame the West for not stepping in soon enough to prevent the débâcle that unfolded and for failing to help arm the Bosnians. The West, including the USA, did belatedly intervene, yet this failed to prevent a perception of moral equivalence that worked against the Muslims. This failure to intervene quickly and in an even-handed fashion created a vacuum that was exploited by Islam's radical and fundamentalist elements, including the Arab-Afghan battalions and the government of Wahabi Saudi Arabia, in financing mosque reconstruction. In Iraq, of course, the West is blamed by Islamists and Muslim leaders more generally for being too quick to interfere in the matters of a Muslim sovereign state, and the US and British occupation is cited as evidence of an attempt to bring Muslim lands under *jahilli* 'Crusader' rule. As former Iranian President Rafsanjani declared, 'We never want the US to become victorious in Iraq because the US is more dangerous to us than Iraq. This is our ideological position and our political experience' (Rafsanjani, 2003). Muslim leaders fear the consequences of yet another Western 'occupation' of Muslim lands. Muslim leader Sheikh Qaradawi issued a *fatwa* prohibiting Muslim states from assisting the Coalition powers and reminding Muslims that 'resisting the invaders is an individual duty on all Muslims. If the enemies invade a Muslim country, the people of that country should resist and expel them from their territories' (Qaradawi, 2003). Yet in Iraq Muslim elements were divided in opinion about the foreign intervention. What remains significant, however, is that major Iraqi Shi'a resistance groups, such as the Badr Battalions based in bordering Iran, did not engage in attacks on the Coalition forces as they achieved regime change and occupation of the country. Post-war some leaders of the majority Shi'ite population have joined the ruling council. Other elements, including outside Islamist factions, bitterly oppose the continuing presence of so many foreign troops in their territory. Such a presence fuels radical Islamist hatred. This is evidenced by an al-Qaeda statement in the wake of the war: 'O Iraqi people, we defeated those crusaders several times before and expelled them out of our countries and holy shrines. You should know that you are not alone in this battle. Your *mujahid* brothers are tracking your enemies and lying in wait for them.'

Images of armed Muslim defenders of Bosnia, the Palestinian suicide bombers, the victorious Hizballah battalions, the Arab-Afghan fighters, the fighters of Abu Sayyaf and Chechen rebels are all employed to make propaganda for the radical Islamists. Such images are used to convey a message about the ability of Muslims to rise to the challenge of defence in times of crisis, conflict and tyranny. They also convey a sense that Islam has been hijacked by such groups when resistance turns to terrorism in the name of a faith with over 1 billion adherents. As the rescue teams work among the rubble of bombed offices, bars, restaurants, hotels, embassies, UN buildings, government offices and shopping malls, Islam becomes increasingly associated in the popular consciousness of the West with terrorism, not rightful resistance. Islam, like Judaism and Christianity, is not a faith system based on the fundamentals of terror, but preaches a message of peace and justice under the divine protection and benediction of God. The history of Islam demonstrates the importance attached to such principles. Its golden age is replete with examples of thriving, forbearing, harmonious societies. In the modern age, however, experiences of conflict, suppression, tyranny and authoritarianism have shaped how Islam is interpreted by its supporters. The violent radical fringe dominates, turning the notion of margin and centre on its head. Muslim moderates are berated and denounced as heretics for speaking out against terror in the name of Islam. Fear and silence pervade the political arena dominated by the fundamentalists and the terrorists. A 'fury for God' drove Islamists into a new interpretation of *jihad* that turned it into terrorism: the kind of terrorism that led America to abandon Lebanon and Somalia, the kind of terrorism in the name of Islam that has led to the unjustified killing of thousands of civilians and the dehumanization of conflict that the same radicals accuse their foes of. In many Muslim domains the state has reacted with the same measure of ruthless terror to the Islamist threat, and so the spiral of tyranny deepens. Thus, while it may be true that Egypt or Algeria or Saudi Arabia is increasingly less vulnerable to Islamist terrorism, it is also the case that all their citizens are less vulnerable to the forces of liberal democracy, the rule of law, and human security and safety. Such contexts continue to hinder the prospects for liberal democracy and a Muslim reformation to take hold.

THE MAKING OF MUTUAL ANTAGONISM: ISLAM AND THE WEST

Introduction

On September 11th, 2001, al-Qaeda, the Islamist group led by Osama Bin Laden and based in Afghanistan, launched a series of attacks in the USA. It was not the first time that al-Qaeda had targeted the USA or Americans: they had car-bombed the US embassies in Nairobi and Dar es-Salaam in 1998 and attacked the *USS Cole* off the coast of Yemen in 1999. But the 9/11 attack was the first time that al-Qaeda hit at the heart of the United States of America, in a way that previous attacks outside its sovereign borders had never done. By hitting at the symbolic heart of the USA, al-Qaeda succeeded in making ordinary American citizens experience a sense of fear and insecurity previously unknown to them. The attacks epitomized the depth of antagonism that lay at the heart of Bin Laden's attitude towards the West.

Moreover, the response of Western governments, in appearing to single out Muslim domains for revenge, exposed or underscored what appeared to be a major fault-line between the West and Islam. Many believed that the events of September 11th were concrete proof of Huntington's hypothesis of a 'clash of civilizations' between the cultures of Islam and the West. In reality, what has emerged is a far more complicated picture of a series of relations between Muslim and Western domains. This picture represents and recognizes the breakdown of borders, the impact of Muslim immigrant communities, the apogee of distorting mutual mythologies of the enemy, and a widening gap in perspective or opinion on either side of this virtual San Andreas fault-line.

There exists, however, countervailing evidence that the notion of an abyss between that labelled as the West and Islam is meaningless when measured against a contemporary world interconnected and full of fuzzy lines (rather than hard borders) between and within cultures, nation-states and communities of people. Such a view recognizes the breakdown of trade barriers, transcending technologies, international travel, immigration, population movement as a result of conflict and war and the emergence of a generation of young people with global consumerist aspirations. This works against the foundation of constructed ideological and political barriers that are supposed to exist between that classified as the West and that classified as Islam.

In this chapter I will outline the historical relationship between Muslim and Western domains, beginning with an account of the Crusades. A growth of mutual distrust and suspicion will be demonstrated in the emerging Western scholarship on Islam from the mid-nineteenth century onwards and in the growth of anti-Westernism in Islamist discourse throughout the twentieth century. The debate about the West and Islam is linked to the wider context of the era of European colonialism and the accompanying economic and cultural ambitions over geographic domains in Africa, Asia and the Middle East in which many Muslims lived. Thus the relationship also became empirically determined as a result of direct contact and experience. In this context power was removed from Muslim hands and placed firmly in the hands of European actors. The organization of Muslim voices and political activism as a response to such arrangements of power was a constant and growing phenomenon throughout the late nineteenth and early twentieth century, punctuated by actual conflict such as the routing of the British, including the defeat of General Gordon, by Mahdist forces in Khartoum in the 1880s. Conflict has also come to play a part in the contemporary relationship, with a variety of interesting dimensions. Additionally, one must question whether conflict, collision and mutual antagonism are the defining and dominant features of this particular relationship. The evidence that Islam and Muslims pose a potent threat to Western security interests at home and abroad demands attention with the new threat labelled the 'Green peril', which replaces in many quarters Western preoccupations with the threat posed by communism until the collapse of the former Soviet Union and states in Eastern Europe. The manifestation of the threat in attacks on Western interests by radical Muslim groups has irrevocably altered the tenor and dynamics of the Islam and the West paradigm, making the salience of alternative approaches to the relationship harder to accept.

Caped Crusaders

The Crusades are associated with myth, folklore and fairy tales in which brave knights of medieval Europe liberated Jerusalem and vanquished the barbarian 'Mohammadans' by raising the Cross over the Crescent. In practice, the Crusades are still experienced as a relevant, contemporary phenomenon that defines the relationship in populist discourse between the West and many Muslim domains in the Middle East. The image of the Crusades as relevant and important to the relationship between Islam and the West thus remains pertinent to significant players in the mediation of this relationship. In 1996, the fundamentalist leader of an Islamist group based in Afghanistan issued a *bayan* (statement) calling for a war against the USA. In the statement, the resonance of the past as present was reflected by its author, who was none other than Osama Bin Laden. He declared:

> It should not be hidden from you that the people of Islam had suffered from aggression, iniquity and injustice imposed on them by the Zionist Crusaders' alliance and their collaborators; to the extent that the Muslims' blood became the cheapest and their wealth as loot in the hands of the enemies. Their blood was spilled in Palestine and Iraq. The horrifying pictures of the massacre of Qana, in Lebanon are still fresh in our memory. Massacres in Tajikistan, Burma, Khashmir, Assam, Philippines, Fatani, Ogadin, Somalia, Eritreia, Chechnya and in Bosnia-Herzegovina took place, massacres that send shivers in the body and shake the conscience. All of this and the world watches and hears, and not only didn't respond to these atrocities, but also with a clear conspiracy between the USA and its allies and under the cover of the iniquitous United Nations, the dispossessed people were even prevented from obtaining arms to defend themselves.

He deliberately labelled Western states as 'Crusader' in an attempt to garner Muslim support for his self-declared *jihad*. Bin Laden had previously worked with Western elements in Afghanistan as the *mujahideen* movement fought against the Soviet occupation. Now he labelled the West a 'Crusader' element that was to blame for the endurance of rulers and regimes that Bin Laden actively opposed. In September 2001, as President George W. Bush presided over a nation in shock, which was trying to come to terms with the al-Qaeda assault on their homeland, the word 'Crusades' came to his lips as he spoke of vengeance on behalf of the American people. In a statement less than a week after the attacks on New York and Washington, as President Bush pledged to rid the world of 'evil-doers' he declared: 'This crusade, this war on terrorism, is going to take a long time.' Although the US Administration played down the 'Crusades' reference, the resonance of the statement was not lost in the crowded streets of Karachi or the refugee camps on the borders of Afghanistan. The radical leadership of Islamist organiza-tions ensured that the tenor of history reflected in Bush's statement was understood as an attempt engage in another instalment in the epic conflict between Islam and the West. In Islamist circles a belief grew that the American-declared 'War on Terrorism' was in fact an indication that America was 'ready to battle against the Muslim world...as new Crusaders...supporting dictatorship' (Adwan, 2002). Moreover, there was a notion, according to Islamists, that 'the past is not differentiated from the present as America pursues military expansion into Muslim lands' (ibid.).

As I previously highlighted, in 1095 the leader of Christian Europe, Pope Urban II, called on his subjects and supporters to raise the banner of faith in a call to liberate the Holy Land from Muslim influence and rule. The Pope called upon his followers to liberate their co-religionists in the East from Muslim hands. This call to a Crusade against Islam found military expression in the battles of the following two centuries and left an indelible scar on historical accounts of this period. The Crusades were inspired by imperial and religious ambitions, yet they touched the lives of ordinary Europeans in ways hitherto unknown. By extension, they also touched the lives of those who encountered Christianity's bloody wrath in the Middle East. There is no objective telling of the Crusading episode on either side. The symbol of Christianity, the cross, was emblazoned across the tunics and banners of the Cru-saders, and before long they were drenched in the blood of many thousands of Muslims, Jews and Eastern Christians. By 1095, Muslim rule had extended out of Arabia and across the frontiers of the Near East, including Jerusalem and Bethlehem. The territor-ial dimension of the Crusades rested on the premiss that Christian holy lands should remain in Christian, not Muslim, hands. As a series of wars were launched, other motives may not have been apparent. Pope Urban II had responded to the call from Byzantine Emperor Alexius I to repel the Seljuk Muslim threat in his midst, seeing it as an opportunity for imperial ambition, with Jerusalem the intended jewel in the crown. In his speech at Clermont in France, he is said, by Fulcher of Chartres, to have declared:

> Although, O sons of God, you have promised more firmly than ever to keep the peace among yourselves and to preserve the rights of the church, there remains still an important work for you to do... For your brethren who live in the east are in urgent need of your help, and you must hasten to give them the aid which has often been promised them.... On this account I, or rather the Lord, beseech you as Christ's heralds to publish this everywhere and to persuade all people of whatever rank, foot-soldiers and knights, poor and rich, to carry aid promptly to those Christians and to destroy that vile race from the lands of our friends. Moreover, Christ commands it. All who die by the way, whether by land or by sea, or in battle against the pagans, shall have immediate remission of sins. (Fulcher of Chartres, *www.eduplace.com/ss/hmss/7/unit/act5.lblm.html*)

The religious appeal was explicit in the claim that Muslims, the 'vile race', be expunged from a territory now regarded as part of a divine gift. The Crusade would offer its righteous participants rewards either in heaven or on earth. Additionally, the appeal to religious unity in the face of an external threat was relatively successful. By July 1099, the Crusading knights had achieved some considerable success in launching their Crusades in the Holy Land and by capturing Jerusalem from its Muslim rulers. Irrespective of gender, age, colour or creed, the capture of the city spelt certain death for its inhabitants. As Fulcher of Chartres re-counts, the Crusaders 'joyfully rushed into the city to pursue and kill the nefarious enemies' (1912, p. 109).

> Many fled to the roof of the temple of Solomon, and were shot with arrows, so that they fell to the ground dead. In this temple almost ten thousand were killed. Indeed, if you had been there you would have seen our feet coloured to our ankles with the blood of the slain. But what more shall I relate? None of them were left alive; neither women nor children were spared. (Fulcher, 1912, 115).

It was only a matter of time before Muslim opinion and, more importantly, a Muslim call to defence by arms – a *jihad* – prompted the formation of a body of men prepared to take on the Crusader rulers.

Although divided and tardy in its response, there was a recognition that theological logic as well as changing territorial facts of life would compel Muslims into action. Crusader rule over the environs of Jerusalem, however, would endure for more than eighty years before the city was conquered. Nevertheless, the end result of the campaign was Muslim victory and Christian capitulation. Vanquishing the Crusader rulers, however, was the result of many disparate factors, including internal competitions for power within the Muslim realm, schism and dissent. During this episode of history, it would be a mistake to represent the Muslim domain as a centralized and monolithic superpower. In reality, Muslim rule from its centre in Baghdad was dissipated across the empire. Internal dissent and political violence, as mentioned in chapter 2, was already manifest in the appearance of a dissident movement from within the Ismaili Muslim sect which became known as the Assassins. Indeed, the motive of the Assassins is explicable only by reflecting on the nature of the state in medieval Islam and the internal strains between elements of caliphal authority, the military and the *ulama*. Bernard Lewis describes the Assassins as the 'first terrorists' (Lewis, 1980, p. 129).

The Assassins concentrated on mounting a sectarian and political challenge in the wake of the imposition of military rule under the supposed authority of the Fatamid caliphate. The strategy of violence was political in the sense that it was a final means of defence for a beleaguered sect that was already considered heretical under the rule of the Fatamid caliphs of Cairo. The small group gathered around Sabah were not solely dedicated to violence, but indeed embraced the Muslim obligation of *da'wa* (preaching) common to many thousands of Muslim organizations through time and to the present.

There was no monopoly of violence at this time. The deliberate desecration of holy sites, senseless blood-lust, pillage and violence were the hallmarks of the Crusader campaigns and rule in the Middle East. Such a perspective seems hard to reconcile with some historical records of this period. Yet, as Jones and Ereira assert, 'The fanatical blood-lust...would never be forgotten' (Jones and Ereira, 1994, p. 53). In the Middle East the Christian blood-lust was not forgotten within Muslim or Jewish or even Eastern Christian circles. Some saw the opportunity to wage a *jihad* against the Crusader rulers as an opportunity to bid for power within the Muslim domain as well. An additional motivating force was the extent to which more and more land within the Muslim realm fell into the sphere of Crusader control. Thus those who engaged in the defence of Islam were motivated by additional forces linked to the ferment of the times. As Saunders asserts, the 'long struggle with the Franks...was carried to successful conclusion by three brilliant soldiers and statesmen – the Turk Zengi and his son Nuraddin and the famous Kurd Saladin' (Saunders, 1965, p. 162). The historical echoes of the Crusades seep into, and have infiltrated, history and cultures through time. Yet the reason why their symbolism – irrespective of side – remains alive is because those who shape such cultures and histories employ it for political purposes as myth-bound yet passion-rousing emblem of conflict with the 'other'.

A collapse of empire

The advent of European rule and consolidation over the Muslim lands formerly under the leadership of the Ottoman Caliphate coincided with the end of World War I and the Allied victory over Germany. For the first time in nearly 900 years a metaphorical Cross was raised over the Crescent in the Middle East in an important, if short-lived, eclipse of power that would result in thousands of acres of Muslim land in Africa, Asia and the Middle East coming under the direct or indirect control of European state power. The centres of Islam, including Mecca, Medina and Jerusalem, were once again subject to foreign political, military and economic ambitions. The Ottoman Empire had collapsed, leaving in its wake a region forever fragmented by the new boundaries of nation-states established at the behest of the European powers. The political, cultural and economic force of Islam appeared to be nothing more than a miasma now that the cities of Damascus, Baghdad and Jerusalem were placed under the political control of European states. The nominal unity of Islam was lost in the breakup of control that had gradually dissipated throughout the previous century. By successfully engaging in the classic policy of 'divide and rule', the competing European powers went a long way to ensure that the Muslims of the Middle East, Africa, India and South Asia remained divided among themselves and bereft of a leadership not preoccupied with parochial interests. The legitimacy of Muslim claims to leadership were weakened by internal division, repression and an antipathy for meaningful pluralism in societies where it was easier to ape the repressive character of those they sought to replace. Evidence of this can be found in the state-makers of Pakistan and in contemporary Afghanistan.

Such practices were of course malignly and benignly encouraged by the waning powers of France and Britain and the waxing super-power of the United States of America and the former Soviet Union. There are any number of Muslim domains across Africa, Asia and the Middle East where 'the West', cumulatively symbolized in the latter twentieth century by the Soviet Union and the USA, directly interfered in the domestic political arena, with major consequences. Further, through proxy relationships the former Soviet Union and the United States of America were able to secure their national interests at the expense of the citizens of those Muslim domains that they had steered and influenced. The internal legitimacy of such states, even with an appeal to so-called Islamic credentials, contributed to the generation of systems of coercion and abuse by ruling elites that contradicted the spirit of Islam and projected a distorted and negative image of the faith system. The consequences of this particular engagement with the West were very negative. The Islam and the West interface of high politics promoted a spiral of weakening legitimacy among the ruled Muslim masses in such polities. At the level of low politics in such communities the disson-ance created as a result of this high-level engagement was experi-enced and associated with a loss of rights, abuse and a state of fear. When consciousness was raised, among the masses, the finger of blame was levelled not just at corrupt leaders but at their Western supporters as well. Legitimacy was bestowed on those who claimed to represent the struggle to reclaim those rights. The West became a culprit in the process that had denied Muslims rights.

One arena where this was clearly demonstrated was Afghani-stan. In contemporary Afghanistan the many faces of the West – including the Soviet occupation and American intercession in the ferment of internal politics and conflict – have played an important part in the failure of this particular Muslim polity. In Afghanistan the involvement of the USA, through agencies such as the CIA in arming, training and steering the Afghan fighters against Soviet occupation, was not the issue. The problem lay, following Soviet capitulation and withdrawal in 1989, in the rapid abandonment of Afghanistan while it was still beset by internal civil conflict and instability. As Rashid notes, 'For ordinary Afghans the US with-drawal from the scene constituted a major betrayal, while Washing-ton's refusal to harness international pressure to help broker a settlement between the warlords was considered a double pres-sure' (Rashid, 2001, pp. 175–6). In the former Yugoslavia the West was blamed for its failure to address the rights of and support the claims and arming of Bosnia's Muslims as they sought to defend themselves against a Serbian strategy of ethnic cleansing. In Chechnya the campaigns against cities like Grozny by the Russian authorities have further hardened Islamist rhetoric against the West. The chief target of the vitriol circulating in Islamist tracts, sermons and publications was popularly referred to by the late Ayatollah Khomeini of Iran as the 'Big Satan' – the United States of America. These examples, and more, are cited and recited in mantra-like fashion by hundreds, if not thousands, of commentators across the globe, including in Muslim domains, as evidence of American complicity in a war or Crusade against Muslims. One Islamic Jihad leader proclaims: 'All we see from America is enmity. The US is our enemy... Yes, we understand that our enemy is killing us with its US weapons' (Shammi, 2002). Whether the intent of successive American administrations is such a conflict becomes irrelevant when measured against the collective perception and experience of the American power in such communities across the globe.

The emergence of the United States of America and a recognition that since the early 1990s it has been enjoying a unipolar moment have also left it without a fig-leaf when its democratic credentials both at home and abroad are assessed. Maintenance of the 'unipolar moment' has become the defining feature of American national interest, even if this means sacrificing or slicing away at the edifice of democratic principles that is supposed to underpin the project. Such factors provide an explanation for hostility and distrust of American power and its exercise in many parts of the world. They address the many contexts of conflict that one way or another have embroiled Western powers. They address the causes of conflicts as part of an international order that embraces rights-driven discourses on self-determination, resistance and independence. They expose the linkage and tensions associated with economic prosperity in the West and increasing disparities of poverty in other domains, including those where majority Muslim populations are found. They do not address, however, the appropriation of such causes of conflict or tensions by the relatively wealthy, educated and hate-motivated cadres of al-Qaeda, who undertook their campaign of international terror.

Worlds apart

I do not believe this is a clash of civilizations. This may be what they believe in the West but from our point of view Islam has always tried to achieve partnerships between civilizations and not a clash.

Dr Abdel Aziz Rantisi, Hamas leader

If it had been thought that the struggle for geo-political power epitomized by the historical saga of the Crusades had passed into the dusty annals of history, then the events of September 11th, 2001, jolted the Western public and its political leaders awake to the fact that, in the minds of some, the memory of such ancient power struggles remained alive. In the tenth century the locus of geo-political struggle was the Middle East, but in the twenty-first century the arena of the battle was transferred to the heart of the United States of America, and was designed to demonstrate to ordinary Americans, as well as their leaders, the so-called consequences of their involvement in regions far removed. The Bush Administration-inspired 'War on Terror' echoed the epic clash of the past as one between civilization 'as we know it' and the desire of 'our enemies' to destroy and eradicate it. In this highly charged atmosphere, individuals or parties on either side of a cultural and political fault-line were at pains to point out that the American-led War on Terror should not be seen as targeting Islam. British Prime Minister Tony Blair spoke publicly of his reading and respect for the Qur'an, and echoed the call of British Muslim community leaders to damp down the flames of blame against Muslims. Yet in a variety of domains across the globe there was a perceived logic to singling out Islam, or rather its extremists, as the cause for current global distress. In the United States of America the right-wing, dominant, conservative mainstream had already identified Islam as a menace to American national interests. Such national interests linked to the principles of democracy and economic determinism inherent in most American foreign policy approaches lay at the heart of a fear of Islam. This in turn was bolstered by a particular religious antipathy at the heart of many conservatives against Islam as the enemy of Israel. From this perspective Muslims stood in the way of American desires to 'access all areas' in the pursuit of democracy and national interest across the globe. Influential US figures have declared that they want a dialogue with Muslims, particularly those who are moderate and aspire to the same values as the USA and other Western states.

On the other side of the fault-line the 'War on Terror' has been interpreted by Muslim malcontents and their leaders as further evidence, if it were needed, of an attempt by the USA to dispossess and disrupt the Islamic continuum forever. In the crowded refugee ghettos of Rafah and Beit Hanoun, as thousands of refugees and their families sat imprisoned in fetid camps, local Islamists blamed the American-led 'War on Terror' as a war on Islam and evidence of American double standards when it comes to the legitimate rights of Muslim populations. As a senior Hamas figure remarked,

Is it a war against terrorism or Islam? If you look at the targets, this would indicate that the battle of America is against the Muslim world. The declaration of President Bush at the beginning of this battle about the new crusades may have been an accident, but actually it is a new Crusade if you look at what America has done on the ground.... There are great similarities between the Crusaders of the past and the present. (Adwan, 2002)

From these two alternative perspectives the clash between civilizations appears inevitable, with the maximal visions of both sides leaving little room for any kind of position that is more accommodating of the global realities of interconnection. Nevertheless, other factors need to be introduced into this black-and-white equation if the real factors accounting for the dissonance are to be understood. Huntington's paradigm, predicated on a fixed rather than variable assumption that the West and Islam are civilizations with distinct values and characteristics – one the opposite of the other – is now taken seriously as a measure or way of viewing the world. As Turner has pointed out, however, this version of Islam is 'defined by a limited, but highly persistent, bundle of interpretative themes which have the effect of bringing into question the authenticity of Islam as religion and culture' (Turner, 1994, p. 67). From this paradigmatic perspective, Islam is a threat to the West. As Lewis suggested, 'the Muslim world is again seized by an intense – and violent – resentment of the West. Suddenly America has become the arch-enemy, the incarnation of evil, the diabolic opponent of all that is good and specifically for Muslims, of Islam' (Lewis, 1990, p. 47). One of the interesting dimensions that Lewis introduces to this debate is an equation within the 'Muslim world' of the West with America. Indeed, this leads one to question whether Muslim opposition to the West is really just that, or rather a new form of anti-Americanism?

The snake head: anti-Americanism

In this respect one has to ask whether it is a consequence of hyper-power status to be regarded with hostility by other nations or global groupings who regard the monopoly of such power as threatening. There are certainly forms of radical Islamism in which anti-Americanism is a primary focal point for hostility and antipathy. Not only that, but there is evidence aplenty that America has become a direct target of the campaign of violence and terrorism undertaken by a variety of radical Islamist groups across the globe. This gives some important credibility to the fear that radical Islamist elements constitute a world-wide threat to American interests. But this is not the same as imputing such sentiments to all Muslims. This, however, is what authors such as Ajami contend:

> The anti-Americanism blows at will – an alibi for socio-economic ills with deep roots, a simplifying answer for populations drawn to a civilization they can neither master nor reject. Preachers, the wholesalers of terror, make of this country [the USA] a demon. The U.S. Navy monitors the Persian Gulf, the Arabian Sea, and the eastern Mediterranean, protecting the flow of oil. Raging on those shores, though, is an unyielding hatred of America. Places once remote have been hurled into an uneven modernity. (Ajami, 2001)

Ajami depicts populations of Muslims and their wholesaling preachers of terror as culpable for anti-Americanism and its manifestation in terrorism.

In the past, American interests abroad were the focus of campaigns by militant Islamist groups, yet at the same time other groups within the fold worked alongside US agents to bring down common enemies. In the 1990s, however, America's vulnerability was exposed on the domestic front. Radical ideologues, such as Sayyid Qutb and Mawlana Mawdudi, were always deliberately anti-Western and in some respect anti-American specifically. Sayyid Qutb, the radical ideologue of the Egyptian Muslim Brotherhood, had spent time in the United States of America in the 1950s, but returned to his native Egypt with a negativity that coloured his subsequent writings. In addressing the USA and the Soviet Union, his critique rested on the notion that when societies abandoned religion, they lost their *raison d'être*. 'Superficial differences,' he proclaimed, 'are insignificant as long as the social orders and the schools of thought in all these countries do not derive their inspiration from the Divine ideological ideal' (Qutb, 1978, p. 70). This raises an 'ideological' matter that has also been identified by writers such as Huntington and Fukuyama, but in fact is about establishing an artificial distinction between that labelled and valued as Islamic or that as American. In reality this is just too difficult to maintain. America is not an ideological monolith centred around a set of core values that remain ideal and pure; nor is Islam. The vagaries of political life and the internal struggles for power in any society ensure that such so-called core values are under constant threat from a variety of sources.

There is, though, a hostility to that labelled as representative or symbolic of American power and the ways it is experienced in Muslim domains. When the interpreters of such experiences are drawn from the Islamist pool, then certain shades and hues are exaggerated for political effect. Indeed, Rubin contends that anti-Americanism in Muslim domains is not a question of American misdeeds or suffering as a consequence of Americans; he contends that the USA has engaged in policies that are of benefit to such regions and that others have greater cause for grievance against the USA. Rather, it is a question of 'animus [that] is largely the product of self-interested manipulation by various groups within Arab society, groups that use anti-Americanism as a foil to distract public attention from other, far more serious problems within those societies' (Rubin, 2002, p. 73). Islamist leaders, however, are usually on the margins of society, representing popular elements that are excluded and denied their rights by the elite. Islamist leaders not only construct a critique of America, or rather what it represents; they engage with other sources of grievance such as poverty in Muslim heartlands. Such discourse is not about compatibility but about recognition of the profound differences between the ideological manifestation of liberal democracy and that of modern Islamism in the twenty-first century.

The Muslim menace: anti-Muslimism and the spectre of Islamophobia

The notion of a Muslim menace is, according to some perspectives, made manifest in a number of ways, including terrorism, as well as being a cultural or 'civilizational' menace against the principles and values that underpin the democratic traditions of Western nation-states. Such a perspective is encapsulated in the words of Daniel Pipes, who asserts, 'To me every fundamentalist Muslim, no matter how peaceable in his own behaviour, is part of a murderous movement and is thus, in some fashion, a foot soldier in the war that Bin Laden has launched against civilisation. They are barbarians and must be treated as such' (Sutherland, 2002, p. 1). In this way the menace and threat posed by Muslims through their attachment to Islam challenges religio-cultural dimensions of Western identity. From this standpoint the threat emanates not just from the terrorists who attack but from those whom the terrorists claim to represent: the entire Muslim *umma*. The Muslim faith and Muslims are understood as anti-plural, anti-democratic and authoritarian. The West becomes defined in opposition to the values believed to characterize Islam. The Muslim domain, as Said has argued, becomes distilled and essentialized through a set of threatening and frightening stereotypes symbolized by Khomeini, Bin Laden and Saddam Hussein. The essence of Islam becomes threatening, as it is not only understood as the diametrical opposite of that characterized as the West, but because Muslims threaten to bring their agenda to the West in an attempt to destroy, not co-exist. Hence a clash – culturally, economically, militarily or otherwise – is inevitable. And if the West is to keep Islam from its door, and prevent the perpetration of terror on its doorstep, the notion of a pre-emptive strike becomes salient and acceptable. Additionally, the mission of the West as it confronts the threat in Muslim domains is to promote change, and change through a process of accepting Western norms and values as salient. Deep in the heart of those who seek to confront Muslim authoritarianism and tyranny is an explicit belief that at the end of the day Muslims must accept the values that define the West. As Wolfowitz proclaims, 'The larger war we face is the war of ideas – a challenge to be sure, but one that we must also win. It is a struggle over modernity and secularism, pluralism and democracy, real economic development' (Wolfowitz, 2002). The fear is that Muslims can only ever pretend to accept such norms and values, for to actually accept them would be to abandon the faith that defines them. In the past the West – through the conduit of European and later US national interests in such regions as the Middle East and Asia – ensured that some leaders would be compelled to alter their societies and remake them in the image of the West. Reza Shah Pahlavi of Iran, for example, sought to remove the traditional power of the clergy in Iran in the public sphere and impose Western-style reforms on his subjects that had fundamental consequences. Western values were imposed on society by diktat, including Western-style dress. In 1936, in furtherance of his pro-Western agenda, he banned the wearing of the *hijab* (veil) by women in Iran. The issue here is whether, as contemporary historical record tends to demonstrate, the export of such values by diktat from above as the embodiment of an attempt to rid society of its 'backward' attachment to the clergy and Westernize actually embodied the spirit of democracy and pluralism. It seems likely that if Westernization is equated with the removal of Islam from the public domain as part of a policy from above then it is inevitable that tensions will be encountered and conflict will occur. In locations where Islam has always co-existed with the norms and values of other cultures, including polytheistic ones, the outcome is not so apparent.

Steeds of war

The events of September 11th, 2001, transfixed a global audience, as television-viewers, radio-listeners and Internet-surfers watched an act of terrorism unfold live before their eyes. More than 3,000 victims were created in an attack that was also designed to target what symbolized modern-day America and, by extension, the West. Those symbols were commercial, military and, some believed, political. The World Trade Centre, an icon of Western, capital-based economy, had been a target of Islamic extremists in the past. In February 1993 Ramzi Yousef, a veteran of the war in Afghanistan, and his accomplices drove a car bomb to the World Trade Centre in an attack that left carnage. This act of terror was not an extension of the *mujahideen* campaign in Afghanistan, but a direct assault on America as a target of extremist hostility. Two years later, when the Alfred P. Murrah building in Oklahoma was car-bombed, it was initially believed that the same anti-American Islamist extremists were at work again. Although home-grown extremist elements proved to be the culprits, further attacks on US government institutions and military targets continued abroad. These included the 1996 Khobar towers attack in Saudi Arabia, the 1998 bombing of the American embassies in Nairobi and Dar es-Salaam, and the attack on the *USS Cole* near Yemen in 2000. On September 11th, 2001, the attackers directed a US airliner at the heart of the American military complex by targeting a plane on the Pentagon in Washington. This attack was an attempt to demonstrate that even the Pentagon was no longer invulnerable to the reach of an extremist coalition led by Osama Bin Laden.

As the events of the day unfolded, the extent of Osama Bin Laden's wrath and organizational capability was experienced in all its devastating consequences. Interpreted by the Bush Administration as not just an attack on the American people, but rather as a full-scale assault on the West and the values it enshrines, Osama Bin Laden atop a terror network known as al-Qaeda was identified as the chief culprit. Yet Islam, the well-spring of Osama Bin Laden's extremist vision, was also singled out. Bin Laden, a wealthy, privileged son of one of Saudi Arabia's most prominent commercial families, had turned his back on ostentation when drawn, like so many other young Muslims of the time, into the maelstrom of the Afghan theatre of war in the early 1980s. Bin Laden's experiences in Afghanistan are said to explain his Muslim fervour and, by association, that of many thousands of other Arab-Afghan *mujahideen*. The war in Aghanistan had erupted as a result of Soviet territorial ambition on its Eastern frontier with the country, culminating in the act of occupation in 1979. Bin Laden claims he was a kind of Saudi emissary, and along with his American colleagues he claimed that 'the weapons were supplied by the Americans, the money by the Saudis... but we had to fight on all fronts, communist or Western oppression' (Rashid, 2001, p. 132).

Subsequently the Afghan theatre of war became symbolic of the difficult relationship between Islam and the West, as well as demonstrating the expediency of foreign policy during the Cold War era. Prior to the Soviet invasion of December 1979, Afghanistan was characterized by conflict that mostly centred around tribal and clan-based interests and tensions. In 1979 Afghanistan was a Muslim state that also bordered other Muslim domains, including the newly established Islamic Republic of Iran, headed by Ayatollah Khomeini, and Pakistan. Multi-ethnic, multi-tribal and strategically placed, Afghanistan was important in Muslim circles across the globe. The Soviet invasion was interpreted by Afghanis as a major assault on their faith system, obliging Muslims to engage in defence of Islam through *jihad*. For policy-makers in Washington, the implication of the Soviet invasion lay in Cold War calculations, not Islam. The American objective in Afghanistan was defined in opposition to the Soviets, and the Americans were prepared to use any means to oust the Russians from Kabul. In other words Afghanistan became an extension of the Cold War between the USA and Soviet Union. In this context the Arab proverb 'My enemy's enemy is my friend' became apt as part of the short-term strategy to circumscribe Soviet occupation. Evidence of an attempt to measure the long-term consequences of an American alliance with an ill-assorted array of Muslim *mujahideen* forces against the democratic principles underpinning the state is difficult to find in assessing this relationship.

Cold War realism in foreign policy-making circles in Washington largely excluded any attempt to include other foreign policy perspectives, including Wilsonian or Jeffersonian ones. It appears that in American policy-making circles few were troubled in the early 1980s by the contradiction inherent in a Western secular nation-state aligning, supporting and encouraging Islamist forces who were obliged on the basis of religious duty and political motive to expel a foreign infidel invader of Islamic lands. Eliminating Moscow from Kabul, however, would not be easy, and pulled the USA further into the maelstrom created by the Afghan and Arab *mujahideen* in their guerrilla campaign. As the occupation and re- sistance progressed throughout the 1980s, the involvement of the USA and other regional actors such as Saudi Arabia in supporting the *mujahideen* became a significant factor in the military campaign, contributing to the advantage that these fighters had over their Soviet foes and local proxies. In 1988 Moscow had given its assent to an agreement between Pakistan and Afghanistan ending ten- sions and conflicts on the country's southern frontier. Additionally, the agreement included a commitment to 'non-interference' that was binding on both Moscow and Washington and a timetable for Soviet withdrawal. By 1989, as the collapse of the Soviet Union began to unfold, Moscow threw in the towel and withdrew its demoralized troops from Afghanistan. The casualties of this decade-long war in which a Muslim-led motivated, organized guerrilla force defeated a superpower included 1.3 million dead and 5.5 million Afghans internally displaced or made refugees. The country was littered with dirty munitions, and mine contamination was rife.

In this turbulent environment the *mujahideen* forces, including an increasingly prominent Osama Bin Laden, were dangerously mar- ginalized from the resolution agreements. This marginalization can be regarded as a fatal error, for exclusion also led to a refusal to recognize the terms of the 1988 agreement, and the civil disputes that had beset Afghanistan before and during the Soviet occupation were unleashed again in 1989. The country remained destabilized, and the *mujahideen* forces now faced each other across the plains and mountains of the country. The USA, having achieved its ob- jectives quickly, exited from the Afghan theatre, leaving President Najibullah to his fate at the hands of the *mujahideen*. By 1992 a new *coup* had brought the ethnic force of the northern Uzbeks to power in Kabul, backed by *mujahideen* factions who then engaged in another round of fighting against their former allies and comrades in other *mujahideen* factions. Ethnic southern Pashtun control of Kabul had been lost to the northern Uzbeks. The loss of a common enemy was the spark for an internecine war that paralysed the country.

The fate of one of the most important groups in the Afghan theatre, that of the Arab *mujahideen*, however, appeared mixed. It was estimated that the Arab *mujahideen* was composed of around 30,000 volunteers from across the Middle East. This experience and transnational fraternity through guerrilla struggle allowed them to operate in an environment permeated by an ethos of resistance as a form of religious struggle and *jihad*. These *mujahideen*, portrayed in thousands of newspaper, magazine, film and television images distributed across the Muslim domain and among Muslim immigrant communities in Europe and North America, increased the import of the Afghan element in Muslim politics. The power of the rhetoric was made meaningful by the Arab volunteers willing to die for the liberation of Afghanistan from Soviet rule in the name of Islam. In addition, the war became associated with a transnational Islamist argument that centred on the conflict in Afghanistan as the first step in the liberation of the whole region from Western-inspired and supported tyranny. When it came to the export of revolution, the Afghan success against the Soviet superpower was deeply symbolic, and perhaps more so than Iran to Sunni Muslim communities. Some Arab-Afghan elements remained in Afghanistan or Pakistan, playing a role in the internal battles which by 1996 had led to the consolidation of the power of a new force in the Afghan theatre known as the Taliban. Others, who subscribed to the export thesis, returned to their home states preparing to take the battle with them. Others still moved to other arenas of conflict, including Bosnia, Algeria and Chechnya. In Afghanistan, these men, including Osama Bin Laden, had played a part in achieving real change and victory against one of the world's most formidable military superpowers. While Soviet forces may have beaten the Germans, and crushed Czechoslovakia, they were unable to vanquish the *mujahideen*. Through an Islamist-inspired agenda, the *mujahideen* had played an important part in changing the geostrategic power balances of the world.

The Taliban – pupils of the *madrassas* in Pakistan – and a mainly Pashtun-composed *mujahideen* movement also rose out of the post-Soviet landscape in a quest to assert power over the descent into anarchy that prevailed in the early to mid-1990s. Supported by Pakistan, by 1998 the Taliban, in addition to occupying Kabul, had exerted its authority over 90 per cent of the country. With this degree of control established, under the Taliban leadership, headed by Mullah Mohammad Omar, himself a fighter and spiritual leader, their project to Islamicize the country was implemented. Their attachment to an extreme fundamentalist interpretation of Islam was imposed on the population with major consequences for the country. The perpetration of major human rights abuses, particularly in relation to women, was no compensation for bringing the illegal production of opium in the country under control.

Yet this descent into the dark was largely ignored by the international community. The shelter offered by the Taliban leadership to extremist elements, including Osama Bin Laden, was underestimated. In a mutually beneficial arrangement Bin Laden provided financial support to the Taliban (as he had done previously to the Islamist regime of Sudan) in return for protection.

Bin Laden had allegedly formed al-Qaeda ('the Base') as early as 1989, drawing around him a tightly knit group of supporters and fighters. Bin Laden, subscribing to the radical extremist agenda of Islamist thinkers like Sayyid Qutb and Abdullah Azzam, identified the USA as the chief enemy of Islam, yet also singled out Arab regimes, including his native Saudi Arabia, for his wrath. In a *fatwa* published in 1996, Bin Laden declared:

> My Muslim Brothers of The World: Your brothers in Palestine and in the land of the two Holy Places are calling upon your help and asking you to take part in fighting against the enemy your enemy and their enemy the Americans and the Israelis. They are asking you to do whatever you can, with one's own means and ability, to expel the enemy, humiliated and defeated, out of the sanctuaries of Islam. Exalted be to Allah as said in His book: and if they ask your support, because they are oppressed in their faith, then support them!

The *fatwa* was a declaration of war – with America identified as the chief target. In the *fatwa* America was blamed as an 'occupier' of holy places in Saudi Arabia, and the Saudi regime was castigated for its compliance. Muslims were called to rally under the banner of Islam. In 1998 it was alleged that al-Qaeda had bombed the US embassies in Nairobi and Dar es-Salaam. The US government retaliated by launching a cruise missile attack against Bin Laden in Afghanistan. Bin Laden escaped, and further attacks on the USA abroad were blamed on al-Qaeda. These included attacks on American military forces stationed in Saudi Arabia and elsewhere in the Arabian Gulf. Additionally, the influence and growing support for Bin Laden and al-Qaeda were identified as important factors in internal dissent and criticism of the Saudi regime. The ruling family of Saudi Arabia, long-time conservative Gulf allies of the United States of America, experienced levels of internal dissent that had the potential to threaten and undermine their legitimacy and possibly to destabilize the Kingdom. The consequences of allowing free rein to such dissent was unthinkable if America were to maintain its long-standing commitment to ensure the free flow of energy sources out of the region and into US capital-based markets. In this respect the Bin Laden phenomenon was not just confined to the dirty work and debris of the Afghan theatre but posed a major threat to American national interests in the Middle East.

In the wake of September 11th, 2001, the leadership of the Taliban refused to expel Bin Laden and al-Qaeda and end its support for international terrorism. The USA and its allies began a campaign on 7 October 2001, aimed at both Bin Laden and his supporters, as well as the Taliban. By 13 November Kabul had fallen, and the Taliban had disintegrated. Yet both the leadership of the Taliban and al-Qaeda succeeded in escaping the Allied forces. The precarious nature of interim multi-ethnic rule in Afghanistan, constructed at the behest of Western powers, however, is no guarantee that extreme radical Islamist forces will not garner enough support to destabilize the country again and bring further conflict. There are no guarantees in Afghanistan, and unlike the scene in *Rambo III* where the American general reminds his Russian captor about the lessons of history and the price for ignoring them, it would appear that the lessons remain unheeded.

Additionally, the new phenomenon of international terrorism manifest in the amorphous linkages of extremist Islam, in the guise of al-Qaeda, gave rise to a new dimension in the diametric opposition of the West and Islam. Here the issue relates to the extent to which Muslim ownership of the al-Qaeda and Taliban phenomena are credible. How 'representative' of Muslims and Islam are the attacks of unprovoked international terrorism perpetrated by al-Qaeda and its offshoots? Also, the evidence or criteria invoked to demonstrate such links should be judiciously employed and questioned. The motive of state power aligned with national interest must likewise be factored into any appraisal of policy. The extent to which al-Qaeda and Osama Bin Laden are 'representative' of something inherently and essentially Muslim or Islamic can, I would suggest, be measured in at least two ways. The first is the extent to which Muslim clergy and community representatives, across the globe, either condoned or condemned the al-Qaeda attacks of September 11th, 2001, in America. On 11 September 2002, as British Muslims gathered to commemorate the attacks, one leader declared, 'The world is well aware that those who carried out the attacks in the United States apparently attribute their actions to Islam itself. This attribution was, and continues to be, grossly offensive to the overwhelming majority of the three million Muslims in the UK and one billion Muslims across the globe who practise their religion peacefully and see no justification in the taking of innocent life' (*Huddersfield News*, 13 September 2002). The largest and most significant representative organization of fifty-seven Muslim countries, the Organization of Islamic Conferences, immediately condemned the attacks on September 11th as entirely un-Islamic. Their secretary-general, Dr Abdelouahed Belkeziz, declared just one day after the attacks that the OIC denounced and condemned the attacks as events that ran counter to all covenants, humanitarian values and divine religions foremost among which was Islam. 'Our tolerant Islamic religion,' he said, 'highly prizes the sanctity of human life and considers the wilful killing of a single soul as tantamount to killing humanity at large' (OIC, press release, 12 September 2002, Jeddah). The OIC includes member states as varied as the Islamic Republic of Iran and Morocco. In Iran, Ayatollah Kashani, speaking on behalf of his country, deplored the attacks by al-Qaeda as 'catastrophic'. In Sunni circles the most senior cleric and rector of al-Azhar University in Egypt, Mohammad Tantawi, condemned the attacks, declaring them un-Islamic. In general, then, Muslim leaders condemned the killing of innocents, and the attacks of September 11th, 2001, were also seen as an attack on Muslims and unrepresentative of the faith system. Muslim clerics have not condoned, but rather condemned, the attacks, arguing that they will create more harm. Islam has a long tradition of tolerance and respect for others. The majority of Islam's leaders seek only to remind their followers and Western audiences that such principles underpin their faith system. But such words fail to convince many in the West when popular media outlets depict countless examples of Muslim domains or Muslims themselves who engage in acts that display a contempt for human rights or respect for universal norms of freedom.

The second method or criterion relates to the theological and political force of the argument behind al-Qaeda's campaign. Can it be argued that there is a theocratic and political legitimacy to the attacks waged by this organization, to which millions of other Muslims subscribe? Do they deserve the *jihad* moniker or even a label that indicates some legitimacy to their cause as part of resistance? First, it is useful to remember that the religious character of Osama Bin Laden and his most senior associates, when compared with the *madrassa*-drilled cadres and leader of the Taliban, has not been formed through classical religious study in any of the leading academies of the Muslim world. Bin Laden and senior associates like Zahrawi are not religious scholars, but revolutionary radicals who have forged a world view from engagement in the *mujahideen* war in Afghanistan or other locales such as Egypt or other North African countries. In Afghanistan the war directly involved the superpowers and exposed their credentials. Bin Laden's and, therefore, al-Qaeda's agenda centres on a number of issues. Some of these issues do in fact reflect the concerns of other Islamists, as well as other anti-global and rights-based organizations. They are highlighted in the following articulations and formulations of a range of views on the West, the Palestinian issue, strategy and the obligations of the Muslim community (*umma*) relayed in a series of al-Qaeda statements.

The new Crusaders

Antipathy towards the West is a central tenet of al-Qaeda thinking. The modern nation-state actors of the West are constructed as part of a seamless historical fabric that resurrects the Crusades and the motives of the Crusaders as relevant. Additionally, by employing this motif, there is a direct appeal to Muslims and a prospect of meaningful 'victory' symbolized in the past by Salah Eddin's victory against the Crusaders. Chief among the targets for vitriolic expression is the United States of America. As a statement declares, reflecting on the US-led campaign in Afghanistan in the autumn and winter of 2001:

> We now live under this Crusader bombardment that targets the entire nation. The Islamic nation should know that we defend a just cause. The Islamic nation has been groaning in pain for more than 80 years under the yoke of the joint Jewish–Crusader aggression. The Islamic nation must also know that the US version of terrorism is a kind of deception. Is it logical for the United States and its allies to carry out this repression, persecution, plundering, and bloodletting over these long years without this being called terrorism, while when the victim tries to seek justice, he is described as a terrorist?

Additionally, al-Qaeda makes its position clear regarding the implication of becoming a target of al-Qaeda. An explicit linkage to *jihad* as a method of meeting the challenge posed by the 'enemy' is clearly outlined:

> Let the United States know that the Islamic nation will not remain silent after this day on what it is experiencing and what takes place

in its land, and that *jihad* for the sake of God today is an obligation on every Muslim in this land if he has no excuse.

The presence of American troops and foreign policy actions across Muslim domains is singled out in statements such as this:

> These storms will not calm until you retreat defeated in Afghanistan, stop your assistance to the Jews in Palestine, end the siege imposed on the Iraqi people, leave the Arabian Peninsula, and stop your support for the Hindus against the Muslims in Kashmir.

The response or reaction is measured in terms of the Muslim community – a community portrayed as ready to wage a *jihad* against America:

> The Americans should know that the storm of plane attacks will not abate, with God's permission. There are thousands of the Islamic nations' youths who are eager to die just as the Americans are eager to live. They should know that with their invasion of the land of Afghanistan, they have started a new phase of enmity and conflict between us and the forces of infidelity. We are confident that we will achieve victory thanks to our material and moral strength and confidence and faith in Almighty God. The Americans have opened a door which will under no circumstances be shut.

The appeal and call to arms is made explicit as part of a propaganda ploy directed at the Western audience and designed to project fear and play up the threat posed by al-Qaeda:

> I [Osama Bin Laden] address the US Secretary of State, who cast doubt about my previous statement and downplayed what we said that there are thousands of Muslim youths who are eager to die and that the aircraft storm will not stop, God willing. Powell, and others in the US administration, know that if al-Qaeda organisation promises or threatens, it fulfils its promise or threat, God willing. Therefore, we tell him tomorrow is not far for he who waits for it. What will happen is what you are going to see and not what you hear. And the storms will not calm, especially the aircraft storm.

The Palestinian–Israeli conflict receives important symbolic attention from Osama Bin Laden and al-Qaeda ideologues. While Israel and Israeli targets have not been the principal preoccupation of Bin Laden, Israel is still projected in al-Qaeda literature as a partner in the 'Crusader–Zionist' Alliance that they oppose.

Palestine is a focus of the wider commitment to a global *jihad*. A *jihad* undertaken in other domains such as Afghanistan or Iraq is represented as part of the wider struggle for liberation that will embrace Palestine. The liberation of Palestine from Israeli occupation is represented as a key symbol of the struggle, and central to the renaissance of Islam that underpins *salafi* thinking on this issue.

al-Qaeda's strategy

How it plans to engage in the achievement of certain political or other aims should tell us something about the fundamental mores and values that shape a movement or organization. In this context the commitment to terrorism implies an explicit contradiction to orthodox Islamic texts, which do not advocate attacks on civilian targets in any conflict but propound strict rules or laws of war in such contexts. Yet al-Qaeda advocates such violence:

> Carrying out terrorism against the oppressors is one of the tenets of our religion and Shari'ah.

> God Almighty has said: Then fight in God's cause, thou art held responsible only for thyself and rouse the believers. It may be that God will restrain the fury of the unbelievers, for God is the strongest in might and in punishment.

> The actions by these young men who destroyed the United States and launched the storm of planes against it have done a good deed.

> Against them make ready your strength to the utmost of your power, including steeds of war, to strike terror into the hearts of the enemies of God and your enemies.

Yet Islam is deployed to legitimize such deeds, as Bin Laden himself declares:

> Finally, I thank Almighty God who enabled us to engage in this *jihad* and fight this battle, which is a decisive one between infidelity and faith. I ask Almighty God to grant us victory on our enemy, make their machinations backfire on them, and defeat them. In this regard we greet the *mujahideen* youths who knew their role and the way to respond to the aggression of the unjust, and killed them.

The point here is that Bin Laden pretends to speak in the name of Islam, but he is not a cleric; he did not study in Muslim seminaries;

nor does he have any theological writings or treatises to his name. Thus he is no Sayyid Qutb, and he will leave no legacy of writings or philosophical reflections. Bin Laden has always relied on others for such inspiration.

Appeals to the Muslim community (*umma*)

Yet in seeking to create or exploit the fissure between what is labelled 'the West' and what is labelled 'Islam', Bin Laden employs Muslim rhetoric and appeals to the concept of community (*umma*) in an effort to rally those outside his immediate circle:

> I address this message to the entire Muslim nation to tell them that the confederates have joined forces against the Islamic nation and the Crusader war, promised by Bush, has been launched against Afghanistan and against this people who have faith in God.

> I address Muslim youths, men, and women and urge them to shoulder their responsibility. They should know that the land of Afghanistan and the *mujahideen* there are really facing an all-out Crusader war which is aimed at eliminating this group which believes in God and fights on the basis of a creed and religion. Thus, the nation must shoulder its responsibility. It would be a disgrace if the Islamic nation fails to do so.

He attempts to appropriate Muslim protest and politics as support for al-Qaeda and its strategy of terror. He, like many commentators in the West, conflates the genuine concern of Muslims regarding contexts where conflict and human rights abuses take place with support for the al-Qaeda agenda:

> We also greet the Muslims, both in the East and West, who staged demonstrations rejecting this criminal aggression, repression, and injustice.

> US interests are spread throughout the world. So, every Muslim should carry out his real role to champion his Islamic nation and religion. Carrying out terrorism against the oppressors is one of the tenets of our religion and *shari'ah*.

Saudi Arabia

Within extremist Islamist discourse promoted by Osama Bin Laden and therefore al-Qaeda, the critique of prevailing Islamic state rule – primarily under Wahabi-driven Saudi Arabia – is a unique pre-occupation. Aspects of the critique do remain relevant to concerns about continuing authoritarian rule in a number of Arab Gulf states, and Saudi Arabia in particular. Additionally, internal dissent does have the potential to threaten the stability of the Kingdom and the dominance of the al-Saud family. A precarious Saudi Arabia will of course engage Western state actors, and primarily the United States of America, as it seeks to protect national interests by securing energy resources. The maintenance of a US presence in Saudi Arabia, at the invitation of the ruling family, animates extremist Islamist elements, who interpret this as further evidence of 'Western occupation'. Their position is made clear in the following excerpt.

> Al-Qaeda organisation orders the Americans and the infidels in the Arabian Peninsula, particularly the Americans and the British, to leave the Arabian peninsula. If the mothers of these need their sons then they should ask them to leave the Arabian peninsula, because the land will be set on fire under their feet, God willing. The Arabian Peninsula is being defiled by the feet of those who came to occupy these lands, usurp these holy places, and plunder these resources.

Hatred for Jews and Christians

Religious prohibition of contact and co-operation with Jews and Christians cannot be considered to be rooted in general Muslim discourse, but instead is evidence of anti-Semitism and anti-Christianism legitimated by an extremist fundamentalist clerical clique. This further qualifies the *raison d'être* of the movement as both questionable as transparently Islamic and fundamentally anti-Western.

> We thank Almighty God, who said in his holy book: Ye who believe, take not the Jews and the Christians for your friends and protectors. They are but friends and protectors to each other. And he amongst

you that turns to them is of them. Verily God guideth not a people unjustly.

We support the religious rulings issued by senior clerics in the Kingdom of Saudi Arabia, led by His Eminence Shaykh Humud Bin-Uqlah al-Shu'aybi, who said that it is impermissible to co-operate with Jews and Christians and that he who co-operates with them and gives them his opinion or takes actions in supporting them becomes apostate and revokes his faith in God and his Prophet, may God's peace and blessings be upon him.

It seems that the notion of a gulf between that understood as Islam and the West remains relevant to those ideologues on both sides of the so-called divide and their supporters. In some respects the notion of a divide seems wider than ever, and is persistently exacerbated by terrorism, political violence and the responses to it. The chasm between those on the radical, extreme fringes of political Islam who advocate the annihilation and removal of Western and particularly American influence and (or) interference in their domains and the extremes of US right-wing Christian conservatism has never been wider. These extreme groups sometimes dominate the discourse and the critique, so that moderate mainstream voices are lost. The dissonance of conflict rings true at the level of international dialogue. ·Yet there is some evidence that in the midst of this gulf there are cultural elements within Western societies and Muslim domains that share common values. There is evidence in a variety of Muslim domains, particularly those in South Asia, where encounters between indigenous cultures, Islam and aspects of Westernization have occurred without significant conflict or descent into violence. The slowly evolving acculturations of indigenous cultures with Islam in a symbiosis unique to·a country or region does have the potential to be employed as evidence that the hard border between Islam and the West can be tested. Additionally, within the West, the presence of significant and growing Muslim minority populations and their contribution to the development of such societies undermines the myth that there is a chasm between Islam and the West. We can only make ourselves safer if we tackle the real causes of legitimate Muslim grievance. Mutual trust and understanding need not be an impossible ideal, but this is not the same as making a case for a peaceful fusion between and within cultures so as to produce a multi-cultural global phenomenon. In the American-led 'War on Terror', the war in Iraq must be placed within the context of addressing the sources of terrorism, and not its symptoms. Addressing the sources of terrorism requires long-term not just short-term military-inspired effort and activity in many dimensions of global life. It also requires states to address the rules-based dimensions of the international environment symbolized by international organizations like the United Nations. This implies difficult decisions for a variety of modern nation-states, their definitions of national interest, and the way in which this influences foreign policy-making. It means that irrespective of power, economic strength or geo-strategic location, the leaders of modern states can no longer pick and choose among issues of compliance and participation.

One of the most significant outcomes of the war that took place in Iraq in 2003, and the subsequent US-led occupation, was the manifestation and appearance of new *salafi jihad* groups who directly oppose and attack the occupation and its agents. Radical Islamism, fermented by outside elements, has appeared as a new dimension of Iraq's multi-ethnic and sectarian state. A locally based insurgency against a Western presence in a Muslim domain has been exploited by those who promote a global aggressive *jihad* against the West.

CONCLUSION: ISLAM AND POLITICS, A TWENTY-FIRST-CENTURY CHALLENGE

> Everyone thinks of changing the world, but no one thinks of changing himself.
>
> *Leo Tolstoy*

It has been argued that the modern discourse of both the West and Islam can be reduced to the examination of a series of myths that can be exposed and critiqued. There are dangers behind the adoption of such myths in a modern globalized international order that compels interaction, rather than isolation, between diverse communities (Halliday, 1996, pp. 6–7). Once one concedes the rich and textured reality of societies in the contemporary world as dynamic, fluid and faulty, with a multiplicity of political, economic, ideological, cultural and social configurations, then the place of Islam as something with a set of political dimensions can be grasped. In relation to political culture, for example, Islam has to be perceived as part of a series of imagined and signified constructions moulded by a variety of actors. Some of those actors are Muslims who are politically active; some are preachers, some are worshippers and some are not worshippers, but the Muslim dimension of their identity compels them to address the political. Some actors are not actively Muslim but see in Islam a threat, a challenge and an alternative ideological agenda that clashes dangerously with their own. The ideological dimension of Islam as political culture is instantiated within such contexts and is influenced by them in ways that make them relevant to potential subscribers. Potential subscribers are Muslims who recognize a condition in their own society that works against their aspirations for freedom, security and wealth. This suggests demands for a very real attachment to social conditions and relations that make up the sum of the Muslim experience in a variety of domains across the globe.

Hence political Islam in the twenty-first century can be understood as part of the emergence of an alternative political road-map in an age in which ideology has been declared defunct and is supposed to have been rendered meaningless by the apogee of democratic liberalism. As an alternative, it inevitably places emphasis on protest, opposition and antagonism to prevailing hegemonic orders. Islam additionally, as a faith system, offers the prospect of surmounting the barriers of nationalist ideologies represented by the modern nation-state as a transnational alternative to a geographically diverse audience. Such an approach also attempts to jettison old ideological frameworks founded on differing views of the economic imperative that governs society and offers a faith system – religion as the foundation for a new political order. Much that is represented as political Islam in the contemporary world is in fact an amalgam of 'imagined communities' constructed around myths that have been deliberately built in to the pursuit of power. The religious foundation cannot, however, be ignored. By proffering faith as *the* alternative, it is almost inevitable that a tension is established with a political vision founded on secularism.

The dynamic of societal relations and orders in many Muslim domains has throughout the twentieth century been subject to great upheaval and change. The traditional has been replaced by the modern, religious functions by secularization, and social orders have been subject to breakdown and reconfiguration. This fluidity has created new and continually changing social orders subject to the pressures wrought by reconfiguration. In this way socio-economic factors, normally state-led and secularized, have changed the contexts in which Muslims experience political life – as part of a marginal or alienated set of communities. This alienation, exclusion from power and a sense that Islam has been lost from the public (including the political) realm are profound in a variety of Muslim domains, including some in the West. Political Islam, then, becomes representative of a reassertion of what is considered to be authentic or indigenous. This reassertion often takes place in the face of political rule that is understood as alien, foreign and not of the making of Muslim peoples. This search for the authentic representation of Islam as 'true' rather than 'alien' mirrors the search for authentic national identities and constructions that occurred in a variety of settings throughout the twentieth century. The difference, of course, is the proposed outcome in terms of the political colour of the state. In this sense political Islam, or the Islamists, claims to be a voice for the 'dispossessed' and 'excluded'. Islam is the alternative for a variety of opposition elements to rally around. In this respect the revolutionary impulse in Iran in 1979 against the authoritarian dictates of the pro-Western Shah, which was harnessed (in competition with other social and political forces) by Ayatollah Khomeini and his supporters, is put into context. If the only way to restore Islam to the public realm is through revolution, then Islamists will seek to engage in a battle against the secularizing ideologies of their political elites.

Yet the nation-state – the edifice of the modern international political order – has largely survived the Islamist onslaught. Only Iran, Afghanistan and Sudan were significantly altered by successful revolutionary overthrows of existing authoritarian elites, only to be replaced by new Islamist authoritarian elites. Most Muslim majority states have resisted the clamour for radical or revolutionary change that echoes in Islamist circles by engaging in the promotion of a series of repressive measures that have resulted in an abuse of rights that extends to whole populations and alienates them further from their rulers. Most of these states have not admitted such groups into the political arena through measures of genuine political liberalization or democratization. Politics is still contested, but rarely in a democratic and plural fashion. Islamists have addressed themselves to the concept of the state, particularly in its modern manifestation. Where Islamic credentials are claimed in the name of the state, the emergent polity is subsequently found to be at odds with an international order being reshaped by the driving force of particular liberal-democratic visions.

Islamist discourse comes in all sorts of varieties. Some of them are pure breed and sanctioned by orthodox schools of jurisprudence, whereas others are more hybrid in character, reflecting a variety of acculturated influences that are fashioned and labelled as 'Islamic'. This discourse reflects many conflicting identities and positions fashioned by a diverse range of ideologues. It seeks to address, grapple with and provide alternative routes to contemporary political dilemmas. By necessity, this demands the ability to compete against other ideologues, to counter their positions and arguments, and offer an alternative that has mass appeal. This is a tall order, and has in truth been difficult for Islamists to achieve. In the West Bank and Gaza Strip, for example, the Islamist movement has emerged as an alternative player on a political landscape dominated by a myriad of secular nationalist organizations. It has not, however, succeeded in eclipsing them – even when the nationalists have demonstrated such devastating incompetence in the field of self-rule.

At the end of the twentieth century a split became apparent among those who saw a threat in the phenomenon of political Islam. Some argued that Islamists – particularly in their radical guises – had by and large failed to wreak revolution and topple regimes across the Middle East and beyond. By the year 2000 such forces had succeeded in snatching the reins of control only in Afghanistan, Sudan, Somalia and Tehran. Other attempts to snatch control of the state were thwarted, as in Egypt, Algeria, Jordan and Saudi Arabia. In other domains the achievement of power was the result of the accidents of fate and history more than anything else. It was believed that the apex of the challenge had been reached, with the nation-state enduring as a largely secular phenomenon in most Muslim locales. It is true, though, that concessions were wrought; that successes in terms of the Islamification of society were notable and worried those who resisted such restrictions over their lives. Islamification was often state-led, but rarely state-initiated. By this I mean that the state often adopted the guise of Islam as a means of regime preservation, crudely maintaining legitimacy and meeting the Islamists on the same turf. Even the leaders of states that had previously claimed the most secular and nationalist of credentials, such as those of Ba'thist Iraq, were prepared to play the Islamic card in the belief that it would establish legitimacy at home and among Muslim opinion elsewhere. This was most tellingly illustrated when Saddam Hussein, following his ill-fated invasion and occupation of Kuwait in August 1990, placed Islamic verses on the Iraqi national flag and began to refer to himself as the new Saladin. But the Islamists weren't convinced. For Saddam also engaged in decades of persecution of Iraq's Shi'ite population, murdering thousands, including its top clerical classes. In this respect there are many more skirmishes to take place. In opposition to this view of the phenomenon was the expression of the opinion that the threat posed by Islam was growing and increasingly real. The authors of such views pointed to acts of terrorism as all the evidence needed to underline this perspective. The events of September 11th, 2001, seemed to substantiate this view. Yet such a viewpoint adds credence to the idea that Muslim domains are now defined as Islamic to the exclusion of all other ideologies and belief systems.

In the twenty-first century it is worth asking, Will political Islam remain so important to the international political arena and the politics of regions such as the Middle East, Asia and Africa? There are a number of dimensions to any answer to this question. It is important to reflect, however, on the following key aspects: (a) Islamism as a threat to the *status quo*, (b) Islamism and the project of democracy, (c) Islamism as local, transnational and immigrant, and finally (d) Islam and terrorism. An understanding of Islam with respect to these key themes should do more than hint at the challenge of and to Islamism in the future. Throughout the twentieth century Islamism was manifest as a form of protest and challenge to the prevailing *status quo* in a variety of Muslim domains. Islamism became a vehicle for expressing opposition to the negative impact of modernity, globalization, colonial intrusion, secularization and authoritarianism in Muslim domains. Islamism was an expression of discontent with the system and its elites. In some Muslim domains Islamism is the only vehicle for the expression of opposition to injustice, human rights abuses and repression. In some Muslim domains Islamists have exploited and manipulated such grievances to foist violence on their own societies under the pretext of *jihad* and the overthrow of unjust *jahilli* rule. Violence has been directed not only against the state and its personnel but also at ordinary citizens and civilians who are perceived as transgressing the social rules that are constructed in the name of Islam by radical Islamists. The *status quo* has thus been challenged at the level of both state and society. Radical Islamists seek to do more than change the prevailing political order. Most academics would agree, however, that despite concerted and fundamental efforts to change the *status quo*, the majority of Islamist movements have failed and continue to fail to inspire revolution or regime change. Most Muslim majority states have endured as secular entities, though it is notable that many endure because they are supported by powerful non-Muslim friends.

Islamist overthrow and regime change have been limited phenomena in Muslim domains, and the probability of further achievement in such contexts is limited. In the domains where regime change and revolution occurred in the name of Islam – Iran, Sudan and Afghanistan – the durability of such projects is questionable. In large part this is because of a democracy deficit and the emergence of Islamist governance in authoritarian form. In Afghanistan the Taliban manipulated Islam to rule but not to construct a state or work to redevelop a country ravaged by decades of conflict and foreign occupation. The Taliban used

Islam to make Afghanistan a state of failure and isolation. Regime change in Afghanistan will not alter the propensity of the country's dominant conservative warlords for manipulating Islam in this way. Islam will be used to establish and legitimate tribal and patriarchal structures that deny rights to all but a privileged few. In Iran, more than two decades of theocracy have brought the country to the brink of change that may well usher in a more plural but still Islamic political system. Moreover, the threat of Islamist overthrow in other domains has resulted in existing regimes engaging in strategies that seek to exclude the formal organization of Islamist parties or to co-opt them in such a restricted fashion that they are emasculated within the system. Islamist elements enjoy very little political legitimacy in terms of the domains they operate in or in the international community. Most elements of the international community regard the political project associated with Islamism as a significant threat. Although Islamist groups are able to exploit popular grievances or opposition to the policies of secular nationalist regimes in Muslim domains, they have been unable to build a coalition of the willing among popular elements that translates into revolutionary momentum and overthrow. In the twenty-first century regime change in Muslim domains is far more likely to be an outcome of Western and external machinations than internal Islamist ones.

Regime change that is not Islamist-inspired is not the same, however, as assuming that Islamist groups won't remain an important part of the political landscape in Muslim domains. Where Islamist groups have been tolerated, legalized and incorporated into the fabric of the political system and the state, there is evidence of long-term sustainability and endurance in terms of the shaping of political discourse. In Pakistan, for example, although Islamism is mitigated by the presence of the military core in the state, it still represents a fundamental aspect of the ways in which political consciousness is expressed across a range of issues that affect governance and power. Leaders of the regime, even if they themselves are not Islamist ideologues or supporters of such ideologies, still acknowledge the important legitimating dimension that Islamist discourse brings to their political projects. The same is true in other Muslim domains, such as the former Soviet Muslim republics and other states in South Asia. This in turn highlights the interface between such elements and those who promote the secular liberal project.

It is acknowledged that with the end of the Cold War the 'democratization project' has taken on certain universal or even hegemonic qualities. Yet, within this framework societies may flourish as plural structures founded on principles of equality. Put this way, it is difficult to understand why so many Islamists have chosen to represent themselves as anti-democratic. Yet, Tibi hints at the paradox here when he asserts, 'Egalitarianism can never be based on cultural uniformity, be it the kind of US-style McWorld or – in reverse – an envisaged Islamic universalism. Both prescribe a missionary universalist vision to others, which they do not need' (Tibi, 2001, p. 93). The strategy that so many incumbent nationalist secular or monarchical regimes in Muslim domains have adopted to thwart the fundamentalist threat, however, has also squeezed the political space for other elements in society. Such strategies mitigate against pluralism, and power is rarely subject to rotation as a result of elections. Authoritarian rule prevails, and the voice of opposition is subdued by the preoccupation of such regimes with their own survival through the extension of a major coercive strategy against their citizens. States that resort to emergency powers, state security forces, the military, and criminalization of political activity, while claiming to protect the tender buds of democracy from the grasp of Islamic fundamentalists, do nothing more than reinforce authoritarianism. The democratic era in Muslim domains is a false dawn when the monopoly of power remains in the hands of one party. Yet, with the demand to democratize or be damned, the paradoxical pressure is maintained by Western states as part of their agenda for combating terrorism of the new Muslim variety. There was international consensus, after September 11th, that the fundamentalist al-Qaeda-supporting Taliban regime had to be changed. President Bush spoke of the liberation of Afghanistan in terms of bringing democracy to its poor benighted people. Moreover, throughout the summer of 2002 there was evidence in US policy towards other Muslim domains that a new version of regime change for the sake of democracy would be advocated for the Palestinians (even though their president had been elected on a popular mandate), Iraq, Syria, Iran and other countries. The 'War on Terror' was increasingly equated with the rhetoric of a war to bring democracy to such domains. Yet at the same time US policy-makers were demanding that the elites of Muslim majority regimes such as Egypt, Saudi Arabia and Algeria crackdown on society in order to vanquish the Islamist threat.

Bringing democracy to Muslim domains has been recognized as a dimension of the 'War on Terror' which, it is hoped, will eventually eliminate the threat that Islamists pose. Yet integral to this vision is the demand for an even-handed approach that respects the outcome of popular mandates even if they are not to the likes of the incumbents of the White House. Muslim friends as well as foes have to voluntarily sign up for the democracy project. In reality, as the democratization experiments of the 1990s demonstrated, there is little hope of such an outcome when democracy is posited or understood as the nemesis of Islamism in its contemporary guise. Nevertheless, the achievement of regime change in Iraq and the allied occupation of the country in 2003 were also promoted as an opportunity for Iraq to become a beacon of democracy in a region of Muslim majority states. For democrats who subscribe to this vision, one major element that has the potential to thwart such ambitions is Islam. For many Islamists there is a lack of conviction that in practice democracy offers them any hope of achieving power through a popular mandate. In Egypt, for example, democracy, despite the manufacture of political liberalism by the incumbent regime, is a chimera or fictive construct propped up by the West. As a construct put in place in Muslim domains, democracy is highly circumscribed and limited in manifestation and expression. The democratic experiment is tightly stage-managed by the elite of the incumbent regime, and is largely designed to exclude Islamists along with whole swathes of others in the political spectrum. Only the state regulates the tempo of the democratic march. Yet when Islamists compete more freely in other political arenas, such as professional associations or student union ballots, they have demonstrated that they can convert their support into a popular mandate that is far stronger than that of their opponents. Islamists have become consummate actors in electoral processes the world over, and a failure to accommodate and absorb the import of such engagement is potentially dangerous.

For in this respect Islamism has demonstrated an ability to endure at the level of the local, the transnational and within Muslim immigrant communities across the globe. This has been partly facilitated by the process of exile (forced or voluntary) and the technological revolution that has been harnessed by so many Islamist organizations to great effect. The internal displacement and migration of large numbers of Muslims, as a result either of war, conflict or for economic reasons, has generated new diasporas that by the latter part of the twentieth and early years of the twenty-first century included prominent elements of radical Islamism and Islamism more generally. There are relatively few Muslim domains, and barely any in the Middle East and South-West Asia, where the modernity project has not impacted and played a part in establishing the large-scale migration of Muslims within regions and between them. In North Africa migration and exile have become a feature of modern Muslim communities, and transnational connections have been established, facilitated and bolstered by travel, communications, and the growth in the dissemination of media and literatures. As Burgat notes, 'The Islamist diaspora has moved not so much to Afghanistan as to Europe – especially Britain, Sweden, Germany, Belgium and Switzerland – the Islamic republics of the former Soviet Union and the US, Canada, Malaysia and Indonesia, in addition to some parts of the Arab world' (Burgat, 2003a, p. 175). While it is true that migrant or diaspora communities have amongst them exiled elements of radical Islamism who grab the headlines and claim to speak in the name of Islam, there is a silent majority who have reworked Islam in accommodation with the prevailing socio-political context in which they find themselves. Hence the majority of Pakistani Muslim migrant workers in the Gulf states of the Arabian peninsula have been duly informed by conservative Wahabi and other fundamentalist doctrines that have altered and acculturated dimensions of their Muslim identity. Moreover, for the majority of Palestinian Muslims living in the USA, their identity formation is altered by the liberal-democratic principles so strongly cherished within the American political culture. Where such communities remain vulnerable to the message of enmity that the radicals preach is on the margins, where they are denied a place in the polity and the rights that would thereby be accorded. It is the process of deliberate exclusion and marginalization of migrant communities that gives rise to vulnerabilities that are exploited by those with an alternative, hostile agenda.

The terrorism of Osama Bin Laden and al-Qaeda has been denounced by a variety of leaders within the Muslim community as unrepresentative of Islam and its teachings. Bin Laden has been condemned from within for the 'harm' he has 'inflicted on Islam'. While it may appear that in the twenty-first century, Muslims have a monopoly on terrorism, the truth of the matter is that ideologues, religious fanatics and others have always invoked their creed as a justification for violence – particularly if it is part of a struggle for power. Fanaticism of the type that leads to terrorism in the name of religion is nothing new. Indeed, the origin of the word in Latin refers to a religious place of worship and carries with it connotations of fundamentalist religious attachment. But in terms of contemporary manifestations, many Muslim domains that were tainted by terrorism throughout the twentieth century experienced it initially as a non-Muslim phenomenon. Indeed, early encounters with terrorism originated in nationalist not Islamist struggles in such domains. Yet on the threshold of the twenty-first century an explosion of Muslim terrorism does appear to have scorched the globe and dominated the headlines, inducing new dimensions of fear. It will take a long time to eradicate such fear, and terrorism in its Muslim incarnation will preoccupy and demand the attention of policy-makers and politicians across the globe for the foreseeable future. The interface between Islam and politics remains, for the time being, coloured by terrorism and violence. The threat in this respect is not exaggerated, but should be recognized as profound and menacing in some quarters. Osama Bin Laden and al-Qaeda represent a real threat. Hamas and Islamic Jihad represent a real threat. Abu Sayyaf represents a real threat. But the question here is whether this means, as many American neo-conservatives assert, that Islam itself also represents a real threat. Moreover, if a threat is recognized, the next question is what strategies should be adopted to thwart it. It is here that the contest and struggle for power will endure. The radical end of the Islamist spectrum is populated by a variety of figures who contend that they are patient and willing to take time in their battle to usurp orders that are unjust and un-Islamic. Countering this threat can take a variety of forms, military, economic, social and political. Moreover, it is important to remember that even if the root causes of this kind of terrorism are identified, this does not necessarily mean that they can be solved overnight. As the revenge motive enters the equation, countering terrorism becomes equally more difficult. In this respect, I would contend, it is impossible to win the 'War on Terror' in its Islamic guise. Terrorism is impossible to eradicate, and the optimum aspiration is a balancing of the demand for security in the modern world and the preservation of liberal-democratic orders. The place of Islam in the twenty-first-century political scheme is permanent. It is unrealistic to attempt to remove it from the political fabric of so many domains and communities. Living with Islam as a political phenomenon is a certainty for the foreseeable future.

GLOSSARY OF ISLAMIC TERMS

Allah	the Arabic word for God that all Muslims use
Allahu Akbar	God is Great
amir	prince, or commander
ashura	the commemoration by Shi'a Muslims of the martyrdom of Imam Hussein at Karbala
Ayatollah	Shi'a religious leader
bai'a	oath of allegiance
bayan	leaflet or circular issued as a form of communication
burqa	form of dress completely covering a woman's body
caliph(ate)	successor to the Prophet Mohammad (the institution of Islamic government after Mohammad)
chadour	clothing worn by women to cover themselves according to Qur'anic instruction
dar al-harb	abode of war
dar al-salam	abode of peace
da'wa	call or preaching to Islam
dawla	the state
dhimmi	People of the Book accorded protected status
din	religion
Eid al-Fitr	celebration of breaking the fast, marking the end of Ramadan
faqih	jurisconsult. A man with good comprehension of the technicalities of Islamic jurisprudence
fard ayn	individual obligation (to undertake *jihad*)

fatwa	a religio-juridic verdict or counsel issued by a religious scholar
fez	traditional Turkish headdress for men
fitna	internal disorder or chaos including civil war
hadith	commentary and report of the Prophet Mohammad
Hajj	annual pilgrimage to Mecca, one of the five pillars of Islam
hakimiyya	governance
halal	permitted, sanctified
haram	prohibited
hijab	headscarf worn by women
hijra	the emigration of Prophet Mohammad and his followers from Mecca to Medina
hodna	form of ceasefire during holy war
ijma	consensus
ijtihad	independent reasoning, or interpretation with regard to religious issues
ikhwan	brethren
imam	the leader of prayers in the mosque
iman	profession of faith
islah	reform
Islam	submission or surrender to Allah
Ismaili	Shi'a sect whose members are followers of Ismail Jafar; two main elements: Nizari and Bohras
jahiliyya (jahilli)	originally total pagan ignorance during pre-Islamic era; used in the contemporary era to characterize all societies not considered genuinely Islamic
jihad	exertion, striving, struggle by all means, including military
jizyah	poll tax on *dhimmi*
Kaba	shrine in Mecca
kibla (Qibla)	the direction of Mecca
kufr	an unbeliever
madrassa	religious place of learning
mahram	close male relative allowed to accompany Muslim women in public
majlis	council
majlis al-shura	consultative council
masjid	mosque
mawalis	non-Arab Muslims

mihrab	niche in a mosque pointing in the direction of Mecca, where the *imam* leads the prayers
minaret	the tower of the mosque where the call to prayer is broadcast
minbar	the pulpit in a mosque
muezzin	the man who calls the people to prayer
mufti	Muslim legislator
mujahid(een)	fighter(s) for Allah in *jihad*
mullah	local religious leader
Muslim	follower of Islam
mutawwa	religious police
purdah	exclusion of women from public space
Qadi (Kadi, Qadhi)	Muslim judge of *Shari'a* law
Ramadan	Muslim month of fasting
riba	usury
salafi	relates to the example and inspiration of the Prophet Mohammad and the four rightly guided caliphs; fundamentalist in inspiration
sawm	fasting
Shari'a	Islamic law
sheikh	honorary term with religious connotation
Shi'a	party of Ali – followers of Ali
shihada	profession of faith
shura	consultation
sunna	the sayings and actions of the Prophet Mohammad
Sunni	major sect within Islam
tajdid	revival
taqlid	imitation
tawhid	unity
ulama	scholars or people trained in religious sciences
umma	community
usulia	fundamentalist
vilayat al-fiqh	governance by Islamic expert in Shi'a Islam
Wahabi	movement within Islam based on puritanical teachings of ibn-Abd-al-Wahab
zakat	tax for raising dues for the poor, one of the five pillars of Islam

BIBLIOGRAPHY

Abu Shanab, Ismail 2002: Interview with author, Gaza, September.

Adwan, A. 2002: Interview with author, Gaza, September.

Affendi-al, A. (ed.) 2001: *Rethinking Islam and Modernity*. London: Islamic Foundation.

Afshar, H. 1998: *Islam and Feminisms: An Iranian Case Study*. Basingstoke: Macmillan.

Ahmad, A. and Donnan, H. (eds.) 1994: *Islam, Globalization and Postmodernity*, London: Routledge.

Ahmad, E. 1999: A Jihad against time. *al-Ahram Weekly*, no. 415, February, pp. 4–6.

Ahmed, L. 1992: *Women and Gender in Islam*. New Haven: Yale University Press.

Ajami, F. 2001: The furies of foreign lands. *US News*, 14 September.

Alavi, H. 2001: The constitution of Medina. *The Dawn*, 20 July, pp. 3–4.

Arberry, A. (tr.) 1955: *The Koran*. London: Allen and Unwin Ltd.

Auda-al, Sheikh, S. 1996: *Open Letter. www.sundhouse.com/dissidence/letter_from_salman_al_auda.htm*

Ayubi, N. 1991: *Political Islam, Religion and Politics in the Arab World*. London: Routledge.

Azmeh-al, A. 1993: *Islams and Modernities*. London: Verso.

Azzam, A. 1996: *Join the Caravan*. London: Azzam Publications.

Badawi, Z. 2001: *Zakat, a New Source of Development Finance.* www.io.ie.

Barr, C. W. 2001: A suicide bomber's world. *Christian Science Monitor*, 14 August, pp. 1–4.

Barry, J. 1999: *Rethinking Green Politics: Nature, Virtue and Progress*. London: Sage.

BBC: *Faces of Islam* Documentary Series Roneden, 2000.

Beck, L. and Keddie, N. (eds.) 1978: *Women in the Muslim World*. Cambridge, MA.: Harvard University Press.

Beinin, J. and Stork, J. (eds.) 1997: *Political Islam: Essays from Middle East Report*. London: I. B. Tauris.

Bhatia, S. 1998: Legal challenges in Pakistan. *Observer*, 6 September, p. 11.

Bin-Laden, O. 1996a: *Declaration of War Against the Occupiers of the Two Holy Places*. Al-Quas al-Arabi, 1 August.

Bin-Laden, O. 1996b: Interview. *Nida'ul Islam*, October–November.

Bodman, H. L. and Tohidi, N. (eds.) 1998: *Women in Muslim Societies, Diversity Within*. Boulder, Col.: Lynne Rienner.

Bojnordi, Ayatollah 1998: Interview with author, February.

Burgat, F. 2003a: *Face to Face with Political Islam*. London: I. B. Tauris.

Burgat, F. 2003b: Veils and obscuring lenses. In Esposito and Burgat, pp. 17–41.

Dessouki, H. 1982: *Islamic Resurgence in the Arab World*. New York: Praeger.

Diamond, L. 2003: Can Iraq become a democracy? *Hoover Digest*, no. 2, (Spring).

Djerejian, E. 1993: US State Department. *http://www.hrw.org/reports/1993/WR93/Mew-01.htm*

Donner, F. M. 1991: The sources of Islamic conceptions of war. In John Kelsay and James Turner Johnson (eds.), pp. 31–69.

Duncan, F. and A. C. Krey (eds.) 1912: *Parallel Source Problems in Medieval History*. New York: Harper and Brothers.

Easwaran, S. E. 1999: *Nonviolent Soldier of Islam: Badshah Khan, a Man to Match his Mountains*. Blue Mountain: Nilgiri Press.

Ehteshami, A. 1995: *After Khomeini: The Iranian Second Republic*. London: Routledge.

Eickelman, D. and Piscatori, J. 1996: *Muslim Politics*. Princeton: Princeton University Press.

Esposito, J. L. 1984: *Islam and Politics*. Syracuse, NY: Syracuse University Press.

Esposito, J. L. 1992: *The Islamic Threat: Myth or Reality?* Oxford: Oxford University Press.

Esposito, J. L. 1994: *Islam: The Straight Path*. New York: Oxford University Press.

Esposito, J. L. and Burgat, F. (eds.) 2003: *Modernizing Islam, Religion and the Public Sphere in Europe and the Middle East*. London: C. Hurst & Co.

Esposito, J. L. and Piscatori, J. 1991: Democratization and Islam. *Middle East Journal* 45(3) (Summer), pp. 427–40.

Ezzat, H. R. n.d.: *Women and the Interpretation of Islamic Sources*. n.p.: Islam 21.

Fadlallah, Sheikh 2000: Interview with author, Beirut, April.

FBIS 1992: *Trial against Shubailat*. Washington: FBIS.

Fnaysh, M. 2001: Interview with author, Beirut, April.

Freedom House 2001: *Annual Survey of Political Rights and Civil Liberties*. New York: Freedom House.

Freedom House 2002: *Annual Survey of Political Rights and Civil Liberties*. New York: Freedom House.

Fukuyama, F. 1989: The end of history. *The National Interest*, 16, (Summer), pp. 3–18.

Fukuyama, F. 2001: The West has won. *The Guardian*, 11 October. *www.guardian.co.uk/waronterror/story/0,1361,567333,00.html*

Fulcher of Chartres 1912: Gesta Francorum Jerusalem Expugnantium. In F. Duncan and A. C. Krey (eds.), pp. 109–15.

Ghannushi-al, R. 2001: On the dilemma of the Islamic movement. In A. el-Affendi (ed.), pp. 109–22.

Guazzone, L. (ed.) 1995: *The Islamist Dilemma: The Political Role of Islamist Movements in the Contemporary Arab World*. Reading: Ithaca.

Gurr, T. and Harff, B. 1994: *Ethnic Conflict in World Politics*. Boulder, Colo.: Westview.

Haass, R. 2002: The goal becomes Muslim democracy. *International Herald Tribune*, 11 December.

Halliday, F. 1996: *Islam and the Myth of Confrontation*. London: I. B. Tauris.

Hamas 1988: Covenant of the Islamic Resistance Movement. n.p.: n.p.

Hamas 1998: *Hamas Statement*.

Hammami, R. 1997: From immodesty to collaboration: Hamas, the women's movement and national identity in the Intifada. In Beinin and Stork, pp. 194–210.

Hatem, M. 1993: Toward the development of post-Islamist and post-nationalist feminist discourses in the Middle East. In Tucker, 1993, pp. 29–48.

Held, D. 1996: *Models of Democracy*. Cambridge: Polity.

Hoffman, B. 1995: Holy Terror: the implications of terrorism motivated by a religious imperative. *Studies in Conflict and Terrorism*, 18, pp. 271–84.

Hourani, A. 1991: *A History of the Arab Peoples*. London: Faber and Faber.

Howe, J. 1992: The crisis of Algerian nationalism and the rise of Islamic integralism. *New Left Review*, 196, pp. 85–101.

Hunter, S. 1995: The rise of Islamist movements and the Western response: clash of civilizations or clash of interests? In Guazzone, pp. 343–70.

Huntington, S. 1984: Will more countries become democratic? *Political Science Quarterly* (Summer), pp. 193–218.

Huntington, S. 1993: The clash of civilizations? *Foreign Affairs* (Summer), pp. 22–49.

Jalal, A. 1991: The convenience of subservience. In Kandiyoti, 1991, pp. 77–117.

Jawad, H. 1998: *The Rights of Women in Islam: An Authentic Approach*. Basingstoke: Macmillan.

Joffe, G. n.d.: Political Islam. *Outtherenews.com*

Jones, T. and Ereira, A. 1994: *Crusades*. Harmondsworth: Penguin Books.

Kandiyoti, D. 1991: *Women, Islam and the State*. Basingstoke: Macmillan.

Karam, A. 1998: *Women, Islamisms and the State: Contemporary Feminisms in Egypt*. Basingstoke: Macmillan.

Kedourie, E. 1992: *Politics in the Middle East*. Oxford: Oxford University Press.

Kedourie, E. 1994: *Democracy and Arab Political Culture*. London: Frank Cass.

Kelsay, J. and Johnson, J. T. (eds.) 1991: *Just War and Jihad: Historical and Theoretical Perspectives on War and Peace in Western and Islamic Traditions*. Westport, Con.: Greenwood Press.

Khameini, A. 1994: *Summary of statements. www.khameini.de/news/news1994/nov1994.htm*

Khan, M. 2001: Islam's compatibility with democracy. *http://www.ijtihad.org/isladem.htm*

Kramer, M. 1993: Islam vs. democracy. *Commentary* (January), pp. 35–42.

Kramer, M. (ed.) 1997: *The Islamism Debate*. Tel Aviv: Moshe Dayan Centre.

Lapidus, I. M. 1988: *A History of Islamic Societies*. Cambridge: Cambridge University Press.

Lawrence, B. 1998: *Shattering the Myth: Islam beyond Violence*. Princeton: Princeton University Press.

Lewis, B. 1980: *The Assassins: A Radical Sect in Islam*. Oxford: Oxford University Press.

Lewis, B. 1990: The roots of Muslim rage. *Atlantic Monthly*, September, pp. 47–60.

Lewis, B. 1993: *Islam and the West*. Oxford: Oxford University Press.

Lewis, B. 2002: What went wrong? *Atlantic Monthly*, January, pp. 47–60.

Luciani, G. (ed.) 1990: *The Arab State*. London: Routledge.

Marsden, K. 2001: An economist's view: poverty did not cause the terror attacks. *Transition Newsletter*, World Bank, July–September 2001.

Marty, M. E. and Appleby, S. R. 1991: *Fundamentalism Observed*. Chicago: University of Chicago Press.

Marty, M. E. and Appleby, S. R. 1993: *Fundamentalisms and the State*. Chicago: University of Chicago Press.

Matinuddin, K. 1999: *The Taliban Phenomenon*. Karachi: Oxford University Press.

Mawdudi, M. n.d.: *Selected Speeches and Writings. www.jamaat.org/overview/writings/html*

Mernissi, F. 1983: *Beyond the Veil: Male–Female Dynamics in Muslim Society*. London: Al Saqi Books.

Miller, J. 1993: The challenge of radical Islam. *Foreign Affairs*, 72(2), pp. 43–56.

Milton-Edwards, B. 1994: Jordan and facade democracy. *British Journal of Middle Eastern Studies*, 20, pp. 191–203.

Milton-Edwards, B. 1996a: *Islamic Politics in Palestine*. London: I. B. Tauris.

Milton-Edwards, B. 1996b: Political Islam in Palestine in an environment of peace. *Third World Quarterly*, 17, pp. 199–225.

Milton-Edwards, B. and Hinchcliffe, P. 2000: *Jordan: A Hashemite Legacy*. London: Routledge.

Minces, J. 1978: Women in Algeria. In Beck and Keddie, (eds.), pp. 159–71.

Moghissi, H. 1994: *Populism and Feminism in Iran*. Basingstoke: Macmillan.

Molyneux, M. 1991: The law, the state and socialist policies with regard to women: the case of the People's Democratic Republic of Yemen 1967–1990. In Kandiyoti (ed.), pp. 237–71.

Moussalli, A. S. 1999: *Moderate and Radical Islamic Fundamentalism – The Quest for Modernity, Legitimacy and the Islamic State.* Gainesville: University Press of Florida.

Nakanishi, H. 1998: Power, ideology and women's consciousness in post-revolutionary Iran. In T. L. Bodman and N. Tohidi (eds.), pp. 83–100.

Norton, A. R. 1993: The future of civil society in the Middle East. *Middle East Journal*, 47 (Spring), pp. 205–16.

Pape, R. A. 2003: Dying to kill us. *The New York Times*, 22 September.

Pervez, S. 2002: Muslim Youth Islamic Circle of North America. *www.icna. com/youth/stories_youth.htm*

Peters, F. E. 1994: *A Reader in Classical Islam.* Princeton: Princeton University Press.

Peters, R., 1984: *Islam and Colonialism: The Doctrine of Jihad in Modern History.* The Hague: Mouton.

Peters, R. 2001: Stability, America's enemy. *Parameters* (Winter), pp. 5–20.

Pfeifer, K. 1997: Is there an Islamic economics? In Beinin and Stork, 1997, pp. 154–65.

Pipes, D. 2002: What is jihad? *The New York Post*, 31 December.

Qa'ouk, Sheikh 2000: Interview with author, Sidon, Lebanon, April.

Qaradawi, Sheikh Yusuf 2003: *Fatwa*, 7 March.

Qutb, Sayyid 1978: *The Milestones.* Beirut: IIFSO.

Rafsanjani, Ayatollah 2003: Friday sermon, 4 April.

Ramage, D. E. 1997: *Politics in Indonesia: Democracy, Islam and The Ideology of Tolerance.* London: Routledge.

Rashid, A. 2001: *Taliban, the Story of the Afghan Warlords.* London: Pan Books.

Rodenbeck, M. 1998: *Cairo, the City Victorious.* London: Picador.

Rodinson, M. 1971: *Mohammed*, tr. Anne Carter. London: Allen Lane, The Penguin Press.

Roy, O. 1994: *The Failure of Political Islam.* London: I. B. Tauris.

Rubin, B. 2002: The real roots of Arab anti-Americanism. *Foreign Affairs*, 8(6), p. 73–85.

Ruthven, M. 2002: *A Fury for God: The Islamist Attack on America.* London: Granta.

Saad-Ghorayeb, A. 2002: *Hizbu'llah, Politics and Religion.* London: Pluto Press.

Sadowski, Y. 1997: The new orientalism and the democracy debate. In Beinin and Stork 1997, pp. 33–50.

Saftawi, A. 1989: Interview with author, Gaza, March.

Said, E. 1978: *Orientalism.* Harmondsworth: Penguin.

Said, E. 1997: *Covering Islam: How the Media and the Experts Determine How We See the Rest of the World.* London: Vintage.

Salame, G. (ed.) 1994: *Democracy without Democrats? The Renewal of Democracy in the Muslim World*. London: I. B. Tauris.

Saunders, J. J. 1965: *A History of Medieval Islam*. London: Routledge and Kegan Paul.

Shammi, A. Sheikh 2002: Interview with author, Gaza City, September.

Sidahmed, A. S. and Ehteshami, A. (eds.) 1996: *Islamic Fundamentalism*. Boulder, Colo.: Westview.

Siddiqi, D. M. 1998: Taslima Nasrren and others: The contest over gender in Bangladesh. In T. L. Bodman and N. Tohidi (eds.), pp. 205–28.

Sivan, E. 1985: *Radical Islam: Medieval Theology and Modern Politics*. New Haven: Yale University Press.

Stowasser, B. 1993: Women's issues in modern Islamic thought. In Tucker, pp. 3–28.

Sutherland, J. 2002: Campus watch. *Guardian*, 7 October.

Tibi, B. 2001: *Islam: Between Culture and Politics*. Houndsmills: Palgrave.

Tucker, J. (ed.) 1993: *Arab Women: Old Boundaries, New Frontiers*. Bloomington: Indiana University Press.

al-Turabi, H. 1998: *Islam, Democracy, the State and the West*. London: The Sudan Foundation.

Turner, B. 1994: *Orientalism, Postmodernism and Globalism*. London: Routledge.

UNDP. 2002: *Arab Human Development Report*. New York: UNDP.

US State Department. 2000: *Patterns of Global Terrorism*. Washington: *www.state.gov/s/ct/rls/pgtrpt/2000/*

Utvik, B. O. 2003: The modernizing force of Islamism. In Esposito and Burgat, 2003, pp. 43–67.

Vatikiotis, P. 1987: *Islam and the State*. London: Routledge.

Watson, H. 1994: Women and the veil: personal responses to global process. In A. Ahmed and H. Donnan (eds.), pp. 141–59.

Whalley, L. C. 1998: Urban Minangkabau Muslim women: modern choices, traditional concerns. In T. L. Bodman and N. Tohidi (eds), *Women in Muslim Societies: Diversity within Unity*, Boulder, Colo.: Lynne Rienner, pp. 229–49.

Wolfowitz, P. 2002: Bridging the dangerous gap between the West and the Muslim world. *US Department of Defence*, 3 May.

X, Malcolm 1965: *The Autobiography of Malcolm X*. Harmondsworth: Penguin.

Yassin, Sheikh Ahmed 2003: Statement, *As Sabeel*, September.

Zahar, M. 2002: Interview with author, Gaza, September.

Zubaida, S. 1993: *Islam: The People and the State*. London: I. B. Tauris.

Zuhur, S. 1992: *Islamist Gender Ideology in Modern Egypt*. Albany, NY: State University of New York Press.

INDEX

Abbasids 42
Abduh, Mohammad 28, 164
Abraham 12
Abu Bakr 16, 41
Abu Shanab, Ismail 111, 171–2
Abu Zayd, Nasser Hamid 29
adultery 136
Adwan, A. 183, 190
al-Afghani, Jamal a-din 28
Afghanistan 32; Bin
    Laden 200–1; Bush 214;
    civil conflict 187, 195;
    fundamentalists 21, 176;
    Islam 36; Islamists 32, 211;
    Islamization 21; *majlis al-
    shura* 136; Pakistan 196;
    protest 84; refugees 196;
    regime change 94;
    revolution 210, 212; Soviet
    occupation 76, 187, 195, 196,
    197; US intervention 187;
    women's status 120–1; *see also
    mujahideen*; Taliban
Afshar, H. 123, 126, 127, 138
Ahmad, E. 166–7, 170
Ahmad Khan, Sayyid 164
Ahmed, L. 119
Aisha 124, 125–7, 137
Aisha'a rebellion 107

Ajami, F. 191
Alavi, Hamza 39
Alawite Muslims 11
Albania 78
Alexius I 184
Algeria: civil conflict 93;
    democracy 113;
    democratization 117;
    FIS 72, 91, 111; FLN 72–3,
    91; France 78, 91–2;
    Islamism 47, 48, 72–3; oil
    reserves 72; radicals 35;
    West 117
Ali (Mohammad's son-in-law) 16,
    41
Ali, Mohammad (boxer) 11–12
Ali, Mohammad (Pasha of
    Egypt) 106
Allah: *jihad* 157;
    Mohammad 9–10;
    sovereignty 53, 108, 114
Amman 13
anti-Americanism 32, 190–2,
    201–2
anti-democracy 91, 93, 94, 101,
    103, 113–17
anti-Semitism 205–6
anti-war coalition 2
Appleby, S. R. 29

al-Aqsa Brigades 171, 175
al-Aqsa mosque 14, 45
Arab–Israel war 27, 90
Arabia 37–8, 122
Arabic language 9
Arabs/Persians 17
Aramco workers' strike 75
al-Ashmawi, Mohammad Said 29
ashura 17
Asia, Central 27
Asia, South 206
Assassin sect 47, 172, 185
Associated Press 85
Ataturk 73
Atta, Mohammed 171
al-Auda, Sheikh Salman 76, 77
authoritarianism: developing
    world 20; educated
    young 153–4;
    Indonesia 115–16;
    Islamists 93–4, 116–17;
    legitimacy 93; Muslim
    majority states 214
Ayub Khan, Sayyid 28
Ayubi, N. 29, 167
Azerbaijan 27, 90
al-Azhar University 28
al-Azmeh, A. 59
Azzam, A. 163, 166, 198

Badawi, Zaki 14
Bader Meinhof 152
Badr Battalions 178
Baghdad UN headquarters 171
Bahrain 81
Bali bombing 171
Bangladesh 48, 89, 96, 139
banking 54
al-Banna, Hassan 69, 104, 109–11,
    168
Barr, C. W. 174
Barry, J. 67
Ba'thists 17, 211
Baybar, Sultan 42
Bazargani, Mehdi 66–7
Belkeziz, Abdelouahed 200

belly-dancing 142
Ben Ali, Zine 112
Benin 50, 78
Benjedid, Chadli 72
Bhatia, S. 16
Bhutto, Benazir 54, 134
Bin Baz, Sheikh Abdullah 60
Bin Laden, Osama:
    Afghanistan 200–1;
    fatwas 198; Islam 152, 194–5;
    Islamophobia 192; Israel 35;
    jihad 47, 182–3, 203–4;
    Muslims views on 21; protest
    politics 77–8; Qutb 198;
    radicalism 200–1; Saudi
    Arabia 35, 51, 60, 198–9;
    Soviet Union 182–3;
    stereotypes 193;
    Taliban 198; terrorist
    attacks 1, 180; as threat 217;
    umma 204; see also al-Qaeda
Blair, Tony 189
Bojnordi, Ayatollah 103
Bosnia 78, 176, 178, 187–8
Bosnia-Herzegovina 47
Boumedienne, Houari 72–3
boycotts 81–2
Burgat, F. 72–3, 74, 216
burqa 120, 139
Bush, George 67, 90
Bush, George W. 151, 183, 189,
    190, 204, 214
Byzantium 10

Cairo earthquake 85
caliphate: early 16, 42;
    ending 87; Fatamid 185;
    function 19; Mawdudi 53;
    Mohammad 106;
    politics 22; Shari'a 19; and
    state 40
capitalism 82, 96
Carter Administration 30
chadour 139, 140
Chechyan movement 45, 48, 171,
    176, 178, 188

China 78
Christianity: Crusades 154, 183–4;
    evangelical movements 25;
    feelings against 205–6;
    fundamentalism 26, 64; Holy
    Lands 45, 154, 183–4;
    Islam 162; politics 18;
    radical Catholic priests 67;
    women's status 135
citizenship 39, 55, 80
city-state 39
civil conflict: Afghanistan 187,
    195; Algeria 93; Islamic
    state 42; Lebanon 176;
    liberalization 93;
    poverty 188; sectarian
    differences 69
civilization, clash of 98–9, 180–1,
    188–9
clerical rule 19; elites 74;
    Mamluk 43; Ottoman
    state 44–5; political
    activism 62; reform 77;
    Shi'a Muslims 22, 30; Sunni
    Muslims 44–5; Taliban 48,
    57; see also theocracy
Coalition powers 177–8
Coca-Cola 81
coercion 35
Cold War 7, 175–6, 195–6, 213–14
USS Cole 180, 194
colonialism: aftermath 113–14,
    115; Egypt 165;
    hegemony 166;
    Indonesia 154; Islam 19,
    110; modernization 92
commodification of women 122–3
communism 95, 96
community, imagined 209
community of believers: see umma
conscientious objectors 12
consumerism 61, 81–2, 141, 145
converts 11–12
corruption 61, 75, 76, 107
councils: see majlis
Crusaders 26, 154, 177, 201

Crusades: Christianity 154, 183–4;
    Hizballah 157; Holy
    Lands 183–4; Islam's
    successes 155–7;
    Jerusalem 184, 185;
    jihad 184–5; al-Qaeda 157;
    Qutb 157; symbolism 182–3

Daily Star 150
dar al-harb 166
dar al-Islam 166
Dar es-Salaam 180, 194
dawla 40, 49, 50–2
The Dawn 39
debt rescheduling 89–90, 98
democracy: Algeria 113;
    Bangladesh 96;
    capitalism 96; Egypt 112,
    215; Indonesia 89, 115–16;
    intellectuals 103–5;
    Islam 6–7, 53, 89, 91–2, 96;
    Islamists 92; Kramer 101–2;
    Muslim Brotherhood 111;
    Muslim majority state 89,
    97–8; Pakistan 96; Qutb 104;
    secularism 114;
    sovereignty 107–8;
    theocracy 114;
    vocabulary 104–5;
    women 108; women's
    rights 146; see also
    anti-democracy
democratiyya 104–5
democratization: Algeria 117;
    Cold War 213–14;
    international financial
    institutions 98;
    liberalization 3; Soviet
    Union 94–5; War on
    Terror 214–15; West 88–9,
    90
despotism 106
Dessouki, H. 24
Diamond, L. 88
dictatorship 44
dissent 71–3, 192

divorce 124, 133, 136–7, 144
Djerejian, E. 117
documentary films 136
Dome of the Rock 45
Donner, F. M. 164
Druze Muslims 11

East Timor 48
Easwaran, S. E. 65
economic factors 81–5
education:
    authoritarianism 153–4;
    women 130, 138, 139, 146
Egypt: Ali 106; Cairo
    earthquake 85;
    colonialism 165;
    corruption 107;
    democracy 112, 215;
    divorce 136–7, 144;
    hijab 141–2; Islamism 48;
    Jihad organization 50;
    Muslim Brotherhood 104,
    111; Nasser 70–1, 136–7, 146,
    167; OIC 50–1; personal
    status 136–7; radicals 35;
    re-Islamization 144;
    revivalism 140; women's
    status 119, 140, 141–2, 144
Ehteshami, A. 58
Eickleman, D. 3, 138, 141
Eid al-Fitr feast 14
11 September, 2001: see terrorist
    attacks
elites 25, 51, 71–2, 74
empowerment: hijab 138, 139–42;
    women 134–5, 146–7
End of History thesis 95
enfranchisement 133
Enlightenment 155
Erbakan, Necmettin 73
Ereira, A. 185
Esposito, J. L. 18–19, 51, 53, 74,
    169, 170
ethnic cleansing 188
ethno-national conflicts 176
Eubank, Chris 12, 14

European Union 45, 84
evangelical movements 25
exile 215–16
exploitation 119, 141, 142
Ezzat, H. R. 134

Fadlallah, Sheikh 177
Fahd, King 60, 77
Faisal, Toujan 133
faith 21–2, 24–5, 119–22, 151, 155
fanaticism: Islamists 24, 32–3;
    suicide bombers 173–4;
    terrorism 171, 216–17;
    Western view 3, 159
Farag, Abdel Salam 170
fard ayn 163
Fatah movement 175
Fatamid caliphates 185
Fatima 124, 126, 137
Fatima, from Cairo 141
fatwas 82, 177–8, 198
federalism 23
female infanticide 122–3
feminism 11, 134–5, 144–5
fez 73
FIS (Fronte Islamique du
    Salut) 72, 91, 111, 143
FLN (Fronte de National
    Liberation) 72–3, 91
Fnaysh, M. 26
foreign policy 195–6
France 108; Algeria 78, 91–2;
    hijab 79–80, 113;
    Muslims 104, 119;
    revolution 106;
    secularism 35, 79–80, 113;
    women 119
Freedom House 89
Friday as holy day 12, 13
Fukuyama, Francis 95, 158, 159,
    191
Fulcher of Chartres 184
fundamentalists 29–33, 205–6;
    Afghanistan 21, 176;
    Christianity 26, 64;
    Hindu 22, 26, 64, 170–1;

identity 30; India 170–1;
Iran 30; Islam 192;
jihad 165–7, 170;
liberalism 11; Muslim
migrants 24; revival 143;
Saudi Arabia 76–7; Shi'a
Muslims 99; Sunni
Wahabi 59; women's
movements 143–4

Gama Islamiyyah 157, 167
Gaza Strip 13, 21, 68, 111
gender: equality 76, 122, 127–8,
137; faith 119–22;
identity 130–1; Islam 6–7;
politics 3; relationships 123,
134; segregation 124–5, 139
geo-politics 31, 189
geo-strategic factors 22–3
Germany 78, 80, 104
al-Ghannushi, Sheikh Rashid 91,
112
al-Ghazali 43–4, 47, 69
al-Ghazali, S. 127, 131–2
al-Ghazali, Z. 146–7
globalization 7–8, 20, 92–3, 97–8
Gordon, General 181
governance 40–1, 83–4
Guardian Council 105
guest-workers 80
Gulf Crisis 94
Gurr, T. 176

Haass, Richard 90, 91, 93, 96
hadith 10; *jihad* 161–2;
Mohammad 131; *Shari'a* 16;
women 119, 124
hajj 14–15, 75
hakimiyya 104
halal 11
Halliday, F. 24, 31, 208
Hamas (Islamic Resistance
Movement) 68–9;
Covenant 48–9, 156;
feminism 144–5; Holy
Lands 165–6;

martyrdom 172, 174, 175;
PLO 111; suicide
bombers 171; as threat 217;
War on Terror 189–90
Hammami, R. 68, 145
Hamza, Abu 25, 51
Hanafi school 16, 162
Hanbali school 16, 108, 162
al-Haq, Zia 54
haram 11
Haram al-Sharif 14
harem 139
Harff, B. 176
Hatem, M. 132
al-Hawali, Sheikh Safar 76, 77
hegemony 94–6, 110, 166, 188, 214
Held, D. 95
hijab 119; as act of
empowerment 138, 139–42;
Egypt 140, 141–2;
France 79–80, 113; Iran 193;
Palestinians 68, 145; political
factors 141; Turkey 73, 146
Hinchcliffe, P. 133
Hindu fundamentalists 22, 26, 64,
170–1
hip-hop stars 12
Hizb al-Tahrir (Liberation
Party) 22
Hizballah: Crusades 157; Islamist
propaganda 178; *jihad* 170;
Lebanon 102, 111, 149–51;
religion/violence 26;
Shi'a 102; terrorism/freedom
fighters 151, 152; West 152
Hobbes, Thomas 43, 159
Hoffman, B. 173
Holy Lands 45, 154, 165–6, 183–4
holy places 59–60, 185
Holy Sepulchre, Church of 156
honour killings 133
hostages 30, 163
Hourani, A. 44–5, 106
Huddersfield News 200
human rights 16, 132, 197, 200, 212
humanitarianism 97

Hunter, S.   30
Huntington, Samuel   7, 86, 92,
    98–9, 180–1, 191
Hussein   16–17, 42
Hussein, King   111, 133
Hussein, Saddam   17, 193, 211
Husseini, Safiya   23

Ibn Hisham   124
Ibn Khaldun   44–5
Ibn Taymiyya   38–9, 43, 163
identity: civilization   98–9;
    fundamentalists   30;
    gender   130–1; Islam   10;
    Muslims   12, 15–16, 34, 45, 67,
    81; national   73–4;
    political   66
ideologues   12, 52, 55, 191, 208–9,
    216–17
idolatry   168
ijtihad   56, 164
illiteracy   128
Imam Sadr Foundation   130
imamate   13, 17, 18, 56
iman   12
India: democracy   89;
    fundamentalists   170–1;
    Jamiaat al-Islami   52, 143;
    Muslims   78, 164; UK   65,
    164; violent politics   170–1
Indonesia:
    authoritarianism   115–16;
    colonialism   154;
    democracy   89, 115–16;
    economic growth   85;
    Islamization   176;
    secularism   153;
    women   119–20
inheritance   124, 132, 136–7
intellectuals   29, 103–5
international financial
    institutions   34, 84, 89–90, 98
Internet technology   2, 109–11
intifada   68, 175
intikabat   104
Iqbal, Mohammad   65

Iran, Islamic Republic of: American
    hostages   30;
    consumerism   145;
    fundamentalists   30; Guardian
    Council   105; hijab   193;
    Islamic Republic   105;
    Islamists   48, 211;
    Khomeini   31, 55–8, 66–7;
    OIC   50–1; political
    activism   134; resurgence   56;
    revivalism   56;
    revolution   30, 66–7, 94, 210,
    212; secularism   145, 153;
    Shari'a   57–8; Shi'a
    Muslims   17, 131–2;
    theocracy   55–8, 105, 213; on
    UK   84–5; US   84–5, 177;
    vilayat al-fiqh   18;
    women   134, 145
Iraq: Ba'thists   211; Islamism   48;
    Kuwait   60, 76, 211; post-war
    reconstruction   88; resistance
    groups   178; Shi'a
    Muslims   178, 211; US-led
    occupation   177–8, 207; War
    on Terror   206–7
Iraqi exiles   22
Ireland, Northern   84, 157
Islam   3, 9–10; Afghanistan   36;
    anti-democracy   101, 103; Bin
    Laden   152, 194–5;
    Christianity   162;
    colonialism   19, 110;
    converts   11–12;
    Crusades   155–7;
    democracy   6–7, 53, 89, 91–2,
    96; faith system   5–6, 9, 11–16;
    five pillars of   12–15;
    fundamentalists   192;
    gender   6–7; identity   10;
    Jews   201, 202; jihad   26, 55,
    161–2, 166; media   2, 24;
    Pakistan   36, 51; politics   2–3,
    4–6, 18–27, 32, 209–10; Saudi
    Arabia   36, 51; sectarian
    differences   16–18, 40, 41, 63,

108; socialism 82–3;
sovereignty 108; state 3, 44;
statehood 36;
stereotypes 193; suicide
bombers 152; terrorism 173;
violence 7, 26, 151, 154–61;
West 2, 155;
Westernization 193–4
Islam, Yousef (Cat Stevens) 12
Islamic Action Front 112, 133
Islamic courts 136–7
Islamic Ideological Council 54
Islamic Jihad: *jihad* 170;
martyrdom 174, 175;
Qutb 167; suicide
bombers 171; threat 217;
Zionists 156
Islamic Resistance
Movement 48–9
Islamic states 41–2, 43–4, 46, 61,
84, 100–1
Islamists 210–12;
Afghanistan 32, 211;
Algeria 47, 48, 72–3; anti-
democracy 93, 94;
authoritarianism 93–4,
116–17; democracy 92;
discourse 210–11; Egypt 48;
exile 215; fanaticism 24,
32–3; feminism 144;
Hizballah 178; Iran 48, 211;
leaders 26; Lebanon 48;
liberal democracy 192;
martyrdom 171–2; media 3;
Pakistan 33, 48, 52–3, 213;
protest culture 85–6;
radicalism 64, 79, 160, 178,
190–2; Saudi Arabia 48;
Somalia 211; state 35–6;
state creation 97;
statehood 6; Sudan 211;
transnational conspiracies 86;
US power 8; violence 212;
West 195–6; women 119
Islamization 21, 36, 113, 135–6,
211, 212–13

Ismaili Muslims 11, 172, 176
Israel: Abu Shanab 171–2; Bin
Laden 35;
Lebanon 149–51; US
support 81–2, 202;
wall-building 175
Israel Defence Forces 149
Israeli–Palestinian conflict 48, 68,
174–5, 202–3
Italy 78

jahiliyya 115, 123, 167–8, 177, 212
Jalal, A. 130
Jamiaat al-Islami 52, 53, 54, 71,
111, 143
Jawad, H. 123, 129–35, 132, 137–8
Jerusalem: Crusades 184, 185;
holy site 14, 156;
Ottomans 45; suicide
bombers 171; Urban II 155
Jesus Christ 12
Jews 201, 202
jihad 160–4; Allah 157; Bin
Laden 47, 182–3, 203–4;
Crusades 184–5; faith 151;
fundamentalists 165–7, 170;
hadith 161–2; Hizballah 170;
Islam 26, 55, 161–2, 166;
Islamic Jihad 170;
modernism 164–5; al-
Qaeda 161, 170, 201–2;
Qutb 165, 167–9;
terrorism 178–9;
violence 212
Jihad al-Islami 170
Jihad organization, Egypt 50
Jinnah, Muhammad Ali 52
jizyah 162
Joffe, G. 159
Jones, T. 185
Jordan 111, 112, 133
Judaism 10, 12, 100
judges 16, 53
jurisprudence 16
jurists 19
justice 44, 136–7, 145

Karam, A. 137, 146
Karbala, battle of 16, 42
Kashani, Ayatollah 200
Kashmir 48
Kazakhstan 27, 90
Kedourie, E. 43, 53, 92, 99–100, 106, 168, 170
Kemalists 73
Khadija 124, 125, 137
Khalafalla, Mohammad Ahmad 29
Khameini, Ayatollah 84–5, 126
Khan, Badshah Guffar 64–5
Khan, Muqtedar 114
Khobar towers attack 194
Khomeini, Ayatollah: death 57–8; Divine law 57; ideologue 12, 52; *ijtihad* 56; Iran 31, 55–8, 66–7; revolution 31, 210; stereotype 193; theocracy 105; US 188; *vilayat al-fiqh* 18, 56
King, Martin Luther 64
Kramer, M. 31–2, 92, 101–2
Kurds 17
Kuwait 60, 76, 211

labour force 147, 148
Lahoud, Emile 150
Lapidus, I. M. 42
Latin America 67
law 129; *see also Shari'a*
Lawal, Amina 23
Lawrence, B. 161
leadership: Islamic state 41–2, 43–4, 61; Islamists 26; legitimacy 46–7; *majilis* 107; rejection 47; Taliban 197
League of Nations 34
Lebanon: civil conflict 176; Hizballah 102, 111, 149–51; Islamists 48; Israel 149–51; Shi'a Muslims 130; US 152
legitimacy 39, 46–7, 93

Lewis, B. 26, 100–1, 153–4, 171, 185, 190
liberal-democracy: humanitarianism 97; Islamists 192; Lewis 100–1; Muslim minority states 78–9; radicals 116; secular states 35; US hegemony 95–6
liberalization 3, 93, 97–8
Libya 48

mahram 120
majlis 53, 104, 105, 107
majlis al-shura 53, 54–5, 136
Malaysia 85
Mali 78
Maliki school 16, 162
Mamluk state 42–3, 44
marriage 130, 131
Marsden, K. 85
Marty, M. E. 29
martyrdom: Hamas 172, 174, 175; Hussein 17, 42; Islamic Jihad 174, 175; Islamists 171–2; Qutb 167; respect for 68; suicide bombers 152, 171, 173–4
Matinuddin, K. 136
matrilineality 120
Mawdudi, Muwlana 52–5, 167, 169, 191
Mecca 12, 13, 14–15, 38, 59, 75
media: Islam 2, 24, 25, 26–7; Islamists 3; stereotypes 158; women 118
Medina 14, 37, 59, 124–5
Medina state 38–40, 48, 49, 56–7
Memorandum of Advice, Saudi Arabia 77
Mernissi, F. 124, 125, 131, 142
Middle East 31–2
Middle East Times 81
migrant workers 148, 216
migration 5, 24, 215–16
Miller, J. 25, 158, 159–60

Milton-Edwards, B.   133
Minangkabau Muslims   120
misogyny   131, 137
Mitterrand, François   119
modernist trend   28, 108, 139, 164–5
modernization   19, 50, 82, 92, 153
Moghissi, H.   132
Mohammad, Prophet: Allah   9–10;
    caliphate   106; death of   40;
    hadith   131; life and
    sayings   10–11; Mecca   15;
    Medina state   38, 48, 56–7;
    relationships with
    women   123, 124;
    successors   16
Molyneux, M.   142–3
Mongols   42
monotheism   10, 100, 152
Montazeri, Hussein-Ali   105
Mos Def   12
Moses   12
Motahari, Ayatollah   132
mourning, day of   17
Moussalli, A.   109–10, 136, 137
Mu'awiya   16, 41, 42
al-Mu'ayyad Sheikh   43
Mubarak, Hosni   25, 112, 119, 140,
    144
muezzin   12
mujahid   161
mujahideen   47, 76, 182–3, 195–7
Musharaff, Pervez   107
Muslim Brotherhood: al-
    Banna   109–11;
    democracy   111; Egypt   104,
    111; Hamas   69; Nasser   70;
    welfare   85
Muslim League   52
Muslim majority states:
    authoritarianism   214;
    democracy   89, 97–8;
    Islamists   211–12;
    modernization   153;
    radicalism   160; reform   117
Muslim minority
    populations   78–9, 80–1

Muslims: anti-Americanism   190–2;
    Bosnia   187–8; condemnation
    of terrorist attacks   199–200;
    democracy   6–7, 103–5;
    feelings against   31; France
    104, 119; governance   40–1;
    human rights   200; identity
    12, 15–16, 34, 45, 67, 81;
    India   78, 164; migration   5,
    215–16; oppression   176–7;
    rights   189–90;
    self-government   93–4;
    UK   189; US   90–1, 157–8,
    190; violence   157–8,
    West   63–4, 83, 190

al-Nadha movement   112, 113
Nairobi   180, 194
Najibullah, President   196
Nakanishi, H.   126
Naseem, Prince   12
Nasrallah, Hassan   150
Nasser, Gamal Abdel   70–1, 136–7,
    146, 167
nation-states   45
national resistance fighters   151
nationalism   27, 53, 70, 211
nepotism   106
New World Order   67, 97
Nigeria   23, 33, 35, 48, 78
non-Arab Muslim states   85
non-violent protest   64–5
Norton, A. R.   88
Nurhaysim, Amrozi   171

oil   72, 75, 90
Oklahoma car-bombing   194
Old Man of the Mountain   172
Oman   104
Omar: *see* Umar
Omar, Mullah Mohammad
    197
opium   197–8
opposition politics   6, 62–3
Organization of Islamic
    Conference   45, 50–1, 200

Othman 16, 41, 106
Ottoman Empire 41, 43, 44–5, 70, 87, 186
ownership 129–30

Pahlavi, Reza Shah 193
Pakistan: Afghanistan 196; Bhutto 134; democracy 96; Islam 36, 51; Islamic Ideological Council 54; Islamism 33, 48, 52–3, 213; Islamization 113; Jamaat al-Islami 71; *majlis al-shura* 107; Mawdudi 52–5; Medina model 39; migrant workers 216; radicals 35; *Shari'a* 16
Pakistanis in UK 78
Palestinian Authority 85
Palestinian Liberation Organization 69, 144–5
Palestinians: feminism 144–5; Gaza Strip 21; Hamas 48–9, 111; *hijab* 68, 145; *intifada* 68; Islamists 174; suicide bombers 178; *umma* 166; uprising 82; in US 216; women 145; Zionists 156; *see also* Israeli–Palestinian conflict
Pape, R. A. 173–4, 175
patriarchy 46, 122, 126–7, 138, 140–1
Paul, Saint 135
Persians 17, 30, 42
Pervez, S. 11
Peters, F. E. 162
Peters, R. 158, 164
Philippines 70, 78, 176
pilgrimage 14–15
Pipes, D. 161, 192
Piscatori, J. 3, 138, 141
political activism 24, 62, 68, 132–4, 214
politics 27, 35–6, 64; Arabia 37–8; caliphate 22;

Christianity 18; consciousness 66; faith 155; *hijab* 141; identity 66; India 170–1; intervention by West 187; Islam 2–3, 4–6, 18–27, 32, 209–10; religion 18–19, 26, 53, 71; women 68, 125, 132–4, 143; *see also* protest politics
Popular Front for the Liberation of Palestine 152
poverty 64, 83–4, 188, 192
Powell, Colin 202
protest 58, 64, 68, 75, 81–6
protest politics 6, 62–3, 67–9, 70, 77–9, 87
Punjab 65

Qadi's 16
al-Qaeda 198; anti-Americanism 201–2; Crusaders 201; Crusades 157; *jihad* 161, 170, 201–2; Saudi Arabia 205; terror campaign 188; terrorist attacks 1, 20–1, 63, 180, 183; as threat 217; *umma* 201; violence 203–4
Qa'ouk, Sheikh 149–50
Qaradawi, Sheikh Yusuf 122, 124–5, 177
Qumi, Hassan Tabatibi 105
Qur'an 11; inheritance 132; *jihad* 161–2; law 129; *Shari'a* 10, 16; state 40; women 119, 122, 123, 124, 137
Qutb, Sayyid: Bin Laden 198; Crusades 157; democracy 104; influence 167, 169, 170; *jihad* 165, 167–9; martyrdom 167; Mawdudi 55; Muslims/ Islam 30; *Shari'a* 115; *shura* 114–15; West 84, 191

radicalism   35; Bin Laden   200–1;
    Catholic priests   67;
    Islamists   64, 79, 160, 178,
    190–2; liberal democracy   116;
    Muslim majority states   160;
    politics   27, 35–6, 64
Rafsanjani, President   177
Rahman, Sheikh Omar   25
Ramadan   14
Rantisi, Abdel Aziz   188
Rapoport, D. C.   173
Rapper Q-Tip   12
Rashid, A.   176, 187, 195
Rashidun companions   41
Refah (Welfare) Party   73, 74
reform   28, 77, 117
regime change   94, 213
religion/politics   18–19, 26, 53, 71
respect   134
resurgence: faith   21–2, 24–5;
    Iran   56; Muslim
    women   138; protest
    politics   87; status quo   5;
    Sunni Muslims   31;
    women   120–2
resurgence movement   26
revivalism   6; Egypt   140;
    faith   21–2;
    fundamentalists   143;
    Iran   56; Islamic state   46;
    religion/politics   20; status
    quo   5; Sunni   43
revolution   30, 66–7, 94, 106–7, 210,
    212
Rida, Rashid   165
ritual washing   13
Rodenbeck, M.   43
Rodinson, M.   39
Roy, O.   25, 144
Rubin, B.   192
Ruhani, Muhammad Sadiq   105
Russian Revolution   106
Ruthven, M.   61

Saad-Ghorayeb, A.   102
el-Saadawi, Nawal   144

as-Sabah, Hasan   172
sacralization   68
Sadat, Anwar   50, 140, 170
Saftawi, A.   13
al-sahifa   38
Said, Edward   4, 154, 193
Saladin   42, 156–7, 201
salafi fundamentalists   154, 165
salafi jihad   207
Salame, G.   94
salat   12–13
Saudi Arabia   58–61;
    authoritarianism   61; Bin
    Laden   35, 51, 60, 198–9;
    elites   71;
    fundamentalists   76–7; holy
    places   59–60; Islam   36, 51;
    Islamism   48; Khobar towers
    attack   194; Memorandum
    of Advice   77;
    mujahideen   196; oil
    reserves   75; polarization of
    population   75;
    al-Qaeda   205; US troops   60;
    Wahabi clerics   74, 75, 147;
    women's rights   78, 147–8
Saunders, J. J.   155, 186
sawm (fast)   14
Sayyaf, Abu   178, 217
secessionism   45
seclusion   139
sectarian conflict   69, 157
secularism: democracy   114;
    differences   16–18, 40, 41, 63,
    108; France   35, 79–80, 113;
    Indonesia   153; Iran   145,
    153; Islam   28; rejected   170;
    state   142; Turkey   73–4;
    US   35
seeyada al dawla   104
Seljuks   42, 172, 184
Serbs   176, 188
sexuality   119, 131–2
Shafi school   16, 108, 162
Shammi, A. Sheikh   188
al-Sharawi, Sheikh   127–8

Shari'a 104; caliphate 19;
　hadith 16; Iran 57–8; Islamic
　states 46; Mamluk state 43;
　Mawdudi 53; Nigeria 23;
　Ottoman state 44–5;
　Qur'an 10, 16; Qutb 115;
　state 45, 49–50;
　terrorism 204; Turkey 73–4;
　Zakat funds 14
Shari'ati, Ali 57, 66–7
Sharif, Nawaz 16, 54
Shi'a Muslims: Ali and
　Hussein 16–17; clerical
　rule 22, 30;
　fundamentalists 99;
　Hizballah movement 102;
　imamate 56; Iran 17, 131–2;
　Iraq 178, 211; Islamic
　states 46; Lebanon 130; and
　Sunnis 11, 16–18, 40, 46, 108
shihada 12
Shubailat, Laith 111–12
shura 54, 104, 105–6, 110, 114–15,
　116
Siddiqi, D. M. 139
Siffin, battle of 16
Sivan, E. 28, 168–9
social injustice 65
socialism 82–3, 97
Somalia 47, 84, 211
Sophronius 156
South Lebanon Army 149–50
sovereignty: Allah 53, 108, 114;
　democracy 107–8;
　divine 54; Islam 108;
　state 34–5
Soviet republics (former) 27, 37,
　51
Soviet Union: Afghanistan 76,
　187, 195, 196, 197; Bin
　Laden 182–3; collapse of 37,
　95, 181–2;
　democratization 94–5
state: caliphate 40; coercion 35;
　elites 51, 71–2; Islam 3, 44;
　Islamists 35–6;

legitimacy 39;
　modernization 50; Muslim
　identity 34; nationalism 70;
　Qur'an 40; religion 71;
　secularism 142; *Shari'a* 45,
　49–50; sovereignty 34–5;
　territory 37; types
　(Esposito) 51; violence 58
state creation 37–8, 97
statehood 6, 34, 36, 47, 52–5
stereotypes 3, 158, 193
Stowasser, B. 139
Sudan 48–9, 57, 94, 210–12
Sufi brotherhood 11
suicide bombers 152, 158, 171–5
Sukarno, General 115–16
sunna 10
Sunni Muslims: clerical rule 44–5;
　fundamentalists 59;
　protest 75; resurgence 31;
　revivalism 43; and Shi'a 11,
　16–18, 40, 46, 108; state/
　Islam 44
Supporters of the Shari'a 51
supranational organizations 45
Sutherland, J. 192

tahwid 14
Taif Peace Accord 102
Tajikistan 27, 36, 51
Takfir wa Hijra 170
Taliban: Bin Laden 198;
　clerics 48, 57; human
　rights 197; Islamization 21,
　135–6, 212–13; leadership
　197; opium 197–8;
　US 199; women 120–1,
　135–6, 197
Tantawi, Mohammad 200
tariqa 11
Taurabi, Hassan 91
tawadad 104
technology 2, 29, 109–11, 215
territory 34–5, 37, 42
terrorism: fanaticism 171, 216–17;
　international 199;

Islam   173; *jihad*   178–9;
   national resistance
   fighters   151; religious   173;
   Shari'a   204; theology   167–9;
   umma   192–3; US   178;
   violence   154
terrorism studies   23–4, 103
terrorist attacks: Bin Laden   1, 180;
   11 September, 2001   20–1, 63,
   84–5, 152–3, 157, 159, 194;
   Muslim condemnation   199–
   200; al-Qaeda   1, 20–1, 63, 183
theocracy   48, 55–8, 101, 105, 114,
   213
Tibi, B.   17, 71, 214
Tolstoy, Leo   208
totalitarianism   53
trade   42–3
traditionalists   108
transnational conspiracies   86
Tucker, J.   119, 132
Tunisia   82, 112–13, 132
al-Turabi, Hassan   49, 117, 136–7
Turkey   73–4, 89, 145–6, 148
Turks in Germany   78, 80
Turner, B.   190

ulama   43, 58, 59
Umar   16, 41, 156
Umm Salama   137
umma   50, 66, 104, 163; Aisha   125;
   Bin Laden   204; *dawla*   40;
   Medina   38; Ottoman
   Empire   70; Palestinians   166;
   al-Qaeda   201; Ramadan   14;
   terrorism   192–3; al-
   Turabi   49; United
   Kingdom   81
United Kingdom: India   65, 164;
   Iran   84–5; Muslims   189;
   Pakistanis   78;
   secularism   35; *umma*   81
United Nations   34, 37, 45, 171, 207
United Nations Development
   Programme   128
US State Department   152

United States of America:
   Afghanistan   187; anti-
   American feelings   32, 190–2,
   201–2; as Big Satan   188; Bin
   Laden   35; economic
   growth   85; embassies   180,
   194, 198; federalism   23;
   hegemony   94–6, 188;
   hostages   30; Iran   84–5, 177;
   Iraq   177–8, 207; Islam   12;
   Israel   81–2, 202;
   Khomeini   188;
   Lebanon   152; *mujahideen*
   alliances   195, 196;
   Muslims   90–1, 157–8, 190;
   oil   90; Palestinians   216;
   Saudi Arabia   60;
   secularism   35; Taliban   199;
   terrorism   178; vulnerability
   to attack   191, 194–5; *see also*
   War on Terror
Urban II, Pope   155–6, 183–4
al-Utaibi, Juhayman   75
utopian state   55
Utvik, B. O.   28
Uzbekistan   27, 51, 196

Vatikiotis, P.   70
vilayat al-fiqh   18, 56
violence: ideologues   216–17;
   Islam   7, 26, 58, 151, 154–61;
   Islamists   212; *jihad*   212;
   Muslims   157–8;
   political   70–1, 151; al-
   Qaeda   203–4; state   58;
   terrorism   154
vizirs   44–5

Wahabi clerics   59, 74, 75, 147
Wahid, Abdulrahman   116
war, rules of   164, 174, 175
War on Terror   1, 217; anti-
   Muslims   151, 183;
   civilizations clashing   189;
   democratization   214–15;
   Hamas   189–90; Iraq   206–7

Watson, H.   141, 142
welfare   14, 85, 98
West: Algeria   117;
    democratization   88–9, 90;
    fanaticism, views on   3, 159;
    feelings against   83, 181;
    followers of Islam   4;
    hegemony   110;
    Hizballah   152; Islam   2, 155;
    Islamists   195–6;
    Muslims   63–4, 83, 190;
    oppressive regimes   176–7;
    political intervention   187;
    prejudice   2; terrorism   63–4
West Bank   68, 111
Westernization   193–4, 206
Whalley, L. C.   120
Wolfowitz, P.   193
women: Afghanistan   120–1;
    banned from driving   60; 76;
    Christianity   135;
    commodified   122–3;
    democracy   108; dress
    codes   123, 138, 139–42;
    education   130, 138, 139, 146;
    Egypt   119, 140, 141–2, 144;
    empowerment   134–5, 146–7;
    enfranchisement   133;
    France   119; holy texts   119,
    124; hostages   163;
    Indonesia   119–20; Iran   134,
    145; Islamists   119;
    Jordan   133; justice   136–7;
    labour force   147, 148; legal
    rights   127–8; media   118;
    Mohammad   123, 124;
    ownership   129–30; political
    commitment   68, 125,
    132–4, 143; Qur'an   119, 122,

123, 124, 137; respect from
    men   134;
    resurgence   120–2; sexual
    threat   131–2; as symbol
    of repression   118; 138;
    Taliban   120–1, 135–6, 197;
    terrorized   153;
    al-Turabi   136; Turkey   145,
    146, 148; see also hijab
women's groups   16, 143–4, 145–6
women's rights: Aisha   125;
    contemporary Islam   46,
    119–20, 122; democracy   146;
    documentary films   136;
    inheritance   132;
    Jawad   129–35; modernist
    trend   139; Saudi Arabia   78,
    147–8
Women's Society of the Islamic
    Revolution of Iran   126
World Trade Centre   1, 25, 194
World War I   41, 186

X, Malcolm   11–12, 15

Yassin, Sheikh   172
Yemen   142–3, 180
Yousef, Ramzi   25, 194
Yugoslavia, former   187–8

Zahar, Mahmoud   171
al-Zahrawi, Ayman   50, 156
Zakariyya, Fu'ad   29
zakat   13–14
Zakat Foundation of India   13–14
Zam-Zam   81
Zionists   156, 202
Zubaida, S.   56, 57
Zuhur, S.   125